D0773530

FAITH AND FEAR
IN FLUSHING

FAITH AND FEAR IN FLUSHING

An Intense Personal History
of the New York Mets

Greg W. Prince

Foreword by Jason Fry

SKYHORSE PUBLISHING

www.skyhorsepublishing.com

10 9 8 7 6 5 4 3 2 1

Library of Congress Cataloging-in-Publication Data

Prince, Greg W.
Faith and fear in Flushing : an intense personal history of the New York Mets / Greg W. Prince.
p. cm.
ISBN 978-1-60239-681-4
1. New York Mets (Baseball team)--History. I. Title.
GV875.N37P75 2009
796.357'64097471--dc22
2009001206

Printed in the United States of America

FOR STEPHANIE PRINCE
I'm a big fan.

CONTENTS

FOREWORD

A s you'll soon find out, there are a number of extraordinary
things about Greg Prince.

One of them is his memory. The man remembers *everything*—
not just players, scores of games, and final standings, but when the
games were, who was there with him, and what they talked about
between pitches. So my offhand comment along the lines of "this
reminds me of the night Leiter got the triple and we all laughed"
might be returned instantly with, "It was a Friday night against
the Marlins, last day in August 2001. You and Emily were there on
our regular Tuesday/Friday plan. The night before, we'd beaten
the Phillies to cut the Braves' lead to single digits. Leiter drove in
Agbayani and Rey, and then Fonzie drove him in. We wound up
taking two out of three on the last homestand before 9/11."

It's jaw-dropping the first time he does it (and pretty amazing
the hundredth), but Greg doesn't do it to show off. It's a rare
gift, but not one of which he's particularly exhibitionistic—if
anything, he's a bit shy about it. (Nobody likes being a parlor
trick, even if it's for a friendly audience.) That level of recall is
just something he's always had, and it took him a while to realize
that other people didn't have it too.

I mention Greg's memory because I'm going to tell you how
Faith and Fear in Flushing—the name refers to the blog we both

write as well as the book you hold in your hands—came to be. I'm sure my version of the story is slightly different than Greg's, and given my rather fallible memory, quite likely to be slightly wrong. But tough luck, partner; you've got the rest of the book to tell it your way.

I met Greg in 1994, when we struck up an acquaintance based on being two of the regulars on an America Online message board about the Mets. We didn't meet in real life until a year later, when I moved from Washington, D.C., to New York. We shook hands outside Shea Stadium (like you're surprised), then went inside to watch the major league debut of Bill Pulsipher, a Met lefty who was wild in every sense of the word. Pulse's first big league pitch went to the backstop, and the Mets lost. But our online friendship became a real-life friendship, one that included watching amazingly terrible Met teams lose lots and lots of games.

Between pitches and innings I found out a little more about Greg besides the fact that he'd also seen Edgardo Alfonzo's potential. He had that amazing memory; he adored his cats and his preternaturally wise, patient wife Stephanie; he carried a big, apparently magical bag that contained any mundane object you might need and not a few extraordinary ones you hadn't thought of; and he bore an unapologetic love for the kind of AM pop hits that ought to come with Lactaid. He was also among the kindest, gentlest, most generous people I'd ever been lucky enough to meet. And he was, hands down, the best writer I'd ever known.

For a long time, though, you had to be awfully lucky to know that. Greg would e-mail missives about the Mets' latest tragedies (and occasional triumphs) to a select group of folks —intricate, jewel-box e-mails that would make you nod and smile and laugh and occasionally tear up. They were about the Mets, but they were also about much more than that. They were about being an ambivalent son and a devoted husband and a diehard Mets fan, and how life could tangle those things up so they could never again be teased loose. They cried out to be read by anybody who loved baseball and by anybody who loved good, bracingly honest writing, but how?

We'd both noticed these things called blogs; now and then, during a pitching change or conference on the mound, we'd muse idly that if we ever started one, we'd make a pretty good team. But it was just talk until the winter of 2005. I was making a living as a technology columnist, and I kept writing about the growing blog phenomenon. I'd taken a stab or two at summing up blogs' significance, but I didn't know anything about the day-to-day experience of writing one. So I suggested to Greg that we try our hands at that blog we'd always talked about. We found software we could both use, I thought of a name (Greg wanted to call our blog *Let's Meet at Gate E*, which proves I'm right every now and then), and on the day pitchers and catchers reported to Spring Training in St. Lucie, we put up one post each. At the end of that first day we had 159 page views. I think 150 or so were attributable to the two of us typing in our Web address to verify it was still there, while the other nine came from friends and family who dropped by so we'd leave them the heck alone.

I thought our experiment might last until the end of Spring Training—long enough for me to be able to write with some vague authority about being a blogger. But a funny thing happened on the way to Opening Day—we went from 1,384 page views in the second half of February to 8,882 in March. We had a small but real audience, and we were having fun. And so our little experiment never ended—a couple of thousand posts and nearly twenty-thousand comments and millions of page views later, we're still around. It's led to the book you're holding in your hands.

Like all bloggers, it took a while for us to find what made us different from everybody else out there. We're not a Mets blog dedicated to news or stats or scouting reports, though we love all those things. Rather, we're dedicated to two ideas.

The first is that no game, no season, and no player stand alone—they are part of the unfolding story of a franchise and its fans. When Johan Santana granted the Mets a stay of execution on the penultimate day of 2008, Greg and I walked down Shea's ramps trying to measure his spellbinder against performances by Jerry Koosman and Al Leiter and Bobby Jones. When Ryan Church leapt at the wall and just came up empty against Greg Dobbs and the Phillies last September, we immediately remembered Shawon Dunston against Brian Jordan and the Braves in September '99, and Shawn Green against Scott Spiezio and the Cardinals in October '06. Thinking about Daniel Murphy, we wonder if he could be the second coming of Edgardo Alfonzo, fear he could be a reprise of Mike Vail, and now and then let ourselves fantasize that he'll be neither—that one day it'll be his name invoked when we dream of what some other intriguing late-season rookie callup might do.

It can seem daunting, the sheer breadth of all this Met lore. But you don't need Greg's memory to become one of the Met faithful. All you need to do is listen. Baseball gives you plenty of opportunities to do that. It isn't relentless like football or basketball. It's got spaces, spaces that can be filled up with stories, stories to be passed from fathers and mothers to sons and daughters, between friends and neighbors, among bloggers and readers, until another convert has joined the fold. And, as you'll see, there's no better storyteller than Greg.

And that brings us to the other idea behind our blog: that you shouldn't let anybody tell you it's weird to love the Mets as much as you do. At *Faith and Fear in Flushing*, letting a good chunk of your happiness depend on the outcome of a contest between young superhuman millionaires is perfectly sensible. Taking a pocket radio to the ballet or a friend's wedding so you can hear a Met batter or two every hour is good planning. Lying awake in January fuming about Armando Benitez walking Paul O'Neill is normal. Devoutly hoping someone out there is keying Angel Hernandez's car is above reproach.

At *Faith and Fear in Flushing* we know the truth: You're doing it right, and it's everybody else who needs to get their priorities in order. If that describes you, sit down, put your feet up, turn the page, and meet my friend Greg. You're home. You're gonna like it here.

—Jason Fry
November, 2008

One

ENDINGS HAPPY AND OTHERWISE

I love endings. It may be why I was drawn to baseball in the first place. The first thing I ever read with any recurring sense of purpose was the back page of the *New York Post* in the summer of 1969, when I was six years old. Not the page at the beginning of the paper, but the one at the end. And on the back page, there was, every day, a cartoon featuring a duck in a Mets cap and a bear in a Cubs cap doing some kind of battle I was just beginning to understand as a pennant race. I sided with the duck, which was clearly more lovable and waded in undeniably local waters. That duck was my team, the New York Mets. They became my team then and they stayed my team. Within a couple of months, in the edition my father brought home from the city the evening of October 16, the duck had turned into a world championship swan. It was my first happy ending.

I preferred the backs of baseball cards to the fronts. A picture was a picture. A word picture as painted by Topps told me so much more.

> • *Tom established himself as one of baseball's premier pitchers as he led the Mets to their amazing pennant and World Series triumphs.*

> • *The Mets' 7th pick in the June, 1968 draft, Charlie was born within walking distance of Shea Stadium.*

> • *George likes marshmallow milkshakes.*

I liked the words and I loved the numbers: 25–7. .340. 100–62. Mets in 5. They told me what they told me. I didn't grow up to read anything profound into them that would drain the joy out of them. But I did grow up and remember them.

I don't remember faces that well. Physical description kind of eludes me. I know dates. I know results. I find modern-day stat talk to be numbing, but I know the stats I know. I know who was with me at which game I attended. I might remember what they were wearing if it had a player's name on the back; otherwise, I probably wouldn't. I'd like to think I look into a person's soul before coming to any conclusions about the content of a person's character, but it helps if I can associate that character with a batting average.

I remember seasons after they've ended. I remember much about the journeys within the seasons, but I always remember the destinations, or at least where the journeys wound up after 162 games. Rand McNally would have never intentionally led me to 83–79 in 1970 and MapQuest didn't mean to plot me a course to 89–73 in 2008. Those were places—third and second, respectively—where I definitely didn't need to go. But it's rare that you wind up exactly where you want to be in baseball.

Yet you always wind up at an ending.

* * *

Baseball seasons aren't permanent structures any more than baseball stadiums are. The schedule you lived your life around does conclude. The team you knew inside and out does disband.

Your season comes, your season goes. You live in it when it's here, and you roam around looking at your watch waiting for the next one to arrive so you can move in as soon as they'll let you. You always miss the old one like crazy in the interregnum because, at base, it was the last one you had. Even if it wasn't as wonderful as you'd projected. Even if it ended up falling out from under you without as much as a warning track to protect you.

But you always have it in your head, whether you want it there or not. That goes for the good seasons, the bad seasons, the frustrating seasons, the heartbreaking seasons, the quietly gratifying seasons, the rollicking championship seasons, the historically dismal seasons, and the reassuringly mediocre seasons that are neither good nor bad, just there. All of those are what I like to call Met seasons. So it goes for every season you lived in, live through, and relive over and over. So it goes for every player you've grown attached to or been stuck with. It goes for the Hall of Famers in the making every bit as much as it goes for the marshmallow milkshake drinkers.

It's been that way as long as there have been Mets, which is about as long as there has been me. Hobie Landrith became Jose Reyes; Ray Daviault became David Wright; Jay Hook became Jae Seo. Every blessed one of them who becomes a Met someday becomes a former Met, voluntarily or otherwise. It's hard to fathom while you watch them, cheer them, curse them, encourage them, rationalize them, resist the urge to boo them, spend hours ruminating on them, weigh what you would require to trade them, and rail at management because you might soon be without them. But like the seasons whose moving parts they comprised, so they go.

Even Seo.

Which brings us back to endings. I don't like that baseball seasons have to end, but I do cherish the way they leave us. Honestly, I like them more than beginnings. I like Pitchers & Catchers and Spring Training and Opening Day as any baseball fan does. I like them so much, I can't not type them in uppercase. They are Events—universally recognized touchstones that ought to be holidays. Maybe that's why I like the ends of seasons even more. Not everybody understands the appeal of an ending, of a season's closing day.

Make that Closing Day.

I've long made a habit of attending Closing Day even if it is kind of Opening Day's evil twin. Opening Day is a clean slate and brightening skies and the warmth of the sun approaching . . . all the good stuff we want in life. Closing Day is none of those things. The day after Closing Day is, for all intents and purposes, winter. Somebody I knew only from the ballpark ran into me one Closing Day and told me, "Have a good winter." It was October 3. And I hate winter.

But I do love completion. I love taking it all in. I love putting a cap on my head one final time and putting a cap on a season. For the most part, Closing Day isn't a tough ticket. Every poseur wants to be at Opening Day. Closing Day is a rite for the secret society of baseball fanatics . . . fanatics, not fans. Only the hardcore make an effort to go on Closing Day for the sake of Closing Day. No politician aims to be seen on the last day of the season. Everybody there just wants one more look.

I don't know why more people don't cherish Closing Day as a rule. It's the last chance to trick yourself into thinking it's still summer; to wear a cap for a reason; to eat ice cream out of a helmet; to retreat briefly into this Brigadoon of ours that thrives over a six-month clip. After Closing Day, T-shirt selection loses its meaning. You stop identifying meeting points by Gate. Woodside—the LIRR transfer point for Long Islanders like me who choose not to drive to Mets games—ceases to be the most vital fork in the railroad.

I understand fully that baseball may not be the most important thing in the world, yet in my mind, twelve months out of every year, nothing matters more.

So give me Woodside and the 7 train. Meet me at Gate E. Get me out there one more time. If somebody's kind enough to leave one piping hot final baseball game cooling on the window sill, what kind of idiot would I be to not calmly wander by, furtively grab it, and run like Reyes?

Yet there's no inherent cachet to Closing Day. I don't know why not. It's kind of perfect. Closing Day seals the deal. Every statistic we will see for the rest of our lives—the won-lost records, the earned run averages, the across-the-board totals—go final on Closing Day. Half-games and magic numbers and all loose ends are tidied up for posterity. It provides the necessary sealant before we put a year away, before we put it in the books. We'll take it down from the shelf, peruse it, smile, sneer, and remember that year, its winning, its losing, its drawing. It is what it is, but it's not all that until it's over . . . which it is on Closing Day.

* * *

I experienced some of the greatest baseball days of my life on Closing Day at Shea Stadium. There was '85, my first Closer, the coda to the thrilling Mets-Cardinals duel that didn't quite go our way. My friend Joel and I had waited almost a decade to be at a game with severe pennant race implications. We missed by twenty-four hours, as the Mets were eliminated the day before Closing Day, but 1985's sense of purpose still lingered. Enough time hadn't elapsed for the Mets to morph into also-rans.

All day the B-team wandered on and off the field. No Gary Carter. No Keith Hernandez. No Darryl Strawberry. Dwight Gooden would have gone for his 25th win if the game had mattered (as if there's such a thing as a baseball game that doesn't), but since we weren't going to catch St. Louis regardless of how many the Doctor K'd, we got Bill Latham starting instead. It was his last game as a Met. The transactions box would eventually reveal it would be the final Met bows as well for Larry Bowa, Ron Gardenhire, Tom Paciorek, John Christensen, Ronn Reynolds, and an outfielder named Billy Beane. With two out in the ninth and the Mets down a run, Davey Johnson sent up, as a pinch-hitter, Daniel Joseph Staub. Rusty. We knew this was it for him. He said so. It was his twenty-third season. His first was 1963, the first season I was alive for. Ten years after that, he played in what was, to that moment, the last World Series at Shea Stadium.

Rusty hit a sharp grounder to second. The ball was hit too sharp. The batter was too slow. A long career and an eternal season ended with a one-run loss.

The Mets finished 98–64, three games behind the Cardinals. That should've been that, but 1985 was too good to let go of so quickly.

Our attention was directed toward the Diamond Vision screen, where a highlight montage set to Frank Sinatra's "Here's To The Winners" unspooled. The whole season literally flashed before our eyes. We couldn't help but applaud the immensity and the texture of the thing. Blue and orange balloons went up into the Queens sky. The 1985 Mets—Doc, Darryl, Mex, Kid, Wally, Lenny, Mookie, Roger, Jesse, Rusty . . . the whole bunch of 'em—stepped out of the dugout and onto the field to wave once more. It was a group curtain call demanded for finishing a spirited second.

Then they threw their caps to the fans in the nearby Field Level seats.

Now we could go home.

I would have hated to have gone through my life as a Mets fan and not have been a part of that. I would hate to imagine my life as a Mets fan without Closing Day 1988, which was really a prelude to the playoffs against the Dodgers, a League Championship Series we all assumed was in the bag. The Mets won ten of eleven games between the teams during the year; it's one of those stats a Mets fan never forgets. That Sunday was a milestone party. A

100th RBI for Darryl; and a 100th win for the Mets. Ron Darling upped his record to 17–9, same as Jerry Koosman's in '69 . . . not a round number, but highly Metsian.

The Mets built a 7–0 lead on St. Louis. It all seemed pretty safe. It all seemed worthy of the contemporary hit that played during a pitching change: "Don't Worry Be Happy" by Bobby McFerrin. At the time, my freelance writing career was in the crapper and my mother was fighting cancer. I rather liked the idea of not worrying and being happy.

Giving up a 7–0 lead on an October Sunday at Shea was the stuff of Jets, not Mets. Alas, the Cardinals did put up some impressive yardage late in the game, closing the gap to 7–5, but you never really thought the Mets back then could blow a big lead. And they didn't. It wasn't quite as comfortable as it should have been, but the Mets maintained ball control clear into the ninth. Randy Myers (who made his debut the same day Rusty said goodbye) came on to get the final three outs and was two-thirds of the way home when Mackey Sasser visited the mound and, after a bit of stalling, Davey Johnson jogged in from the dugout.

It looked strange. It was strange. It was, in fact, a setup the likes of which I never saw before and haven't seen again. The Mets cooked up a scheme to lure Davey onto the field so public address announcer Pete Larkin could hail the fantastic job he'd done as manager since 1984 and all of us could be asked to show him our appreciation. And we did, 42,000-some standing as one and applauding. It struck me as being a little presumptuous, but well-deserved. I hoped it wouldn't blow up in our face karma-wise. Randy walked the next guy but the third out was recorded soon enough and the most successful manager in Mets history had his second hundred-win season.

That wasn't it for us, though. We got the final-day video treatment once more. This year's theme was "Back In The High Life Again," one highlight after another showing how 1988 was a lot like 1986 and nothing like the Pendletonian debacle of 1987. On Diamond Vision the Mets swung and connected, pitched and baffled, won and won again. Bobby Ojeda's face materialized and there was an extra cheer. Bobby O nearly cut off his one of his fingertips while clipping his hedges in late September. He would live even if he wouldn't pitch again until 1989. But we had Gooden (18–9) and Cone (20–3) and Darling and Fernandez. We could lose a pitcher and keep winning.

The general adoration morphed into purposeful encouragement. I thought of it at the same time tens of thousands of Met minds did. We chanted it with no prompt from the scoreboard.

"BEAT L.A.! BEAT L.A.! BEAT L.A.!"

OK, so we borrowed it from Boston, from basketball, but it was appropriate to the occasion. We had beaten the Cardinals. We had beaten the Pirates. We had beaten back the disappointment of '87 and avenged the indifference of summer. We bookended that lackluster 41–41 midsection with a 30–11 start and a 29–8 finish. If you put the pieces together correctly, you'd have to say that the 1988 Mets, for half a season, were, at a staggering 59–19, the best Mets ever. Now all we had to do was doom the Dodgers. They had Orel Hershiser and his 59 consecutive scoreless innings, sure, but we had that ten of eleven over them. We had Darryl Strawberry, MVP in waiting. Either him or McReynolds. We had Gregg Jefferies en route to the Hall of Fame. We had it all.

We overflowed with confidence when we left Shea that day. As I headed toward the train, I saw a crowd lined up by the players' parking lot. They were chanting at a bus, presumably a bus that was going to carry the Mets to LaGuardia for a plane that would carry them to Los Angeles from whence they would carry home a couple of formality victories, setting the stage for a pennant to be won at Shea by the next weekend.

"BEAT L.A.! BEAT L.A.! BEAT L.A.!"

I wouldn't be there for that, but I was here for this, this feeling that the Mets couldn't be stopped and couldn't be topped.

They were 100–60, right at the century mark. I still had no career of which to speak. My mother, radiation and remission notwithstanding, still had cancer. 1988 as a year still sucks whenever I think about it. But for a few moments that first Sunday in October, that final day at Shea two decades ago when the Mets adjourned their regular season, I was on top of the world.

Closing Day at Shea had been good to me. It gave me a win on the final day of the 1995 campaign to even my personal record at 7–7 on the year after starting it in the dumps of 0–6. The Mets had limped out of the strike at 35–57 and surged to the finish at 34–18. Me and them together, we came on strong. The Diamond Vision promised that for '96, "We'll be back and we'll be better." They were and they weren't, but none of it detracted from '95. Closing Day gave me another win on the final day of 1997, the year the Mets threw off the shackles of endless incompetence and competed for a newfangled Wild Card well into September. I swear on a stack of Official Yearbooks that no World Series celebration could have felt any sweeter than the sensation I got from the unheralded '97 Mets jogging onto the field after beating the Braves and waving at us while we were waving at them, appreciating us while we were appreciating them. We bonded, them and us. Security might have said different if challenged, but there was no barrier between players and fans when that Closing Day ended. We were a team.

On Closing Day 1999, I gasped as Brad Clontz uncorked a bases-loaded, ninth-inning, tie-breaking wild pitch and Melvin Mora duckwalked across home plate as if channeling Chuck Berry. Brad's poor aim and Melvin's quick reflexes meant the Mets would fly to Cincinnati for that rarest of baseball species, a 163rd game. And when they won that, they'd soon be flying home for my first playoff games ever. You'll postpone an ending if that's what a season's continuation will get you.

On Closing Day 2001, I shivered as, in my ears, Gary Cohen tossed the broadcast not to Bob Murphy or Ed Coleman but to

George Bush. The president was announcing the bombing of Afghanistan. Bush finished speaking, Gary was back on the air, Terry Jones was taking strike one from Glendon Rusch. The Mets lost that Sunday, but in the fall of 2001, loss was everywhere.

On Closing Day 2004, almost everybody said goodbye. John Franco's final pitch as a Met was a popup caught by Todd Zeile —usually a corner infielder, but for that afternoon the starting catcher in deference to his impending retirement. Zeile got to do whatever he wanted this day. He homered on his final swing, a real Toddy Ballgame moment. When his next at-bat approached, Art Howe thought to pull him so he could receive one more ovation. Todd turned and shook hands with home plate ump Angel Hernandez before departing. I don't know what was more remarkable: a player—even a retiring player—reaching out and touching an umpire, or Angel Hernandez, Mets pox, not ejecting Zeile. It was Howe's last game as manager, an 8–1 romp, the kind he almost never managed. For good measure, it was the final game in the history of the Montreal Expos, a franchise whose annals began at Shea in 1969 and whose demise was sad enough to elicit a full-throated "O Canada" out of a lot of us. It was the last time the Canadian national anthem would be played at Shea Stadium. It wasn't all *au revoirs*, however; with one half-inning to go, Howe sent Joe Hietpas behind the plate for his only big league appearance. We saw the sun set all over the place, but we also saw Moonlight Graham in the flesh.

On Closing Day 2005, the Mets were rolled by the Rockies, but the rest of us were moved by Mike Piazza. The Piazzazoic Era ended that day. The seventh-inning stretch extended itself as we stood and stood and clapped and clapped for The Man who stood for everything we liked about ourselves as Mets fans. The Mets applauded their teammate. The Rockies applauded their opponent. The umpires took their eyes off the Armitron clock for as long as they could so we could keep going and going. I'd never seen a game stuck in park for reasons that had nothing to do with

rain or records. Technically, we were saluting the expiration of
Mike Piazza's contract.

I loved Closing Day almost without qualification until
September 30, 2007, which was when 7 up with 17 to play
became codified as the most notorious numerical cue in Mets
history since 6/15/77. On that Sunday afternoon, Closing Day
at Shea Stadium ceased to be a well-kept secret. It became a
flashpoint for anger, disappointment, and, in all but one notable
case, devastation. To say I wouldn't look at the New York Mets the
same way again after Tom Glavine came up tiny on the mound
(0.1 IP 7 ER) and in the clubhouse ("I'm not devastated. . . .")
would be both unremarkable and true. Unremarkable because I
never look at the Mets exactly the same way from one season to
the next—after forty seasons of looking at them, it's the nature
of the business to see things differently year after year. True,
maybe *extra* true, because how can you trust a club that collapses
historically on your head while it declares through its deeds and
words that it's not terribly hot and bothered by its massive failure?
I had a real hard time looking the Mets in the eye from the end of
2007 to the middle of 2008.

And by the end of 2008, I wouldn't look at Shea Stadium the
same way ever again . . . though not by choice.

I love endings. Some, however, end happier than others.

Two

TAKING IT PERSONALLY

Back when we came to be, in 1962, my people and I were dubbed the New Breed. I think that's accurate. Clearly we were bred to be fans of the New York Mets. Our post-postwar version of the Metropolitan Experience tells the tale like PBS might amid a pledge drive.

We were born somewhere we've always been too young to remember. *That's us? We lived there? It's so dark and green ... and who's that funny-looking, gnarled-up old man babbling on about 'Metsie! Metsie!'? He's* related *to me? Really?*

When our family moved out from the inner city to that new development featuring easy access to the highway, we were indulged, if not spoiled rotten. Our new room was done up as if from a box from Crayolas—Burnt Sienna, Goldenrod, Sky Blue—and it even came with a giant globe to amuse us should we get bored with our baseball team. The World's Fair folded up its tents, but something much better was installed in its place: a World Series. It gave us an excuse to play on the grass, and nobody yelled at us to get off the lawn.

Our religious training got underway in earnest after we turned ten. Catechism? Haftorah? Try "You Gotta Believe." It was indoctrinated into us before we reached our teens. This principle tenet of our faith remained our bedrock as we grew older and it allowed us to ward off the corresponding cynicism of maturity.

Adolescence was difficult. It always is. Our best friend—our protector from all the bullies in the National League schoolyard—moved to Cincinnati. The neighborhood became too dangerous to hang out in. The cool kids left. We stayed.

While we were away at college, somebody redid our room. What was Dandelion was now Neon Carrot. It looked good. The block had really been spruced up while we were allegedly learning to be adults. This was the happening part of town again. Everybody hung out here. We couldn't wait to move back home.

Gentrification (not to be confused with earlier Gentryfication) didn't take in the long run (though, come to think of it, neither did Gary Gentry). We invested in this place and now we were taking a beating in the market. Once again, nobody wanted to be here except for us.

Our midlife crisis hit hard as we entered our thirties. We were confused and anguished. We wondered about this life we had chosen, this life that had chosen us. Others seemed happy. Others seemed to be working toward a goal. What was our purpose? What were we doing here?

We were doing what we had always done, doing that for which we were bred. We were being Mets fans and our lives were, as ever, eerily paralleling that of the Mets. As our proxies in uniform approached, reached, and trickled into a fifth decade, their performance veered back and forth between manic and depressive, almost exactly mirroring our moods: frustrated until we could be vindicated; redeemed until we would have our hopes cashed in; sure that every year would be *the* year, yet certain that somehow no year was immune to crumbling on contact—promise became an allergy and Shea Stadium a den of ragweed. Those Mets who were getting old with us would fall through the floor only to rise above their missteps and lift us up with them . . . only to slip again and drop us on our noggins.

After which we cried like the babies you might have figured we'd stopped being in 1962.

We're nearly fifty, the Mets and us. We're still waiting on that growth spurt that will certify us as mature and ready to handle real responsibility. Speaking for myself, I don't think it's coming.

* * *

We Mets fans, as a people, were indeed bred for this, for being Mets fans. Yes, we were a New Breed and after nearly a half-century in captivity, I consider us a breed apart from other sports fans, let alone other life forms. Maybe other fans of other teams, other aficionados of other pursuits even, see themselves that way. I wouldn't know about them. I'm a Mets fan. And I know we're different.

For instance, we take everything personally. It's the Metsopotomian way. Our team is ours in a manner more tangible than the law allows. In Green Bay, Wisconsin, the townspeople own the football team. We technically have no piece of the action, but we act as if we do. It goes beyond the banal pronouns that allow us to figuratively lay claim to victory. Sure "we" win. But we lose and we make no ironic bones about it having happened to us. It simply did. Whatever happened, it's our result. We played a role in it as we've been doing since 1962, the first time we propped up our placards at the Polo Grounds and distracted Casey Stengel from the process of losing 120 games.

Do we border on narcissism? Are we, as if honoring the borough where we settled, drama Queens? The answers are probably, and a little. But you have to remember that it was set up for us this way. We had a stadium built for us—specifically for us, the kids who would grow up inside its three walls, with one end left open so we'd always have something to look forward to. The Mets were two years old when we were presented with a playpen of our very own. It wasn't ancient. It wasn't the Polo Grounds.

It was bright and dazzling, colored in blues and oranges and yellows.

Or is that Lindsey Nelson's plaids-on-stripes sports jacket I'm seeing?

We invented Banner Day. The front office institutionalized it but we brought out the laundry markers and enhanced (some mothers might say ruined) the bed sheets. With management's blessing, we took to the warning track once a year to show off what we were doing in the stands, like our role model the Sign Man. We were made-for-TV, a movie of the week. We saw our fellow travelers on Channel 9 and fancied ourselves a part of it all. When we won our first World Series in 1969 and we stormed the field, now *that* was a banner day. We were world champions? That was great. *We got to go on the field? That was Amazin'!*

We did all that before we as a people had reached our eighth birthday. No wonder we grew up to think the Mets were us, that we were the Mets, that everything we do, we do as them and that everything they do . . . the least they can do for us is win us a few ballgames and maybe another World Series or two.

Yes, it is personal with us. We are the Mets fans.

No, actually, we are the Mets.

We look at the script Mets on those uniforms and that's our name. That's us. However it happened, we became Mets a forever ago. We don't get paid. Doesn't even occur to us how much being Mets costs us in dollar terms let alone man and woman hours devoted to this cause we've made our own across each and every one of our lifetimes. We bleed, we sweat, we cry because, c'mon, what else are we gonna do?

We can do everything for our team except hit, hit with power, run, throw, catch, and pitch. So we do what we can. We wear them and we hope them and we yell them and we live them and, in cases like my own, we write them. We do it with only limited promise and no guarantee of success most years. We do it on the slightest chance that every now and then we can call ourselves the champion of something. It's not a dealbreaker when we can't, but it surely serves as a contract extension into perpetuity for us when we do.

It's been this way since 1962 when the Mets started 0–9. It's been this way since 1964 when Shea Stadium opened, the paint barely dry, the same old Mets one-run losers. It's been this way since we were treated at an early age to a miracle and then cusped our teens with a reward almost as generous for doing something as simple as believing. After 1973's absurdly successful pennant chase, the credo of "You Gotta Believe" was ingrained.

OK, we believe. Now what?

Belief only got us so far as the '70s unfolded . . . or, to be overly accurate about it, unraveled. The Mets were already tumbling toward the depths of the NL East by 1977—and that was from a norm of comforting mediocrity whose official score was a well-pitched 2–1 loss. The trade of Tom Seaver shoved us down a whole other chute, straight into irrelevance where the outside world was concerned. We believed we were doing the right thing publicly sticking by our team, but in our own precincts we weren't really buying into them. How could we? Tom was gone. Cleon was gone. Tug was gone. Rusty was gone. Kooz was as good as gone. We had been on a first-name basis with these guys, a nickname basis even.

Now we were getting to know new Mets, bad Mets, unwanted Mets. But we sucked them up and learned to love them. You give us four Reds castoffs for Seaver? They're Mets now, they're ours. You wedge some reluctant third baseman from somewhere else into the middle of our order and tell us he's the answer, we'll answer, at least until we know better, *Welcome to New York, Richie Hebner.* You tell us Lee Mazzilli is Tony Manero in a tight uniform instead of a white suit and we'll succumb to the fever.

Believe, believe, believe . . . believe the Mets won't always finish last; believe the Mets won't always be buried in the greater consciousness, believe that being a Mets fan won't always have to be worn as a badge of honor, loyalty, and what a friend of mine calls Metsochism.

Believe in Magic! New owners come in and inform us The Magic Is Back. We have a hard time remembering it was ever here, but all right, we'll bite. Win a few games in a row and we'll swallow the whole thing. By the time we digest it, we'll realize we've been had, that there's no Magic inherent in Frank Taveras and Mark Bomback, that it's a few years later and we're still last and buried and Metsochists. But we don't stop believing.

And it works! The new owners, it turned out, *did* know what they were doing. They planted a Strawberry on the farm. They graduated a Doctor. They traded for an MVP first baseman, Keith Hernandez, and then a perennial All-Star catcher. *Welcome to New York, Gary Carter.* Oh, that sounds so much better than Richie Hebner.

And it works! Suddenly, you the Mets fan aren't so rare a species any longer. It's 1986 and you're the smart one for having gotten on the front of this bandwagon when it was an abandoned Rambler. You are rewarded for adhering to force of habit. You weren't going to stop being a Mets fan back in '77 and '78 and '79, you weren't going to stop believing, but you don't have to tell anybody that.

And it works! It takes a little nudge, a wild pitch that should have been called a passed ball but really should have been a hit batsman . . . and then a ground ball to first and beyond, but it works like a charm. You, like your team, are a champion. You deserve it, you earned it, you believed.

Then it stops working, because life with the Mets, like life itself, goes on, and life isn't fair. 1986 melts as 1969 did. In a matter of seasons, it's down the tubes again, and 1993 is 1979 reincarnate and here we go once more, except the Mets aren't so much nonentities as a national joke. David Letterman gets a new late night talk show and he has a ready-made punchline to deliver from the West Side of Manhattan: you . . . the Mets. *"Top Ten New York Mets Excuses: Number 10—All those empty seats are distracting."* The Mets? You? Same thing as far as you're concerned. You and your team have melded into one entity. Again you're being asked what's wrong with you. *How could you be a fan of that team?*

And you think, how could I not?

To up the ante where embarrassment and humiliation and low self-esteem are concerned—because it's not enough that you represent to everyone you know an organization whose left fielder tosses firecrackers at little girls in stadium parking lots (get out of New York, Vince Coleman)—a new variable enters the equation in the mid-'90s.

The Yankees! They're awesome again! And you, as a result, suck!

You went through this once, in junior high and high school, your team out, your least favorite team in. Puberty was already filling you with confidence. And now, 1996? These Yankees are castor oil. The media is intent on shoving them down your throat as being good for each and every one of us.

And you think, *I'm not swallowing this.*

Your Mets actually got better soon after 1996. Pretty good at first and then they got very good. Flirted, in their fashion, with greatness. We brought in a new franchise player, a Hernandez/Carter acquisition for the turn of the millennium, Mike Piazza. Mike Piazza took your breath away. Mike Piazza and a cast of well-meaning supporting players pulled off some unbelievable stunts in the late '90s and early '00s, unbelievable even as you kept believing in them.

Nevertheless, you still sucked because you rooted for the Mets and not the Yankees who were just plain better. You could debate issues of moral superiority and which side had a heart as opposed to a résumé, but you always lost the argument on the field, definitively in 2000.

But you persevered. The Yankees wouldn't win World Series forever. Their aura receded, no thanks to the Mets. The Mets of Piazza crested when their fourth pennant didn't come wrapped around a third world championship. The Mets of Piazza, just as the Mets of Seaver after '73 and the Mets of Hernandez after '88, didn't age well. Sort of like you after forty years of this.

By now, you were too old to change, too stubborn to not believe yet too hardened by events to take everything at face value. Your Mets did you in again. Piazza faded. No one took his place as Met of Mets, at least not immediately. There was no reason to believe it would be anything but another long slog to the abyss before our station improved substantially.

Then, somehow, it halted. The horizon cleared and the tarp was lifted. The Mets, who had followed an almost perfectly Biblical pattern of seven-year increments (more or less) of famine and feast throughout their history, gamed the schedule. The lean times ended and an unforeseen period of abundance commenced around 2005. Those who make the decisions that determine whether you will be happy or sad opted to cheer you up. They started seeking talented players from other organizations, paying them handsomely. Better yet, they decided not to trade away their best youngsters. Who knew they even had any?

This should pull us into the present, the new and rich era of unabashed Mets joy, where championships are at last the rule and disappointment is an artifact from the distant past, no more a part of the Met future than Richie Hebner or, for that matter, Shea Stadium.

Ah, but how often does it ever work like that for us? If the '69 Mets could release Ed Charles and the '86 Mets could let Ray Knight walk as a free agent, why should it surprise anyone that the formidable '06 Mets would cut to the chase and dispense with their heart and soul without bothering to capture a World Series first? In the modern-day Mets' case, it wasn't about getting rid of an essential player in a fit of hubris. It was losing the will to win.

Seventh game, ninth inning, tying runs on, your most lavishly compensated superstar at the plate, a called strike three dropping in at his knees—and that wasn't even the contemporary ending that *really* hurt.

Your 2006 Mets went down, not altogether unlike your 1999 and 2000 contenders, in postseason flames. There was something noble about that. It was, after all, October baseball. Carlos Beltran, you could tell yourself, had a finely trained eye. He knew enough to earn $17 million a year for seven years; surely he knew Adam Wainwright's curve wasn't hittable. You could keep telling yourself that. And you could still, 34 years since you first understood you had to believe, believe in your Mets, believe in 2007.

2007, however, kicked you in the groin. By the time 2007 was over—its statistically impressive yet spiritually unconvincing first-place lead hacked to bits across eighteen helpless September days and nights—you were so over these Mets, these sons of Richie Hebner, these check-endorsing clock-watchers, these acute collapsers who lacked the good grace to admit they had sinned in our name. And 2008? A 2007 tribute band. *Not the original, but an incredible facsimile! And the same kick in the same place!* By the time you got to its ending, you could hardly tell the difference.

Nevertheless, 2007 had one thing going for it that its successor didn't. It had next year at Shea Stadium. 2008 had the Closing Day to literally end all Closing Days. A playoff spot lost on the last day of the season you could handle. A playoff spot lost on the last day of the season *twice in a row* you could handle. At least you had practice.

But this? The ending of Shea Stadium itself? The focal point of your very existence cleared to provide parking for a vanity plate of a ballpark? They could run all the propaganda they wanted in advance of the construction of World Class Citi Field. Nothing prepared you for September 28, 2008, the final Closing Day at Shea Stadium.

You didn't know whether or not to believe anymore.

Oh, who am I kidding? You knew you'd believe. You believed after '07. You believed after all the sour endings before it and amid every misstep that preceded them. You were congenitally incapable of not believing. No matter how much you mourned Shea, you couldn't help yourself.

In whatever facility they stick you after 2008, you know you'll end up sticking with the Mets. You're stuck with the Mets.

You wouldn't have it any other way.

THREE

LIFE BEGINS AT CONTENTION

It's a long season, and I don't mean April through September long or even two too many weeks of 2007 and 2008 long. The baseball season . . . a season with the Mets . . . can't be confined to a single pocket schedule and shouldn't be considered limited to a single calendar year. You buy your yearbook (with your full-color team photo suitable for framing), you collect your cards (high numbers and all) and, if you're like me, you write down the result of every game you attend, but you can never quite put a wrap on it. No, the baseball season . . . a season with the Mets . . . goes on forever.

That's my baseball season, anyway, my Mets season. At the risk of simultaneously channeling Casey and Yogi in some kind of cosmic car crash of common sense, my season started when it started because it had to begin somewhere. It hasn't ended yet. It just goes on amid a time-space continuum that would confound Marty McFly. My baseball season doesn't go back to the future because the past never commenced to being the past. It just kept going until the past became the present, before the future and all its FUTURE STARS OF 1978 could come to fruition, before I realized that every bit of Mets baseball I've ever experienced is an ongoing proposition.

Show me a Met highlight—or lowlight—from any of the allegedly discrete campaigns to which I have voluntarily borne witness and I will fall in immediately to whatever year from which I recognize it. Let's say there's a double-play ground ball hit by somebody in the wrong uniform.

If it's Buddy to Boswell to Clendenon, it's 1970 and I'm seven years old. Those are my guys, my Mets. We have to hold off the Cubs and catch the Pirates. LET'S GO METS!

If it's Phillips to Millan to Milner, it's 1975 and I'm twelve. Those are my guys, my Mets. We'll be in a dogfight with Pittsburgh, Philadelphia, and St. Louis. LET'S GO METS!

If it's Taveras to Flynn to Jorgy, it's 1980 and I'm seventeen and likely kidding myself that those guys, my Mets, have any chance in hell of keeping up with the Phillies, the Expos, and so on. LET'S GO METS!

Whatever the season, I am nothing if not in perpetual midseason form.

Point is it keeps going like that. It starts in childhood; I'm barely able to tie my own shoes but I'm completely tied up in the moon launch that will land us on the first world championship in Mets history. It shoots toward adolescence, when for the first time I'm having funny feelings that have nothing to do with Skip Lockwood. It takes me into high school when my social life is broadcast on Channel 9 and then away to college when I run up bills dialing Sports Phone (fast and first!). I graduate into a real world that is real familiar because my first assignment—career be damned—is following the Mets into a real pennant race and a real shot at a second title. I remain committed even as I grow older in the company of Anthony Young. The '86 Mets become, in far less than seven years I'm sure, the '93 Mets and now I'm in my thirties and the Mets are playing like they were when I was born, which was horrendously. But I keep aging and the Mets keep turning until they turn promising again and I turn to them at the turn of the century as I've never turned to them before, and they reward me in every way but completely. Then they go back to losing, then winning, then historically disappointing, and then I don't know what.

I keep aging but I don't start maturing. I just keep watching the Mets.

* * *

If you're a Mets fan, you know me. How could you not? I'm you. Maybe a little older or perhaps younger, probably a bit heavier, no doubt substantively more weighed down by facts, figures and occasionally accursed memory, but I'm essentially you.

That is if you're a Mets fan. 'Cause that's what I am. And that's what I'm here to talk about.

I can talk about being a Mets fan from the moment they open Gate C for batting practice (if, in fact, we still have a Gate C) 'til the tarp covers the field. I can talk about being a Mets fan through an entire homestand and a couple of road trips. I can talk about being a Mets fan when I'm supposed to be talking about or thinking about anything else. I don't know if it's something to brag about; it's just what I do.

I'm you. I'm a Mets fan. What the hell else are we going to talk about? And this is my life, see? There are other aspects to it, but when disconnected from the Mets, few of them are significant to me, really. Don't pity me, however. I like being this guy. Actually, I like being "That Guy." You know . . .

That guy from work who has all that Mets stuff on his desk and who you can't stump on baseball trivia and always remembers who was traded for whom and when.

That guy from down the block who's always going to or coming back from Shea; I swear he must have like ten different Mets jackets.

That guy at that thing who we thought was hard of hearing and wore an amplification device. Turned out it was an earplug for a radio. He was listening to WFAN the whole time.

That guy. The Mets fan. He's the biggest Mets fan I know.

I don't mean to declare myself a bigger Mets fan than you. That would be impolite and unknowable on my part. I'll give you yourself. You wouldn't be doing your job if you didn't think you were the biggest Mets fan you know. But if you exclude yourself, I think you'll find I'm decent Met company.

Yes, I have my share of bobbleheads and *tchotchkes*, enough overpriced licensed Mets crap to pay for at least one of Johan Santana's warmup tosses. I could probably arrange to function an entire day and never go without seeing orange or blue. But it's not my merchandise that makes me a big Mets fan. Other people have more stuff.

And I am pretty good at remembering the obscure Mets and Mets happenings, partly from a memory which I'm told is exceptional (I wouldn't know; it's the only memory I've ever had), partly from my conviction that nothing about the Mets should be considered obscure. But it's not the knowledge that makes me a big Mets fan. Other people know more stuff.

Can't even say it's because I've been to more games than most Mets fans. I've been to a lot, but I've never been a season ticketholder. I do go out of my way to keep up, pitch by pitch, but it's not my commitment to staying current that makes me a big Mets fan. Other people have seen more stuff.

Yet after forty years as "That Guy," I can't believe anyone takes it more personally than me; that anyone embraces it more fervently than me; that anyone gives it more thought than me; that anyone, even after the final loss of 2007 yielded its mass quantities of devastation upon my psyche, was less willing to disavow it than me. I may grow tired of the Mets at the nadirs when they are less than Amazin', but I never tire of being a Mets fan. And I do love to talk about it with other Mets fans, other baseball fans, anybody who'll listen.

If I'm true to my own self, it's my life. It's how I interact with those I care about most, whether it's my family, my friends, my cats sometimes. It's what I do. It was the case when I was six; it's been the case throughout the long season that's been in progress ever since; it's the case right now. I never got the memo that I was supposed to outgrow these Amazin', Amazin', Amazin' Mets.

I guess I'm just easily amazed.

* * *

One of the supreme ironies of my life as a Mets fan is how often I've felt like an outcast from the world at large for choosing a team that has been known to veer from the beaten path—or stumble onto a road paved with beatings. For when the Mets slip from public consciousness and spiral down the competitive staircase toward the too-familiar finished basement of basement finishes, they take you with them. Eventually somebody unsympathetic to your cause finds you there, your hand clutching a transistor radio, your head screwed into a blue cap emblazoned with a curly NY the color of a Cheez Doodle, and the reaction is inevitably some variation of how unusual it is to find a Mets fan anywhere these days.

The irony for me is I wasn't going for iconoclasm when I decided the Mets were for me. I just wanted to be normal. This was supposed to be my ticket to that.

It hasn't been, not often enough.

* * *

Where the hell did I get the idea that being a Mets fan was my way in with the in crowd?

Well, that duck in the *Post*, the one that tracked the Mets' progress in the first season I ever followed, helped clue me in. It was 1969 and if you were going to be in New York and you were going to like baseball, the Mets were the obvious choice.

But why baseball? Neither my father nor my mother nor my older sister gave a damn about it. My fragmentary understanding of how America worked, however, played into baseball's hands. Baseball was our National Pastime. It was very popular with Charlie Brown, for instance, and I knew Charlie Brown was a popular figure in the late 1960s, albeit not within his own Joe Shlabotnik universe. (Joe Shlabotnik was a utility guy only Charlie Brown would make his idol—like I did with Joe Orsulak in the middle of the '90s.) There was an air of normality to something that was popular. If my family didn't like baseball, it meant we weren't terribly normal.

I wanted to be normal. I pulled together the few scraps within arms' reach—my sister's Peanuts compilations and her mysterious collection of 1967 and '68 Topps cards (purchased under peer pressure, I'd learn later)—and familiarized myself with the concept of baseball. Then the *Post* and the duck and *Newsday* and the standings with all its magical talk of magic numbers and these Mets I just met closing in on a division title . . . it was quite alluring.

The Mets weren't good until 1969, which is when I became a fan. Maybe I'm the original frontrunner. Or maybe it's proof that life begins at contention.

* * *

I've got an alternate theory that says my addition onto the active roster of Team Prince when it occurred was no accident. As snugly as I fit into the New Breed demographic, it's too good to be a coincidence. I was born on December 31, 1962. 1962 means I was on Earth for the first time the same year the Mets were, even if it was after their first sorry season was filed away for posterity and hilarity.

Consider that there are typically as many months in human gestation as there are innings in a regulation baseball game. Subtract back from New Year's Eve '62 and account for the fact that for once in my life I arrived for something early. Late December minus nine months, plus the week or two that I'm told I skipped in the womb . . . and you've got a couple that was so excited about National League baseball returning to New York on April 11, 1962, even if it was with an 11–4 loss to the Cardinals in St. Louis, that their passion overwhelmed them and next thing you knew . . .

I wasn't just born to be a Mets fan—I was *conceived* to be a Mets fan!

But that's just a theory.

* * *

It was appropriate, I suppose, that the first baseball number I ever got my head wrapped around was 1, as in LOOK WHO'S NO. 1! That was the message on the Shea scoreboard on September 10, 1969, the night the Mets moved into first place. The papers picked up on it. The standings took on extra prominence. Our local team was going to try to win its division. The second number I got to know was our Magic Number. It reduced every time the Mets won, the Cubs lost, and the duck took it to the bear.

Wednesday night, September 24, 1969. The Mets are going for it. With one win over the Cardinals (which confused me, 'cause I could swear it was the Cubs we had to beat), the Mets would be National League Eastern Division Champions. There's so much information to process. We're in the National League. . . . We're in the Eastern Division. . . . There's a team in Seattle, which is in Washington and in the Western Division, but there's also a team in Washington that's in the Eastern Division; the pencil case with a map of the United States but no District of Columbia on it, the one I take with me to first grade every day, tells me something is seriously wrong. Before my burgeoning grasp of geography confused me anymore, Major League Baseball would move the Pilots and the Senators. And who cared about the American League anyway? I wanted to watch the Mets clinch—another new word—on Channel 9.

We had two TVs, both black and white. One, rather large, was in my parents' bedroom. It was being used for the viewing of *Kraft Music Hall*, Eddy Arnold hosting, on Channel 4. The portable Sony that my doctor-show-crazed sister, Suzan, controlled was dedicated to the premiere of Chad Everett in *Medical Center* on Channel 2. I was left to receive updates from Suzan who relayed them from her friend Iris over the phone.

"Donn Clendenon hit another home run," I was told. "The Mets are winning 5–0." I was so happy, it didn't even bother me I was being blacked out from seeing for myself the securing of the very first playoff spot in New York Mets history.

* * *

When I figured something out, I was anxious to share it. So it was on Saturday afternoon, October 4, 1969, the Mets and Braves on snowy Channel 4 in my parents' bedroom. I came to a conclusion and I rushed into the kitchen to deliver it to Mom and Dad.

"The Mets are playing in Atlanta! Know how I know?"

"How?"

"When the Mets do something, the crowd boos. When the Braves do something, the crowd cheers."

My parents chuckled. It wasn't pointed out that even on our crappy TV there were different shades of gray to indicate a home uniform from a road uniform, or that it was announced in advance where the game was played. It was cute that I took my circuitous path to observation, I guess. The pattern of benign neglect toward me and baseball was in effect.

Nobody stopped me from watching the Mets win the pennant in a three-game sweep. My father even put on the first game of the World Series from Baltimore when he was driving Suzan and me to the new Times Square Store in Oceanside the following Saturday. It was on Long Beach Road, in a 1963 powder-blue Chrysler Newport, approaching the TSS parking lot, where I was definitively introduced to my favorite player on my favorite team, Tom Seaver. He was the starting pitcher for the Mets. I also made the acquaintance of immediate disappointment when Don Buford of the Orioles hit Tom's first pitch for a home run. My dad put on a show of seeming let down for my sake.

It was never explained to me why I wasn't planted in front of one of the TVs at home.

The Miracle Mets came back after losing Game One. They won three straight and could become World Champions on Thursday afternoon, the sixteenth of October, if they could beat Baltimore one more time at Shea Stadium. School would have to take precedence over baseball, of course.

But going to the doctor, in this case a misdiagnosing eye doctor who recommended a procedure I didn't need and wouldn't get, took precedence over school. Somebody saw the need to schedule me an appointment for Thursday morning, a few hours before Game Five. At first I was uncooperative, fighting the eyedrops. Then my father threatened with a cudgel no parent has been able to wield on any Mets fan progeny on any weekday since:

"If you don't let the doctor put in the drops, you can't watch the World Series this afternoon."

My eyes were wide open.

* * *

I took the drops, got home and turned on the TV in Suzan's room (she was in school . . . ha-ha). I don't remember the most famous play of Game Five, that of the shoe polish ball, the one produced by Gil Hodges to prove Cleon Jones had been hit by a pitch on the foot, the one that set up another Clendenon home run, the one that turned the tide. I do distinctly remember Ron Swoboda doubling home Cleon, and Swoboda scoring on an error shortly thereafter in the eighth inning. I thought the double was a home run because I assumed a run and a home run were synonymous. I also thought an inning was called a hitting. I'd straighten out eventually on the niceties. What I understood immediately was that when thousands and thousands of fans stormed the Shea Stadium field, it meant the Mets were World Champions.

My team! We were the best! This was special. This was like when Neil Armstrong walked on the moon during the summer. Everybody had to be watching it. I had no history, no context, no clue beyond a little on-the-fly explanation from Curt Gowdy that the Mets had pulled off the greatest upset in the annals of professional sports, no concept of how far and how fast the Mets had propelled themselves to this pinnacle, no insight into what Miracle Mets meant. I just knew it was great, and that my father, who had gone into work after taking me to the shady eye doctor, would be coming home that night with the *Post*. I'd be looking for my second quack of the day.

And there it was, on the back page: the duck had become a swan.

* * *

The next morning, I'm mustering in front of my friend Scott's house. His mother, someone you might call crunchy in twenty-first century patois, is about to drive him, me, and our mutual neighbor Jeffrey to school. As we're getting in the car, I transmit a news flash.

"Hey—did you know the Mets won the World Series yesterday?"

They did! They did! Wow, I thought, this Mets thing must be huge. I had never had a baseball conversation with anybody outside my apathetic family before, not even with other kids, not even with Jeffrey from the block. The Mets didn't exist only on TV and in the papers. They took place in real life. Maybe Charlie Brown and the gang were onto something. Maybe baseball really was the coin of the realm in terms of relating to people. If Scott's hippie mother knew about the Mets, there was no telling where this thing could lead.

FOUR

TALK ABOUT YOUR CHILDHOOD WISHES

Given my late-summer callup in '69, I guess my rookie status had been used up prior to the 1970 season, but '70 is where the Mets as a habit really kicked in. It was the first baseball season that I was prepared for. It wasn't a cartoon. It wasn't a theory. It was real and it was spectacular.

It was everywhere.

A little piece of me is always watching the Mets in 1970. Somewhere in the back of my mind it is the first time I've entered April looking forward to a full season, the first time I've anxiously watched the standings fluctuate, the first time I'm immersed in percentages and averages, the first time I have a favorite player, the first time I have something to collect, the first time I have something to look forward to every day, the first time I'm teaching myself the game, the first time I have an identity to go alongside my name.

I am seven and a Mets fan. If baseball isn't everything to me, it is pretty darn close. I couldn't say that before 1970, but now I could.

There were lots of best things about 1970 for a seven-year-old Mets fan. For one, there was 1969. We were defending world champions, me and my team. The fact that we had been the Miracle Mets told me there was something askew at work the year before.

I didn't really catch on until I bought my first pack of baseball cards.

1970 was the year of the card, the first year I was buying them on my own with whatever minuscule allowance I received. The first card I pulled out of the first pack that said WORLD CHAMPIONS. At least it's the first one I remember. It was a team picture of the New York Mets. On the back were all kinds of statistics about the team's history. It had our year-by-year record:

1962: 40–120
1963: 51–111
1964: 53–109
1965: 50–112
1966: 66–95
1967: 61–101
1968: 73–89
1969: 100–62

Hmmm . . . seems we weren't too good before 1969. I couldn't even imagine what that was like. Glad I missed it. Forget the back. Look at the front: WORLD CHAMPIONS. It couldn't be denied. We Were No. 1!

Were. This was a new year. We had to win again. I got that. At seven, I was already assuming nothing.

The Mets didn't win in 1970. They were close. They hung around first well into September. I should have been more disappointed than I was. But it was enough, somehow, that they remained relevant. I liked feeling a part of something that was important to a lot of people, which was talked about by a lot of people. I liked that I was moving into "we" territory, as in "we the Mets" and "our team".

William Leggett wasn't kidding in *Sports Illustrated* when he wrote, in the aftermath of the 1969 triumph, that anyone driving past "candy stores, playgrounds, and lots in Queens and Nassau

County" would see "youngsters by the thousands" mimicking Mets: "throwing phantom baseballs and diving to make catches that really could not be made." That was life on Long Island in 1970 when I was seven. We all aspired to be Tom Seaver, we'd all gladly settle to be Tommie Agee. Every catch I had with anybody, I always asked somebody to throw it so I'd have to dive for it.

I discovered quickly I couldn't play sports worth a darn, but I made for a helluva fan. I was a Mets fan and they were what really mattered. They never mattered more than in late June of 1970. School was just out and day camp hadn't yet started. The Mets went to Wrigley Field to play a five-game series against the Cubs. I didn't know you could play a team that many games at once, but I knew they were all important because the Cubs were in first place, three-and-a-half games ahead of the Mets at the time.

The Mets won the first one. Then the second one. Then two more in a doubleheader. That was four wins in a row.

The night after that game, we went to Nathan's. This was Nathan's in Oceanside, the second one the company ever built. This was Nathan's when it had rides and an endless menu. My sister had the fried chicken. She found a wishbone. We each made a wish and pulled a side. I won.

"I know what you wished for," she said.

She was right. I wished that the Mets would sweep the Cubs the next day. It's the first time I can remember subjugating all other concerns to concentrate on the Mets' well-being.

Oh yes—I got what I asked for from that chicken: 8–3, Koosman beating Holtzman. A five-game sweep. My team was in first place and my priorities were straight. Only one of those facts would stand the test of time.

* * *

The Mets continued to be viable as I matriculated through elementary school. With the great Tom Seaver on the mound every fifth day, any team would have a chance, even one that seemed allergic to scoring runs. The data says differently, but I'm sure every game the Mets won before I turned twelve was 2–1 . . . maybe 3–1 if they were feeling frisky. We had great pitching: Seaver and Koosman; Gentry, then Matlack; the mellifluously named Ray Sadecki. We had so much pitching that we could trade Nolan Ryan. The offense was occasionally tinkered with. Big names from elsewhere were shuttled in. Joe Foy was going to help at third base. When he didn't, Bob Aspromonte. Then Jim Fregosi (for, you know, Ryan). Rusty Staub was a big deal when he wasn't hurting. Willie Mays . . . he was Willie Mays, no matter how old. But the Mets were pitching, not hitting. They were good, not great.

But I was used to it quickly. They were never really out of it in the early '70s, winning 83 games for three consecutive post-championship years, finishing third every time. They never really looked capable of another miracle, but I kept recalling 1969, how they were way back of the Cubs in August, how they stormed the Wrigley Bastille, how they got to be No. 1. I figured there was always the chance they could do that again. They kept me hanging on.

They also kept me wanting more of them, wanting a first-hand look-see for myself. I wanted a trip to Shea Stadium more than anything. With parents who weren't interested in baseball, who didn't impede my burgeoning baseball yen but didn't indulge it (whatever I did up in my room was my business), I wasn't getting there despite being the kind of kid who pulled every wishbone with the Mets in mind.

We drove by it once on the way to somewhere else. It was all blue-and-orange speckled on the outside. It was the Emerald City as far as I was concerned. It was so close, yet I could never quite reach it.

* * *

In fourth grade, the spring of '73, we were given a writing assignment: suppose you knew the world was about to end and you had only one day left on Earth. What would you do with it? Assuming "find the button that reverses the fate of the planet" was out, I methodically worked out an itinerary that showed just how limited my worldview really was. I planned to spend the morning listening to my favorite 45s—the Spinners, Gilbert O'Sullivan, Vicki Lawrence—being played over Long Island's own WGBB. For dinner, I would go to Gino's, Long Beach's pizzeria of choice. The afternoon, however, was reserved for a trip all the way to Queens.

2:00 P.M.: Watch the Mets at Shea Stadium.

I showed my agenda to my sister, who scoffed. "One day left? I'd go to Paris or something. You have no imagination."

Was she kidding? I'd been imagining a trip to Shea Stadium for almost four years now. It was the only way I was going to see it.

Pestering was frowned upon in our house, so I tried not to whine. My passive-aggressiveness almost paid off before contemplating the end of the world. My big break was supposed to come on September 23, 1972, a date that is ingrained in my brain because it was a date I heavily anticipated. This would be it. This would be my first trip to Shea Stadium, not a glimpse from the highway, not through the television, but real and for myself. I couldn't wait.

Except I got sick. I got sick a lot as a kid. I was a pretty good judge of the seriousness of my illnesses. I swear whatever I came down with in the middle of September '72 was no worse than the innocent *faux* virus I cooked up so I could stay home and watch Game Five of the 1970 World Series between the Reds and Orioles. But somehow it was taken as serious and I was taken to the doctor. My pediatrician was an Italian lady, Dr. Insolera. Thick accent. Lots of pets in her home/office. Dogs. Cats. Maybe a monkey. Plus a layer of rubbing alcohol. You could smell it all. If I was sick, I couldn't have smelled anything.

Dr. Insolera examined me. Oh yes, she diagnosed, he's sick. He can't go anywhere this weekend. "Hear that?" my mother asked. "It looks like we can't go the Mets game."

I protested mightily. I indicated that I felt fine, that whatever was ailing me now won't be ailing me then, that this was my first Mets game and you're telling me that you're taking the word of the crazy pediatrician with the stinking menagerie over mine?

Yes, that's what I was being told. And when I later suggested I deserved some kind of make-good for my troubles, I was reminded that I already had it pretty good, that I was a spoiled brat, that I should shut up and like it.

I had no problem completing that "imagine the world is ending" assignment. In the days immediately prior to September 23, 1972, I was certain it had.

* * *

Age ten. A Mets fan since age six. Not a single trip to Shea Stadium. We lived one county over. I saw the stands on TV. I sent away for the 1972 yearbook. There were always images of little kids enjoying their day at Shea. Kids who were younger than I was. A whole new generation was coming up and getting into Shea Stadium before me. What the hell was I going to have to do to step right up and literally meet the Mets?

Get someone not related to take me, specifically the good folks at Camp Avnet, a kosher day camp in Long Beach. Odd that I was pawned off on them for the summer of '73 since we were quite the secular family. It was one of the few places where not being Jewish enough was cause for derision from other ten-year-olds.

But this one time at day camp would prove my salvation in one very important spiritual sense, as on Wednesday, July 11,

1973, it got me to Shea Stadium. We had several field trips. This one was to see an actual field.

It was a muggy, murky morning when we gathered outside the Hebrew Academy on Broadway and waited for the magic bus that would whisk us to my dreamed-of destination. I brought my glove. Every camper brought his glove. Marvin, our counselor, told us to return our gloves to our cubbyholes at once. We'd just lose 'em, he said. Marvin got Willie Mays to sign a twenty-dollar bill in Shea's parking lot at the 1964 All-Star Game. Marvin knew what he was talking about.

We didn't bring our gloves to Shea Stadium. Mindful of Marvin, I never would bring mine. Can't say I couldn't take direction.

First thing I wanted when we were guided to the Upper Deck was the Official 1973 New York Mets Yearbook, a beautiful addition to my baseball library, according to Lindsey Nelson. My baseball library to that point was essentially my Official 1972 New York Mets Yearbook. This would be better because I wouldn't be sending away for it. This would be more official because I'd be buying it at Shea Stadium for seventy-five cents. It was a pleasure to make that my first-ever transaction with a roving vendor.

The cover featured every current Met who had ever been an All-Star, eleven of them in total. The Mets resided in last place at the moment, but nearly half our roster had been All-Stars? *Gosh, I had no idea we were this great!* One of the stellar Mets pictured was Jim Fregosi. Each of Fregosi's selections had been from his days as a Los Angeles or California Angel. Jim Fregosi had done nothing remotely starry since becoming a Met in exchange for Nolan Ryan, whose trade I supported because I never thought he'd amount to anything. (I was eight; what was GM Bob Scheffing's excuse?) Fregosi had been, reportedly, an All-Star shortstop in the American League. We were getting him to play third base. Why would we do such a thing?

That very morning, the Mets sold Jim Fregosi to the Texas Rangers. It was announced on that gigantic scoreboard. It was outstanding news. Fregosi had hit .232 in '72, and was hitting .234 in '73. Ryan was proving me and the Mets wrong. Ryan for Fregosi was already a legendarily bad trade. Only problem was my yearbook was instantly out of date. I somehow expected a revised edition to be made available on the spot.

Besides telling you how green the grass was, people allegedly don't remember what happened in their first game. Hogwash. I remember that the Mets got beat. I'd been waiting five seasons to have a result to count as my own because I was hyper-aware of everything the Mets were up to since discovering them. As great as it was to see this place in person . . . as great as it was to see the cover and the contents of the yearbook come to life in the personages of 1968 and '69 All-Star Jerry Koosman starting, Jim McAndrew in relief, Wayne Garrett taking over for good at third (at last), and erstwhile All-Stars Felix Millan, Rusty Staub, Cleon Jones, Bud Harrelson, and Willie Mays himself (playing first), I distinctly recall it being a lousy game. Down 3–0 in the middle of the second . . . 6–1 by the fourth . . . losing 7–1.

And not being able to eat like a normal person. Remember, we were kosher at Camp Avnet. We answered to a higher authority. We couldn't buy a hot dog or, heaven forbid, an ice cream. We were confined to the box lunches with the salami sandwiches brought from Long Beach, packed onto the bus that morning, being broken out sometime after two o'clock. It had been a hot day. It had been a long day. Those salami sandwiches didn't travel well.

I went home from my very first trip to Shea Stadium and threw up. But at least the world didn't end.

FIVE

BELIEVE IT OR ELSE

Of the 414 games I'd attend at Shea Stadium after that first one on July 11, 1973, I came home *literally* nauseous only one other time (may Citi Field engage a different chicken tender supplier than Shea did in 2004). My post-salami episode was a passing thing, meaning I wasn't allergic to Shea. But the Mets, in that summer of '73, were playing rather sickly as a rule.

They were in last when I went to see them, a full dozen games behind the Cubs. Last place was not part of the pact. I could deal with the mediocrity of third place. Sixth was a different story. Sixth took the wind out of the sails I'd been gliding under since I was six, since '69. Last place was for the back of the team card, that dark and unimaginable section of team history for which I had the good sense not to be sentient. One kid and one kid only in my camp group was a Yankees fan. The Yankees, for the first time since I'd been following baseball, were in first place. The Mets, for the first time since I'd been following baseball, were in last place. The Yankees fan was not content to quietly enjoy his team's good fortune and my team's downturn. This was getting personal.

How could a team with ten All-Stars even after the sale of Jim Fregosi be in last place?

Fortunately the Mets picked exactly the right year to summer in sixth. Trusting the Cubs with first place was like leaving Nixon alone with a tape recorder: it wouldn't end well for either of them in 1973. Right around the day of my Mets-Astros game, the chairman of the board of the Mets, M. Donald Grant (benign-looking sort on page four of my yearbook), gave the team a little pep talk. Tug McGraw, instant legend had it, was overly jazzed by it. He spouted his assent: "You gotta believe!" Grant, as suspicious as Nixon at the height of Watergate, was ready to pencil Tug onto his enemies list. The screwballing reliever had to run up to the front office and swear to Mr. Grant that, no, I'm agreeing with you . . . I believe.

And the rest of my life was, at once, laid out before me, forever enhanced and completely skewed.

You probably know that in late August the Mets were still in last but not an interminable last. The Cubs had given way to the Cardinals. The Cardinals lost Bob Gibson to injury. Nobody was playing very well in the NL East. The Mets were only six-and-a-half games out of first on August 30. Right around then, Berra told the papers that it wasn't over until it was over. I read it and got it immediately. It wasn't over because the Mets still had a chance.

The Mets left last place on August 31. With no world-beaters in their way, they methodically stepped over every divisional opponent. Garrett, Jones, Staub . . . everybody was healthy and everybody was hitting. "You Gotta Believe!" was on everybody's lips. Tug was now extinguishing other teams' rallies like a true fireman. Almost every appearance was a win or a save. He was slapping his glove to his thigh and turning on the stadium, turning on the city. I was turned on until I was glowing.

On the night of September 20, a school night, I stayed up and watched the Mets on the little Sony black and white portable TV that landed in my room for keeps once Suzan decided television wasn't her thing. I watched the Mets and Pirates—the Pirates had become the latest to hold the hot potato of first place—battle into the thirteenth inning. Pittsburgh put a runner, the oafish Richie Zisk, on first. With two outs, Dave Augustine hit a long fly ball to left. The Mets' announcers were always very careful about hesitating to declare fly balls home runs (maybe because the Mets hit so few themselves), but this sure looked, even on the tiny Sony, like it would put the Mets behind 5-3.

Yet somehow Augustine's ball did not clear the fence. It bounced off the top of the wall and directly into Cleon Jones' glove. Jones fired a relay to Wayne Garrett. Garrett, reincarnated for one month as Brooks Robinson, threw a perfect peg to rookie catcher Ron Hodges. Richie Zisk, slow and getting slower, was out in a close play at the plate.

The Ball Off the Wall Play it became known as. Like You Gotta Believe! and Yogi's It Ain't Over 'Til It's Over analysis of the race and Willie Mays' Say Goodbye To America farewell address five nights later, it was living Met history. It was the stuff of 1973, of fifth grade. It was fitting rather than miraculous that Ron Hodges drove in John Milner with the winning run in the bottom of the thirteenth. The Mets, in last place three weeks earlier, were, as midnight approached, a half-game from first.

The next morning at the bus stop, somebody's father asked if any of us had seen that great Mets game last night. I did, I volunteered, right to the thrilling end.

"That's awfully late for you to be staying up," he admonished.

Whoa! We're sharing a moment regarding the greatest Met moment since 1969, one this whole season had been building up to, and now you're judging me and my hours? They threw Zisk out at the plate when the ball didn't go for a home run and you have a problem that I saw it?

So why'd ya ask?

* * *

Nobody's record in the National League East was very good, but right there toward the end, the Mets' was the least worst of 'em all. On the final Sunday, thanks to rainouts, makeups, and general mediocrity, the remote possibility existed that five teams—everybody but the Phillies—could tie for first. It didn't quite happen, but the Mets did have to take their improbable journey into Monday and Wrigley Field. Tom Terrific was a little low on stamina, giving up four runs and eleven hits in six-plus innings, but in came the Tugger and, as I got home from school, he was closing out the Cubs. Three almost perfect innings of relief and the Mets were division champs.

The Mets were champs. Wow! I knew it *could* happen because we were constantly fed the backstory of '69, but for it to *actually* happen? On my watch? Without aid of cartoon ducks but because of Seaver and Koosman and Matlack? Because the Mets lived up to the limited promise of all those 83-win seasons by taking the division with 82 wins? By making a prophet of Tug McGraw?

This was, of course, great. It immediately forgave all the shortcomings of the early '70s. It immediately gave me my own miracle, not one whose coattails I'd barely latched onto. It immediately justified the investment I'd made in my fandom, not just now in 1973, but the so-so years before it. It would pay off even more, if possible, in the coming weeks when the Mets blitzed Cincinnati and nearly toppled Oakland. It would give me something to stick in the face of that fourth-place Yankees fan from camp when next I saw him.

It made You Gotta Believe! a rallying cry for the ages.

You'd think that would be a good thing. In its way, it was. I shouldn't have to think twice. We Mets fans love telling each other that You Gotta Believe! The words and the sentiment lived on with the Mets long after Tug McGraw was traded to Philadelphia, well after Tug McGraw passed on. We've resorted to it at every grim interval in our history when it seemed anything of value was at stake.

Can't beat the Cardinals? You Gotta Believe!

Can't beat the Braves? You Gotta Believe!

Can't beat the Yankees? You Gotta Believe!

Every crappy, crummy collapse and calamity that would befall this franchise for decades to come? Looming disasters at the hands of teams that weren't yet gleams in an expansion committee's eye?

Yeah, yeah, I know the drill.

Didn't matter that we didn't always cash in on our belief. The point was the believing. The act of faith was now and forever ours. Tug invented it, we perpetuated it. The Mets were not shy about marketing it. *Believe* was one of the four words they inscribed on the facing of Shea's press level during its final seasons, right up there with *Amazin'*, *Miracle*, and *Magic*. Only one was a verb. Only one was in our hands.

For the next thirty-five seasons, I would Believe in this team no matter how counterintuitive it struck me, no matter how much it would be killing me.

I hadta.

SIX

REPRESSED MEMORY

I've always thought so highly of the way we won in 1973. The National League Championship Series—the playoffs as we called them then—was the culmination of You Gotta Believe! We weren't supposed to hold a candle to the Big Red Machine, but we had pitching and we had momentum. In Game One, Seaver struck out thirteen at Cincinnati but lost 2–1; OK, so we had pitching. But we got the momentum back the next day when Matlack, in one of the least talked about great starts in Mets history, mowed down the Reds 5–0. Jon gave up no hits to Bench, Rose, Morgan, and Perez . . . just two to Andy Kosco. When the series shifted to Shea, it unleashed all kinds of memorable furor. Pete Rose slid obnoxiously hard into Buddy Harrelson, a melee ensued, Pedro Borbon took a bite out of Buzz Capra's cap, the partisans overlooking left field acquainted Rose with the latest in glassware . . . the Mets nearly forfeited from the fan violence/ exuberance, but came away behind Koosman for a 9–2 win.

Talk about memorable: the Mets scored nine runs!

Rose got his revenge the next afternoon, when he homered in the twelfth to hand the Mets their second 2–1 loss of the series. The deciding fifth game had the good fortune to be taking place in the runup to Sukkot, the Jewish festival of the fall harvest; or kind of a Harry Parker among Jewish holidays when compared with the High Holy Days one-two punch of Rosh Hashanah and Yom Kippur. School wasn't closed for Erev Sukkot, but you could be excused if so inclined. It was all right with my mother who decided me, her, and my sister would drive into the city to meet my father.

I brought along my transistor radio and hung on every pitch. We stopped at a McDonald's (some Sukkot observance) where the girl behind the counter asked me for the score. They broke in with news that Spiro Agnew had just resigned the vice presidency of the United States.

"Hey," I told the McDonald's girl. "Agnew resigned!"

"Who cares? What's the Mets' score?"

The Mets' score was 2–2 in the fifth when the Mets decided to make Sukkot the highest, holiest day of them all. They scored a run, loaded the bases and brought up Willie Mays to pinch-hit for Ed Kranepool. *Wouldn't it be something if Willie got ahold of one here?* It would've been. He swung mightily, chopped one way up in the air and, by the time it came down, everybody was safe. The Mets were up 4–2. They'd lead 6–2 by inning's end, 7–2 when Seaver himself scored in the sixth. We were in the city, in a Lamston's—like a Woolworth's—as Seaver ran out of gas with one out in the ninth. As had become habit when there was trouble, Yogi called on Tug. He retired Morgan, then Dan Driessen to end the game.

I ran outside. On the streets of Manhattan, there was yelling and there was paper falling from the skies. Not an inordinate amount of either, but enough. It was a spontaneous ticker-tape parade. The Mets were National League champions. And to all a Happy Sukkot.

* * *

That's usually, give or take Sukkot, how the story of 1973 climaxes. The Mets come from last place at the end of August, tiptoe through the division, win a pennant. At Shea the fans overtook the field (scaring the hue out of the Reds). In the city, it was joyous. All Mets fans were thrilled. Then, as a footnote, the Mets played the A's in the World Series, challenged them mightily for seven games but came up a little short.

I was always comfortable with that version. Losing the second World Series in team history never bothered me. These were the 82–79 Mets who were kind of lucky to have gotten as far as they did. These were the Mets who stuck it to Pete Rose and validated everybody's belief system. Those were the A's in the middle of an honest-to-Catfish dynasty. Taking them to seven games was victory enough.

For thirty-two years, that was my story and I stuck to it. Then something happened that unhinged me. It was too late to change anything about the outcome in 1973, but it sure made it look different in the rear view.

* * *

Interleague play is basically a hodgepodge where the schedule is concerned. We know we play the Yankee six times every year since 1999, and there's usually some pattern to which American League teams you wind up seeing otherwise, but it's always a little surprising when you actually find them in the same game as the Mets. It turned into a shock for me when the Mets flew west from New York in 2005 to play the Oakland Athletics. It was their first time visiting the A's since the 1973 World Series ended. I thought it would be just another Interleague series.

I was wrong. It dredged up a memory so deep and so piercing that I, who am thought by friends to remember *everything*, had practically forgotten it. It took a long look at Oakland Coliseum (or whatever it was called in 2005) and those green A's caps to bring it all back.

The A's put me in therapy that week.

* * *

"So," my therapist asked, "the Mets are in Oakland for the first time since they played them in the World Series. How does that make you feel?"

"Well the games themselves are no bigger a deal than any other games they play."

"No?"

"The Mets eventually play everybody in Interleague. Oakland's the last team they hadn't played, so it seems reasonable that they finally do."

"What was the first game like?"

"I couldn't tell you."

"Oh?"

"I fell asleep. Missed most of it. I know they lost, though."

"How does that make you feel?"

"What do you mean?"

"Well, it's the first Mets-A's game since 1973, since you were ten years old, and you slept through it."

"I was tired."

"Were you?"

"Yes! Is it a crime that I fell asleep rather than watch the Mets lose to the A's? I don't even know who's on the A's. Why do I have to stay up all night and watch us succumb to guys like Bert Campaneris?"

"Bert Campaneris?"

"What about him?"

"You just said you didn't want to stay up all night and watch the Mets lose to Bert Campaneris."

"I did?"

"Yes."

"I meant Bobby Crosby, their shortstop. I don't watch the American League that much."

"So who's Bert Campaneris?"

"He was the shortstop on the '73 A's. Probably deserved the Series MVP instead of Reggie Jackson. And I still don't see what you're getting at."

"It just doesn't seem like you to miss a game like that."

"It's just one game."

"Yes, but you're very meticulous about things like this. You've been careful to buy a ticket to at least one game against every American League opponent who's ever played the Mets at Shea Stadium."

"That's just a thing with me."

"A thing?"

"The first year they had six-packs, the Mets promoted the one I bought as the 'firsts' six-pack: first Interleague game against the Devil Rays, first Interleague game against the Orioles, like that."

"When was that?"

"In 1998."

"So it wasn't the first game against the Orioles, really."

"No, I guess not. 1969 was the first game against the Orioles."

"In the World Series."

"Sure. So?"

"The Mets won that World Series."

"Tell me something I don't know, Doc."

"You've told me you have very happy memories of the 1969 World Series."

"What little I remember of it, yeah. It was wonderful."

"But you haven't told me much about the 1973 World Series."

"What's to tell?"

"Why don't you tell me? If you're old enough to remember 1969 then I assume you can tell me about the 1973 World Series."

"Fine. It's 1973. I'm ten years old. The Mets are in the World Series. I'm very happy."

"Are you?"

"Why shouldn't I be?"

"Why should you be?"

"Because the Mets are in the World Series. What more could a ten-year-old want?"

"You must've enjoyed watching that Series a lot."

"Sure. I guess."

"You guess?"

"To tell you the truth, I'm kind of hazy on the memories."

"Oh?"

"Well, the main thing I remember about the first game is it was in Oakland and that Felix Millan made the error that set up the eventual winning run to score for the A's."

"Did you know that would be the winning run when you saw it?"

"I didn't exactly see it."

"You didn't?"

"No, I went with my parents to Hills in Island Park while the game was going on. We had to go grocery shopping. I remember the store manager announced the score while we were in the produce aisle."

"Your parents took you grocery shopping?"

"Yeah."

"During the World Series?"

"Yeah."

"With the Mets in the World Series?"

"Yeah."

"How did you feel about that?"

"I don't know. It was more than thirty years ago."

"But you were a big Mets fan even then."

"Sure."

"And you weren't allowed to watch it?"

"Well, I wouldn't say I wasn't allowed."

"But your parents didn't think enough of your Mets fandom to let you stay home and watch it?"

"I don't know. When I was a kid, they didn't necessarily take stuff like that into account."

"What else do you remember about the 1973 World Series?"

"The Mets lost that first game. They won the second game. I seem to recall watching it if that makes you feel any better."

"Uh-huh."

"Then the Mets and A's came back to New York to play the middle three. Seaver pitched great, twelve strikeouts in eight innings, but they lost Game Three in extra innings. Then the Mets won the next two. It was really cold at Shea."

"At that point, the Mets were up three games to two over Oakland."

"Yeah. I remember how exciting it was to feel the Mets were just one win away. George Stone."

"What did you just say?"

"One win away."

"After that. You mentioned a George Stone."

"I did?"

"You did. Who's he?"

"Oh, George Stone. He was the Mets' fourth starter that year. He went 12–3. He should've started the sixth game in Oakland."

"He didn't?"

"No. Yogi Berra decided to start Tom Seaver on short rest."

"How did that work out?"

"How do you *think* that worked out? Tom had just struck out twelve in a night game in freezing Shea Stadium on Tuesday night. Now it wasn't even 96 hours later across the country and Yogi was making him take the ball again. Tom had thrown his heart out down the stretch. He'd do anything you asked, but he was used to pitching on four days' rest. It wasn't right."

"So Seaver didn't win Game Six."

"No."

"What about Game Seven?"

"Matlack pitched. He was also going on three days' rest."

"I take it the result was the same."

"More or less. We lost."

"How did you feel watching that."

"It's hard to say."

"Why is it hard to say?"

"Because I didn't really get to watch much of it."

"You didn't?"

"No."

"How come?"

"Well, that weekend, my parents took me and my sister upstate to the Raleigh, a resort in the Catskills. It was the first time we ever went to one of those places as a family. We'd stayed in hotels before, but my mother said this was different because instead of going somewhere else to eat, they served meals in the dining room to everybody staying there all at once and everybody had to dress up."

"Uh-huh."

"Well, I thought that was kind of stupid. I didn't like dressing up then any more than I like dressing up now."

"Uh-huh."

"But my mother made me promise to bring my sport jacket."

"Uh-huh."

"And I didn't."

"You didn't?"

"No."

"Why not?"

"I don't know. I didn't want to. I rarely acted out as a child but this seemed, to my ten-year-old mind, an unreasonable request. We ate dinner all the time and I never had to dress up. The only time I had to put on a jacket and tie was to go to temple. It didn't seem right to have to do it just to eat dinner."

"How did your mother react?"

"Not well. She was pretty mad once we got upstate and I said I'd forgotten to pack it."

"Uh-huh."

"So she told me because I didn't bring the jacket, I couldn't watch the World Series."

"You couldn't watch the World Series?"

"No."

"How did that make you feel?"

"How the *fuck* do you think I felt? This was the Mets, the only thing in the world I really cared about when I was ten years old and they're in the fucking World Series which was a miracle in itself and I can't watch it?"

"What did you do?"

"To be honest, I managed to sneak enough peeks to see what was going on, that Seaver didn't have it, that Matlack didn't have it, that Reggie Jackson and Ken Holtzman and yes, Bert Campaneris, were doing us in."

"So the punishment didn't really take?"

"Not completely, no."

"Yet you still seem upset about it."

"Look, I was a good kid. I'm a good adult, I think. I don't hurt anybody. I don't gratuitously insult anybody I know. I always say please and thank you. All I wanted to do that weekend was watch the Mets beat the A's in Oakland and not have to wear a stupid sport jacket. Is that so bad? Does that make me a bad person?"

"Do you think it does?"

"No!"

"Well, that's good."

"Why is that good?"

"Because you realize you can't be responsible for your ten-year-old self."

"It's a little late for that."

"No it's not. You're obviously carrying around a lot of animosity for your mother from that World Series. You react to the Mets being in Oakland by tuning them out. You miss their first game there since 1973 by falling asleep. And the second game?"

"I didn't watch. Just a couple of peeks."

"So you can barely stand to look at the TV while they're playing their second game there. Seeing the Mets in the Oakland Coliseum—or whatever it's called now—is painful for you."

"That sounds a little dramatic, don't you think?"

"What do you think?"

"I'd say painful is the headaches I get and the chronic indigestion I have and when my cat Bernie died. The Mets playing baseball isn't painful."

"It's not?"

"All right, I stepped into that one. Yes, it can be painful when they lose a big game to the Braves or the Yankees, or something like that."

"But not the 1973 World Series?"

"I was just happy we got that far."

"You were?"

"Yes. The A's were a great team."

"They were?"

"Yes, they were! Look at all the Hall of Famers and the perennial All-Stars they had. They won the World Series the year before and the year after. They were a dynasty."

"Uh-huh."

"But we could've won."

"Could've?"

"Yes, we could've. If damn Yogi had started George Fucking Stone in Game Six, we could've won. Should've won. Because even if he'd lost, Seaver would've been well-rested and he would've beaten the goddamn A's and we would've been World Champions. Instead, in the *Daily News* the next morning, Bill Gallo drew a cartoon that had Yogi changing the letters in the Mets' slogan from YA GOTTA BELIEVE to YA GOTTA BEREAVE. I had never even heard that word before. God, that sucked."

"You seem upset about it."

"I'm not upset."

"Not upset about losing the World Series?"

"We were just lucky to be there."

"Really? It was enough just enough to win the pennant?"

"Winning the pennant was great."

"But was it enough?"

"All these years, I've looked back on 1973 fondly because of Tug and Tom and the comeback from last place and all that. But . . ."

"But?"

"But I think I've been rationalizing."

"What are you rationalizing?"

"When I was six, the Mets won the World Series."

"Uh-huh."

"And it was the greatest feeling in the world."

"Uh-huh."

"And they were still a good team the next few years."

"Uh-huh."

"They just didn't finish first."

"Uh-huh."

"I knew that was part of the deal, that you couldn't win every year."

"Uh-huh."

"But in 1973, we suddenly had this golden opportunity. And it didn't happen."

"What didn't happen?"

"We didn't win the World Series. We could've, but we didn't. We *should've*, but we didn't."

"How does that make you feel?"

"It makes me feel awful!"

"Why?"

"WHY? WHY? Can you imagine how great it would have been to have won the 1973 World Series? Can you imagine how great it would have been to have grown up with two world championships instead of just one fluky one that I barely remember? Can you imagine what might have happened to this franchise if they had beaten the A's? They were there for the fucking taking and we didn't do it! Maybe everything changes after that! Maybe the whole organization doesn't go into the tank! Maybe somehow Tom Seaver doesn't get traded in 1977! Maybe he gets his no-hitter for us! Maybe everything about being a Mets fan in the '70s is better. Maybe we don't suck for years and years and I'm not reduced to remembering Steve Henderson hitting a stupid home run against the Giants in 1980 as my lone happy moment of being a Mets fan in high school. Goddammit!"

"Anything else?"

"Maybe I should've packed my stupid sport jacket."

"Why?"

"Maybe if I had, I would've gotten to have watched the World Series without having to sneak around like a criminal. Maybe . . ."

"Maybe what?"

"Maybe we would've won."

"Do you really think so?"

"I don't know. I'm not a superstitious person, except when it comes to baseball. Honestly, I've never connected any of this before. I just wish the Mets had won the 1973 World Series."

"But they didn't."

"No, they didn't."

SEVEN

THE MEDIOCRITY LAP

You wouldn't call the mid–'70s a golden age for Mets baseball unless you knew what was coming next. The Mets made me believe in the mid–'70s, just enough to tease me into believing they were good. I guess they were. More like "not bad," I suppose. They made all kinds of deals to prop themselves up after standing pat and falling apart in 1974. It was the most exciting offseason I had ever seen. Out with those whom I perceived as old and tired after a 71–91 sag: Ray Sadecki, Duffy Dyer, Ken Boswell, Teddy Martinez, Don Hahn, Dave Schneck, and even the great Believer himself Tug McGraw. I must have taken an unsentimental pill. Or maybe I was just happy the Mets were in the news so much in winter.

The guys they brought in were an upgrade. They had to be: Joe Torre, Jack Heidemann, Gene Clines, Bob Gallagher, Del Unser, John Stearns, Mac Scarce, and, to top it off, Dave Kingman, secured in a cash deal from the Giants. Kingman had hit a legendary home run as a visitor to Shea, which broke the team bus window. I cut Hebrew School to watch Opening Day. Our new slugger homered. Torre, the latest to try his hand at third, singled in the winning run. Seaver beat Carlton and the Phillies 2–1. Maybe that was the day I gave up religion for secular humanism. I know it was the day I believed '75 was going to be better than '73, even better than '69. Who needed miracles when you had Dave Kingman?

Alas, the '75 Mets could have used a few miracles. They wound up inside their typical range: tied for third, with 82 victories. But I was honestly surprised when they didn't win the National League East. I thought they were a juggernaut. Sky King (he hated being called Kong) broke the team record for homers, Rusty became the first Met to drive in a hundred runs, and Felix Millan played every game. But we weren't really much on offense; it was just not a Mets thing. Tom Terrific, on the other hand, earned his third Cy Young. We always pitched. Many of the non-Kingman acquirees didn't work out. Mac Scarce, for example, threw to exactly one batter, gave up a game-winning hit, and made himself . . . well, you know. Torre was old. Stearns showed promise. Unser sizzled for a while. On the downside, Cleon Jones was released and Yogi Berra was fired. For that matter, Casey Stengel and Joan Payson died. My mercenary unsentimentality—*I actually approved of the Tug McGraw trade?*—was coming back to bite me.

But I recall these mediocre Mets with fondness for two overriding reasons:

1) For about ten minutes, they convinced me they were the real thing. Mike Vail, a throw-in to the inconsequential Martinez-for-Heidemann swap, came up from Tidewater in August and hit in 23 straight games. That was a sign. Seaver shut out the Pirates on Labor Day and struck out his 200th batter for the eighth consecutive season. That, too, was a sign. The *Post* ran a headline on its back page after a particularly rousing late-summer win declaring the Mets were THE GUNS OF AUGUST. I'd always had such good luck with the back page of the *Post*.

2) Before it all went south, sour, and sad, before it occurred to me that Mike Vail was far more than 33 games shy of Joe DiMaggio, I was having a great baseball time that summer. It was, at age twelve, my last summer of being largely unaccountable for my actions. It was, in its way, the last summer when the Mets as an institution, as New York's default baseball option, went unchallenged. Doublemint Gum ran a commercial in '75

with a jingle that borrowed the tune of "Let's Do It, Let's Fall in Love"—you know, *birds do it/bees do it*, etc. In the ad, it was "even those crazy fans at Shea do it!" Shea was being sublet by the Yankees while our guys were on road trips, but the crazy fans in that commercial? Mets fans.

The things one holds onto.

While I wormed out of one more go-round at Camp Avnet (they tried to take us to a Yankees game in Queens; I quit in protest), I signed up for Camp Baseball. It took place every morning, afternoon, and evening as I sat with the *Sporting News* and *Baseball Digest* and every relevant paperback I could find at TSS (*Screwball* by Tug McGraw; *How I Would Pitch to Babe Ruth* by Tom Seaver) and my almost-complete set of 660 Topps cards. I would call Sports Phone every ten minutes. Sports Phone—999-1313—was the Internet before there were computers. You called and there'd be sixty seconds of sports news, baseball mostly. Twice a day there would be a Quickie Quiz. It became my goal to win it and get myself interviewed so the other socially selective twelve-year-olds in the New York Metropolitan area could hear me. One night, on the 7:30 quiz, I got through, fast and first as the Sports Phone slogan went, on a question about American League retired numbers. Host Guy LeBow asked me what current great might someday have his number retired. I said Johnny Bench.

"By gum, Greg," Guy responded. "I think you're right."

My parents (presumably before the phone bill arrived) were quite amused that somebody still said "by gum." I was a little disappointed my victory wasn't cause for us all to go out to dinner and celebrate.

The Princes did pack up the 1970 Chrysler Newport one night in early July '75, however, for a family outing to Shea Stadium. It was the first time all four of us went to see the Mets at once. It was also the second time inside a week that I was at Shea . . . unthinkable! But true! Suzan took me to our second annual

Old Timers Day the previous Saturday (a rain delay scared her off in the second inning of the real game, but I can always say I saw Randy Tate strike out Mike Schmidt) and now, Wednesday night, it was a family affair.

Just like normal people!

Maybe not completely like normal people. I don't know why I kept expecting us to materialize into *The Brady Bunch*. I don't even think I wanted that. But maybe for one night, for one Mets game, we could have all enjoyed together what I so adored by my lonesome.

It wasn't to be. Oh, the game was great. Matlack pitched and won. Torre homered, Unser drove in a run, Millan drove in four. Hooray! But what stood out in family lore was who we were sitting behind: a bevy of large men, all from the same firehouse. Men whose guts attested to their taste for Schaefer, the one beer to have while they were having five or six. Men whose guts were being tended to with care as the Mets played the Cubs.

They liked their Schaefer and they liked their hot dogs and they were upset with the member of their party tasked with fetching the franks because not nearly enough mustard had been secured for their picky palates. So one of them got up and returned moments later with the entire mustard dispenser, a big damn thing. Nobody else on the first base side of Loge would be dressing their dogs, but our heroes were roaring with laughter at the ingenuity of the move. Prime examples of how those crazy fans at Shea do it.

My mother observed this blend of bonding and hijinks with the look of a lady who had stepped in bubble gum.

Maybe that's why the spirit of the evening expired when it was over. I was told that I could look forward to receiving a take-home version of the game in the form of a brand new 1975 Mets cap. As we approached a concession stand, I had the temerity to ask for two caps: the Mets model and a red-billed, blue-domed lid bearing the stylish T of the Texas Rangers. I was briefly enamored of the Texas Rangers when I was twelve and couldn't believe their caps were for sale right there in Flushing, so far from Arlington. I was informed by my mother that I was being greedy and now I would get no cap: no Mets, no Rangers, no nothing. The mustard-stealing firemen apparently tested her baseball goodwill beyond its boundaries.

Then we got back to the car and discovered someone had broken off a piece of the antenna from the Newport. It was the last time all four of us went to see the Mets at once.

The things one holds onto.

EIGHT

I ACCEPT YOUR RESIGNATION

I have an idea as to when it was I became the biggest Mets fan anybody knew. When the Mets were chugging along a bit over .500 and capturing lightning in a bottle once or twice, it wasn't hard to find Mets fans, so I didn't stick out. It was when everybody else began scurrying to other quarters and I was left standing proverbially naked amid a sea of pinstriped frontrunners that I was the acknowledged captain of the sinking ship.

Maybe it was the day in the spring of '77—when I was holding tight to my usual prognostication that with a little bit of hitting Seaver, Koosman, and Matlack could pitch us into a real race—that the phone rang and I should have foreseen what my future held for me.

On the line was a friend with whom I hung around a lot in eighth grade. I'd begin to shake loose of him in ninth because of what we spoke about.

"Hello?"

"Hi, Greg. I'm calling to let you know I'm not a Mets fan anymore. I'm a Yankees fan."

"What?"

"Yeah."

He wasn't kidding. Plus he had two of our classmates with him. They, too, were switching loyalties. To make it official, however, they had to resign their commissions as Mets fans.

To me.

* * *

I don't know if other adolescents all over New York were going through the formality of informing the nearest Mets fan they could find that they were breaking ranks, but the effect was the same and the impact was widespread. In about the time it took to peel the orange wrapper off a Reggie! bar, fourteen-year-old Mets fans were giving up on the Mets.

The key to my thinking was if you're a Mets fan, you stay a Mets fan. Actually, I didn't even think it. It required no thinking. What was there to think about? You had a baseball team, you stuck with it. Team wasn't getting any better? Team was, in fact, getting worse? Team made no discernible moves to improve itself in the offseason? Team at long last wilted under the weight of disinterested, retrograde management?

So what? You're a Mets fan. You feasted on the fruits of victory or at least respectability since 1969 and 1973. Is it really beyond your capability to suck on the rinds of defeat for a little while? Maybe longer than a little while?

If it is, then go on. Go jump on that bandwagon if you can ferret out the space. I'll accept your resignation. But when we get good again, don't come crawling back to me to rescind it.

I needn't have worried there'd be a second-thoughts stampede in the direction of us loyalists. The abandonment of the Mets by almost everybody who used to like the Mets was pretty thorough in 1977. Once they were gone, we wouldn't see them for a very long time.

Fine by me.

* * *

For those of us who took the trouble to dig in and stick up for our Metsies in fair-minded forums like junior high school (because burgeoning adolescence isn't challenging enough), the 1977 Mets rewarded us with . . . well, nothing. Nothing, and then some.

Thanks Mr. Grant!

We should have seen it coming. We should have seen it coming when free agency was instituted in the fall of '76 and the Mets, despite shuffling some papers around in the re-entry draft (a process by which even cheapskates could claim to have "drafted" Reggie Jackson), ignored it. Bereft of activist ownership in the wake of Mrs. Payson's death, control of the team had fallen to M. Donald Grant, and M. Donald Grant didn't care for modern contrivances like free agents and salaries and improvements where players were concerned. The Mets' only acquisition heading into the fateful season of 1977 was a chip to place on the right shoulder of their ace, Tom Seaver.

I grew up in the sweet spot of a cynical age. Vietnam wore on. Watergate blew up. There was no innocence to be lost when the pastoral contours of sports crumbled. Players went on strike. Arbitrators declared contracts void. Nothing was keeping your favorites tethered to your team except mutually agreed upon terms. At any moment, somebody could be headed somewhere else. Those great A's clubs, moustaches and all, were picked apart and redistributed because of money. It was the norm.

All of which explained how it didn't seem all that extraordinary when a buzz arose in the spring of '77 that the Mets might trade Tom Seaver.

It didn't make it any less shocking, however.

* * *

Tom Seaver taught me how to pitch. Not that I *could* pitch, but I knew how, thanks to Tom. I knew how to wind up and how to follow through. I knew my right knee had to touch the ground, that it should be a little dirty when I was done shutting out the Pirates and the Cubs. I knew enough to wear number 41 when they stuck me on the mound in tee ball.

I didn't want to be Tom Seaver as much as I wanted to have him nearby. Every book I'd read about him or "by" him related the electrical charge he shot through his teammates by being a professional when they were all a bunch of amateurs by comparison. Buddy Harrelson was always handy for a quote about how the team played better behind Tom. Buddy may have been Tom's roommate, but it wasn't his bias talking. How was it that a team that struggled to remain a couple of lengths over .500 every year managed to support their ace enough to regularly secure him win totals near, at, or above 20? It's because he made them better.

Tom was the star of the game every game he pitched. When he won at home, he'd go on *Kiner's Korner*. In 1975, when Ralph had to tape one show in advance because he was going to be in Cooperstown, his guest was Tom Seaver. Ralph was going into the Hall of Fame that Sunday. Tom would be going into the Hall of Fame someday. Everybody knew it.

And the Mets were thinking about trading him? That was just business as usual in the jaded '70s. It would have been as unnecessary as it should have been unthinkable, except Grant was grappling with the revocation of the reserve clause and the attendant activity that gave players any power over their own fates. Seaver saw compensation on the rise and his employers taking cover. He spoke up. He wanted his share. He would have also liked Gary Matthews or some free agent south of Reggie Jackson to join the Mets. Grant sicced his *Daily News* mouthpiece Dick Young on him, attacking his character, dragging his wife into it. The Franchise and his franchise weren't a good fit anymore.

One day, June 12, you were watching Tom Seaver pitch and win for the Mets from Houston. Three days later, June 15, you were learning all the rumors were true. The Mets were trading Tom Seaver. From the chintzy chairman Grant, who deported Rusty Staub, it was to be expected. From a humanitarian standpoint, it was almost charitable. I wanted Seaver to have runs scored on his behalf, and surely they would do that for him far more in Cincinnati than they had ever done in Queens.

From being a fourteen-year-old Mets fan in 1977 whose favorite player had always been and always would be Tom Seaver, there is still a searing abdominal cramp at the very thought he was traded.

Twenty-two years later, I was in midtown Manhattan on a Saturday afternoon, bushier than I needed to be. I decided to stop in to the first barber shop I saw, a pricey one attached to a hotel as it turned out. It was an unremarkable haircut, but it did the trick. I went to pay the barber and include a tip commensurate to its ritzy location. Scotch-Taped by the cash register was a recent *New York Times* obituary for M. Donald Grant.

"Was he a customer here?" I asked.

"Oh yes," the barber gushed. "What a nice man!"

I should have stiffed him on the tip.

* * *

Seaver's exile hastened the exodus of however many weak-willed Mets fans remained through that season's first third. I was sad and upset to have lost my baseball idol (along with Dave Kingman in what was instantly dubbed the Midnight Massacre), but I really was kind of relieved for Tom that he wouldn't have to be a part of this corpse of a team anymore. What is sometimes forgotten by Mets fans who point to the trade of Tom Seaver as the signal event in the disintegration of the club is they were already incredibly awful before June 15, 1977. The manager, a minor league lifer named Joe Frazier, punched out for good at the end of May, fired after a 15–30 start (with Grant releasing a statement that everything was going to be fine, we won in 1969 and 1973, you know). The Mets had tumbled with a world of speed into irrelevance in New York. The removal of their manager and the dispatching of their star at least won them some car wreck headlines. Once it became old news, nobody talked about the Mets anymore.

Nobody but me and my ilk, that is. As bad as they had become and as bitter as they were making us, we gave ourselves no recourse but to root as hard as possible for them. Because that's what we did. We were Mets fans. We rooted for the Mets.

It required no thinking.

* * *

In the blink it took to watch Tom Seaver tear up before reporters as he cleaned out his Shea locker, unfamiliar faces flooded Flushing. Who, exactly, were Pat Zachry, Doug Flynn, Steve Henderson, and Dan Norman? They were the flotsam the Reds' Bob Howsam pawned off as ransom to rescue Tom Seaver from the swirling waters off Flushing Meadow. Zachry wasn't a nonentity per se. He had been co-Rookie of the Year in the NL a year earlier. Flynn was a vaguely familiar caddy to Joe Morgan on the Machine. Henderson and Norman, it was sworn, were hot prospects held back only by the immovable object of Cincinnati's rock-solid outfield of Foster, Geronimo, and Griffey.

But really, who the hell were Pat Zachry, Doug Flynn, Steve Henderson, and Dan Norman and what were they doing on the New York Mets?

Zachry took Seaver's turns in the rotation if not exactly his spot. Flynn began putting down roots in the middle infield. Norman was sent to Tidewater for seasoning (a lot of seasoning had been spilled in Tidewater but the steaks never seemed to arrive in New York well done). Steve Henderson was a modest success right away. He won his fourth-ever game with an eleventh-inning three-run blast and had his average over .300 for a while. Maybe he would morph into George Foster eventually.

But they were strangers in what, for us, was becoming a strange land. Three Reds were now on our roster. Tom Seaver wasn't. Two Padres, undistinguished reliever Paul Siebert and washed-up utilityman Bobby Valentine, were now Mets. Dave Kingman wasn't. Joel Youngblood, in the most agate-type transaction ever, had also been acquired, from the Cardinals, the night of the Massacre, replacing backup shortstop Mike Phillips. That meant six players to whom no Mets fan had ever given more than passing thought were now our immediate concern. In the middle of June, no less. If we weren't abandoning ship on behalf of Tom Terrific and Sky King and Mike Phillips even, we would have to get to know them and get used to them. On the off chance that the Mets won a home game, we'd have to look forward to maybe seeing one or more of them on *Kiner's Korner*.

Thirty years after the trade that made him a Met, Pat Zachry reflected for the *Daily News* on being Ralph's guest. As honorarium, Pat received Getty Gas gift certificates. He tried to use them to fill his tank at a station near Shea.

"The attendant," Zachry said, "had no idea what they were and he came after me with a ball peen hammer."

To be a Met in New York in 1977 was not to be a prince of the city.

* * *

Pat Zachry's first summer as a New York Met was my first as gainfully employed. I had taken on a *Newsday* route, delivering papers every afternoon and early on Sunday mornings (if not early enough for most of my customers). In addition to tips and some small percentage of the $1.55 a week's subscription cost, we newsboys received points for every new subscriber we signed up. I signed up one: my dad. He took a Monday–Saturday plan, refusing on principle all seven days because he thought *Newsday* was a terrible newspaper. That didn't stop me from receiving the notices telling me the fabulous prizes I could earn by selling more subs. One was tickets to a Mets-Astros game, hyped as the opportunity to see "Met stars Kranepool & Henderson!"

Had it really come to this? Our stars were a rookie who had been here for ten minutes and a pinch-hitter who had never been a star, not even when he was an All-Star in 1965? No denying he was on the cover of that '73 yearbook in the vicinity of Jim Fregosi, but c'mon . . . Ed Kranepool? Our star attraction?

Had it really come to this?

I didn't make it to *Newsday* Carrier Night but I did put my paper route proceeds to good use. All the change I'd been collecting added up. At fourteen, I was responsible enough for something approximating a job. Surely I was responsible enough to, after finding a fill-in, ditch the job, take one afternoon off and go, without any adult supervision, to a Mets game. I had the coin (literally). I had a comfort level with the Long Island Rail Road. I had my mother's permission.

I was going to a Mets game! On my own!

Well, I did have to drag along two Yankee-sympathetic friends, including the one who called me in March to tell me it was over between him and the Mets, but that was all right. Among the three of us, we weren't going to get lost. As the most motivated of our triumvirate, I was in charge of logistics.

I bought my LIRR tickets, they followed. I got on the train, they followed. The conductor saw our destination was Shea Stadium and asked, "Who's pitching today?"

"Craig Swan," I answered.

I'd been waiting all my life for somebody to ask me that.

It wasn't a very good game. Of course it wasn't. It was 1977. But so what? Five short years before, I had only been driven past the Emerald City. Now I was paying my way into Oz. I went for Field Level seats behind third base, not a tough task given the lack of demand that August. I secured, as had been custom since the Camp Avnet trip, my yearbook. It was the revised edition, new manager Joe Torre on the cover. I saw the need to replace my adjustable plastic batting helmet that my idiot Met-resignation friend had broken a few months earlier. I ponied up a ten-spot, handed it to the vendor at the nearest concession stand and walked away satisfied with my three-dollar purchase.

I'd also walked away without seven bucks until the vendor croaked, "Hey, you forgot your change!"

So I wasn't quite ready for prime time that Wednesday afternoon, but that was OK. Neither were these youthful Mets, advertised in *Newsday* with the chicken salad and lemonade come-on, "Bring Your Kids to See Our Kids!" The ad featured the cream of Long Island youth in a team picture formation with "Lee, 22" and "Steve, 24" and other Met kids mixed in with various Michael, 13, and Karen, 12 types. As of August 10, 1977, I no longer had to be brought to see the Mets' kids. I could take myself. No matter how hard the Mets were to take.

NINE

A VERY MAZZILLI THANKSGIVING

As the Mets descended from public view in the late '70s, my family mostly steered clear of what must have looked like, from the safe distance they maintained, my dangerous loner obsession. Not that my mother was beyond a thoughtful gesture now and then. One night in ninth grade she brought home a miniature batting helmet with a slot in the top: a baseball-style piggy bank. She knew I'd like it, she said, because it's blue with an "NY" painted on it.

I didn't know what to say. It was blue. It did have an NY painted on it. Except the blue was navy and the NY was white. My mother gave me a Yankee batting helmet bank.

"Oh . . ." was all the reaction I could muster before muttering my thanks.

She meant well. I couldn't quite conceal my dismay that all these years of second-hand exposure to the Mets had made no impact, but I hadn't survived to nearly fifteen in our house without learning that pointing out my mother's mistakes could be hazardous to my well-being. I quietly dug up some royal blue construction paper, an orange crayon and some Scotch Tape and salvaged it for display purposes. My mother thought she was getting me a trinket representing my favorite team. In actuality she gave me one bearing a logo I associated with mental cruelty.

It was the thought, I reasoned, that counted.

* * *

I had a replica Mets batting helmet on which to base my patch job, the one I bought at Shea during my first unsupervised outing in '77, the one I forgot to get my change from. That vendor was certainly thoughtful. And, in the grand scheme of things, he was something beside that.

During the offseason that followed, my sister was unusually giddy. She had a new boyfriend she was bringing home to meet everybody. Oh, you're gonna love him, she said. Why, he even worked at Shea Stadium!

It was my vendor, there in my living room. You'd think it would be like bumping into Cow-Bell Man on the way into your bathroom, but we recognized each other immediately.

"I usually keep the change," he admitted. "But I must have liked you."

Mark, en route to becoming my brother-in-law, did not ignore baseball and the Mets the way the members of my family did. He openly despised both. But he had a reason I could respect. Working at Shea Stadium, unless you were one of the players, wasn't much fun (and during this period, being a player there wasn't such a picnic either). He had to schlep sodas up steep flights of stairs. He had no good comeback when, lugging a stack of yearbooks, Bob Murphy asked him, "Carrying a stack of yearbooks, huh?" His conscience screwed him out of seven easy bucks of uncollected change.

But Mark did have interests like mine, or at least parallel universe interests. He was into comics and sci-fi. So he intrinsically understood what it was like to be obsessed with matters not universally taken seriously. I'd almost say he respected it, except, no, if it came from Shea Stadium, where he worked to put himself through college and then came home to deflect questions from neighbors who asked "how'd they do?" (queried one too many times, Mark destroyed a glass door in the lobby of his Flushing apartment building: "*THAT'S* how they did!"), that was too much to expect. But he liked me, he liked my sister a lot more, and to impress her, he used his connections from the vendor job he just quit to get us into a Sunday game in June of '78, just after I finished junior high.

It was more than getting to a game, mind you. Mark got us somebody's box seats, inside of third base. And, because he was a mini-legend among his former peers, he took us backstage, like Henry Hill entering the Copa through the kitchen in *Goodfellas*. We saw where all the vendors gathered (they'd "retired" Mark's Harry M. Stevens button), where all the souvenirs were stored. During a lull in the Pirates' 4-0 shutout of the Mets, he led us deep within the Shea storage closet. Everything that had ever been put up for sale or was left over from a promotional date was crammed back there. Go ahead, Mark said, take what you want.

He was serious. I could take whatever I wanted, as much as I could carry out. Mets stuff. Astros stuff. Padres stuff. If I had still had a yen for that Texas Rangers cap, I could have dug it up.

But I froze. I choked. I couldn't fathom that I was offered this kind of access. So I muttered, nah, that's OK, I dunno . . . until I settled on exactly one item that I had no idea existed: a white T-shirt with red letters and numbers indicating CINCINNATI 41 for Tom Seaver in exile.

"You sure that's all you want?"

"Yeah. But thanks."

This was the first episode of Mark going out of his way to "pander" to my Mets thing, and he wasn't going to be stopped short. Later in the day, he and Suzan went back into the supercloset and emerged with a tote bag full of what can best be described as Mets crap. Great Mets crap. Even the tote bag had a Mets logo.

I could handle a little pandering.

* * *

The greatest extent to which I was pandered by my blood relations came over Thanksgiving weekend 1977. Thanksgiving had always had an *I Love Lucy* feel about it in our house. It was wacky! There was, for example, the year I was eight and I had been cleared of my poultry allergy, so my mother decided to make a turkey; because I had been allergic for so many years, she hadn't made one in my lifetime. It wasn't ready until about a quarter to ten that night. Legend has it that we knew it was ready when "the turkey's ass jumped out of the oven."

Oh, Lucy!

The next year, Mom got ambitious and invited over her relatives who had had us over once for a picture-perfect holiday. Frightened to death of another rearguard bird action that would make her look inadequate in the face of her *balabusta* cousin, she ordered the whole spread from a catering place called, more ironically than I realized at the time, the Happy Hostess. She insisted nobody tell these people she hadn't cooked the dinner. I didn't help matters, though I swear I thought I did, by mentioning roughly every five minutes that this turkey you made, Mom, it's delicious!

With such mildly amusing but ultimately self-defeating calamities in our family album, my parents must have gotten it in their heads that the place to be for Thanksgiving '77 was away—away from home, away from cousins. They liked the Catskills and my dad noticed that Kutsher's, one of the then reasonably thriving resorts up there, found space on its Buddy Hackett/Robert Goulet–type marquee to host a sports weekend. I don't suppose they have those anymore. For that matter, I'm not sure they have much of anything in the Catskills anymore, but back then, these hotels would lure New Yorkers an hour-and-change upstate with the chance to meet famous athletes, active and retired. Sports stars were just getting rich. The middle class among them could use a few extra bucks. It was a win-win.

There were no pitchers at Kutsher's, but three baseball players:

> • Elston Howard, the old Yankee, would be there—I didn't care;
> • Ron Swoboda, the old Met, would be there—I cared less than I would today, maybe because Swoboda hadn't been a Met for seven years (hell, he'd been a Yankee at one point), maybe because seven years is half a lifetime when you're fourteen;
> • Lee Mazzilli, the new Met, the center fielder whose rookie season had just ended, would be there.

That I could get really excited about. Actually, I could get excited about the whole idea of being taken to an event that only I among my father, my mother, my sister, and me had interest in; as excited about it then as I am mystified by it now. Why, after such a long period of benign neglect, was my baseball mania being indulged instead of ignored? Was it because I wasn't such a bad kid after all? Was it because I could have been worse? Was it because, despite my extraordinarily disinterested academic performance that fall (my mother received four pink notices informing her that her son was in danger of failing biology, geometry, Spanish, and gym . . . *gym!*), I had just that month brought honor to the family and distraction from my grades by winning the Long Beach Junior High School spelling bee—*Q-U-A-I-L . . . quail*—as a redshirted ninth grader?

Or was it because they meant well and to this day those who are still here mean well?

I had never been in the same room with a baseball player, let alone a Met, unless you count Shea Stadium as a room. Ed

Kranepool came to our class in sixth grade as a surprise (he knew our teacher, somehow) but I had the bad sense to be out sick that day. Virtually all of my face time with the Mets was via TV, most of that on the five-inch black and white Sony that landed in my room. On the Sony, they all looked very small.

The sports forum was held on Friday afternoon in one of the hotel ballrooms. My sister, who had no interest in baseball but nothing else to do, came with me. The three players plus the two-time heavyweight champion (of boxing, not spelling) Floyd Patterson, a greeter of some sort for the hotel and de facto moderator, sat at a table up front and answered questions. Whatever Howard, Swoboda, and Mazzilli said is lost to the mists of time, though I'm confident they all copped to playing hard and living clean. When they were done fulfilling their contractual obligations, we were encouraged to mill about and collect autographs, which I did from all of them, even Howard and Patterson. I don't remember a lot of eye contact. Maybe I should have made some.

As the crowd thinned, I positioned myself to walk out of the ballroom with Swoboda, the hero of Game Four of the 1969 World Series, the Met who drove in the winning run of Game Five, one of the very first specific baseball memories I'd ever recorded. Ditching Suzan for a moment, I asked him if he would mind if I asked him a question. Hands in his pockets and never breaking stride, Swoboda said, sure, go ahead.

"Whatever happened with your comeback?" I asked.

In the spring of '76, Ron Swoboda, who hadn't played since 1973, announced he would attempt to remake the Mets at the ripe, old age of thirty-one. He had been doing sports on Channel 2 and I remember them gamely tracking his return to St. Petersburg. In retrospect, it was almost a template for Chico Escuela's comeback with the Mets as covered by Bill Murray on "Weekend Update."

"I didn't make the team," Swoboda told me much as he might have told me he hadn't seen *Close Encounters* yet.

I thanked him for his answer, he said sure and he kept walking. At the time, it seemed like a perfectly reasonable inquiry, almost clever. Hey, nobody else asked it. Today I can't believe I wasted my one one-to-one Ron Swoboda question on an aborted comeback that was already forgotten a year-and-a-half after it barely happened. Ron Swoboda defined October 1969 and I'm asking him about March 1976. My sister told me it was probably an insensitive question to ask. She didn't know thing one about baseball, but she certainly understood civility.

She also had a better set of eyeballs on her than I did. For not long after parting ways with Swoboda—maybe we hung around the lobby for a little while—Suzan and I got on an elevator. With us were two young guys. It was a month before *Saturday Night Fever* opened, but these fellas looked like they could've been extras in the 2001 Odyssey scenes. They had this strut about them even as they stood waiting for their floor.

As long as I was on an insensitive roll, I made a face to Suzan, maybe a gesture to indicate that I, fourteen and suddenly a card, thought these guys were too cool for their own good. *Heh-heh.* When we got off ahead of them, Suzan shot me this "you idiot" look.

"Didn't you recognize him?"

"Recognize who?"

She had to spell it out for me, the spelling bee champ. "*That was Lee Mazzilli!*"

Boy was I embarrassed. That and a little concerned that I was going to need glasses one of these days. Wasn't I just in a room with that guy? No, the Sony really didn't do him justice. Funny, I recognized Swoboda, but he did the sports on Channel 2. . . .

Hold it—I was on an elevator with the Mets' center fielder and *made fun of him?* Pantomimed and mocked him? First Ron Swoboda finds me insensitive and now I can't find Lee Mazzilli in an elevator? Sure, I thought it was dopey that Joe Torre sat him down on the last day of the season to protect his .250 average, and that basket-catch bit of his made me nervous, but he was a Met. He was Lee Mazzilli—young, good-looking, a ballplayer in a hotel. Why shouldn't he strut?

Given my keen powers of observation, for all I know the other guy in the elevator was Doug Flynn.

Oy, as they say in the Catskills. We went back to the room and told Mom and Dad what had happened. Dad was amused. Mom said I shouldn't feel too bad—Lee Mazzilli must have recognized my discomfort with the situation. I'm pretty sure Mazz and his bud didn't notice me at all. If they were what I thought they were, they were probably checking out my twenty-year-old sister.

Dinnertime approached. In a place like Kutsher's, everybody ate (and ate voraciously) during the same two-hour window. Meals were on the American plan, which meant your meals were included. Most Catskills vacationers rushed the dining room as soon as it opened for breakfast, lunch, or dinner, killing time between sittings by sitting and noshing in the coffee shop. We, however, were European in our approach to dinner. Our internal clock was set to eat later than most, thus the place was fairly well-packed as we were shown to our table.

And whose table should we pass by? That of Brooklyn's own Lee Mazzilli and his disco dude pal. No doubt he had been recognized by fans more sharp-eyed than me and greeted by dozens of guests since he sat down. But only my mother, upon learning who that young man sitting over there was, felt compelled to tell him, "He's sorry. He didn't recognize you."

Mazzilli nodded, smiled, and proffered a half-wave of the hand. (I don't remember which hand—he was a switch-hitter.) Lee Mazzilli was polite enough to not ask, "Who's sorry? Who didn't recognize me? Who the hell are you?"

We were seated. Directly, a waitress came over with a bottle of champagne. She'd be back to open it in a moment, she said.

Champagne? We ordered no champagne. There was only one logical explanation for this, my mother divined. Lee Mazzilli, having seen my fallen face moments ago, felt so bad about my embarrassment that he wanted to show us there were no hard feelings over my mugging and smirking and failure to acknowledge him (first I failed gym, now Mazz). Thus, as any twenty-two-year-old professional athlete would do on his off time, according to this hastily concocted storyline Mom fervently believed, Lee Mazzilli, the center fielder for the New York Mets, sent our family a goodwill gesture. Yes, that was it! Obviously. My mother waved to him again to thank him. A bewildered Mazzilli waved back.

The waitress quickly reappeared and grabbed the bottle. "Sorry. Wrong table."

So it turned out Lee Mazzilli didn't send us or probably anyone else champagne on Thanksgiving weekend 1977. So it turned out Lee Mazzilli *emphatically* didn't notice me not noticing him in the elevator. So it turned out that me and my family and my team never quite meshed as a unit no matter how well we all meant.

But that's all right. At least no turkeys' asses were harmed in the telling of this story.

TEN

LIKE MAGIC

June 14, 1980. Just to look at that date is to see fulfillment. On June 14, 1980, for one phenomenal Saturday night, the Mets, who had resided somewhere south of sea level for almost three years—20,000 leagues under the NL East—rose up and touched the sun.

That's what it felt like anyway.

It had been coming. The 1980 Mets had been increasingly less embarrassing for about a month, which was the era's equivalent of being on a thirty-day winning streak. That season started badly as most of those seasons did. In a way, it was worse. New ownership was trying to pump up an old product and resorted to sloganeering instead of, I don't know, signing free agents. Their chosen motto: The Magic Is Back.

The Mets, coming off a 63–99 disaster, began the Magic era by going 9–18. Thanks to a transit strike, attendance at Shea was almost nonexistent. It cratered on April 16 when a kaffeeklatsch of 2,052—briefly an all-time low—gathered at Shea for an afternoon date against the Expos. Never mind that the Mets won. Never mind that I anxiously followed every pitch by transistor radio en route to some afterschool project. The Mets were setting new records for apathy. The back page of the *Post*, featuring section upon section of unoccupied seating, referred to Shea Stadium as THE MAGIC GARDEN.

The Magic Is Back was intended to let the mass of New Yorkers who weren't automatically plugged into WMCA's broadcasts and who didn't compose the band of brothers who made up 1979's Shea Stadium attendance (all 788,905 of us) that National League baseball in the city was back. If not returned to its Giants, Dodgers, and 1969 Mets glory, then, well, at least help might finally be on its way . . . eventually. The new ownership group, helmed by Nelson Doubleday and Fred Wilpon, was the first good sign. They replaced Mrs. Payson's daughter, Lorinda de Roulet. Mrs. de Roulet let her daughters talk somebody into letting a mule roam foul territory before games. The mule's name was Mettle.

It was supposed to be precious.

The mule took a hike after '79. So did Richie Hebner, the most outspoken of those Mets who didn't want to be Mets. (THE HEBNER IS GONE would have been a pretty triumphant slogan.) Doubleday and Wilpon hired a new GM, Frank Cashen, who had built the old Baltimore dynasty. Then they hired an ad agency to conjure the bit about the Magic. Then, like true Mets fans, they hoped for the best and that people would stop laughing at them.

What was to laugh at? I wondered. I had grown so accustomed to Mazzilli, Stearns, Henderson, Flynn, Youngblood, Swan, and Zachry that I thought Our Kids were good kids. Fans like me looked past Frank Taveras's deficiencies at shortstop (he was disinterested in playing it) and reveled instead in his speed and occasional flurry of base hits. Tom Hausman, I noted, was quite the middle reliever, and when you combine his skills with those of young Neil Allen and Jeff Reardon, that's quite a bullpen. Mark "Boom Boom" Bomback . . . John Pacella and his uncooperative cap . . . obviously we could pitch. We could always pitch.

As eleventh grade wound down, reality ever so briefly came to match my fantasies. The Mets began to win games. Then they began to win series. They were beating some good teams. Took three out of four from the defending champion Pirates. On the eve of the Regents exams, the big shot Dodgers came to Shea and we swept 'em. Mike Jorgensen ended one of those games with a grand slam in the tenth inning. Instead of being a lousy last-place team, we were now an almost decent fourth-place team. The sweep of L.A. put us one game below .500. Get to .500, I figured, the next thing to happen would be we'd be over .500 . . . a winning record . . . a winning team. As it was, we were only six out in the second week of June. Get a little momentum going and who knew?

The Magic was Back, I'd read somewhere.

* * *

Saturday night, June 14, 1980 did not begin auspiciously. The Giants were the opponent and they jumped all over Pete Falcone, the lefty from Brooklyn who was said to suffer from concentration problems. I always wondered what could distract a major league starter during a baseball game, but whatever it was, Falcone was gone from the Shea mound by the second inning, the Mets down 5–0. John Montefusco, concentration complete, took care of the Mets with little fuss, no-hitting them for five innings. San Francisco added another run off Bomback in the fifth. It was 6–0. It was not going to be a Magic night.

Except Claudell Washington, the first new Met brought in by the new regime, lifted a sac fly to make it 6–1 in the bottom of the sixth.

Except three eighth-inning singles, the last of them of the infield variety by Steve Henderson, made it 6–2.

Except in the bottom of the ninth, with two out and Doug Flynn on second, Mazzilli singled him home to make it 6–3.

Except that after a walk to Taveras, Washington—so new that he didn't yet have his name stitched on the back of his uniform—drove in Mazz to make it 6–4.

Except that Henderson was coming up with two on.

The Giants replaced reliever Greg Minton with Allen Ripley. And Ripley threw a pitch to Henderson. And Henderson swung.

It flew to right field. It kept flying. It flew over the fence, into the Mets bullpen, caught by Tom Hausman.

The Mets won 7–6.

THE METS WON 7–6!

THEY NEVER DO THAT!

I have since learned that the Mets had, before June 14, 1980, come from behind and won ballgames on home runs in their final at-bat. It was unusual behavior, but it wasn't unprecedented. But I swear at the moment Hausman caught that ball—he and I leaped in the air at the same time—I assumed this had never happened before. It couldn't have. My Mets? My Mets come from six runs down? My Mets rally for five in the ninth? My Mets winning on a home run? Any Met hitting a home run? The *Daily News* was having a good laugh already that season tracking the Mets' progress versus Roger Maris from 1961. As a team they were barely keeping pace with his record-setting home run output (the Mets, like Maris, would finish with 61). Things had been looking up in June. We had beaten the Pirates. We had swept the Dodgers. But to do *this*? To be out of it and *win*? To watch Steve Henderson circle the bases, be surrounded by his teammates, be demanded back on the field by the fans for what Bob Murphy called an encore?

I only stopped jumping up and down so I could run from my parents' bedroom where I was watching on the color TV (they were out) to tell Suzan and Mark, breathlessly, about the greatest ending to a Mets game that I had ever seen.

Mark, total deadpan: "Who cares?"

I did.

* * *

I was seventeen that summer. Like Janis Ian, I learned the truth at seventeen.

I learned that advertising slogans are come-ons, not guarantees. I learned that a few dozen wins in the middle of summer does not mean a pennant is in the offing. I learned that every promising story doesn't have a happy ending, just an ending. I learned that the magic isn't back just because somebody says it is.

And I learned that a baseball team isn't all it seems at seventeen.

Ah, but there was a fleeting moment when I was seventeen when I hadn't learned any of that. I was happier when I was that much more ignorant. For a summer, I basked in the momentary sunshine of being three-and-a-half behind and thinking my team was going somewhere.

It did—right back to fifth place when all was said and done. But somehow I'm not fazed by that or by the 95 losses that piled up at year's end or the eventual likelihood that when my team got good, pretty much nobody from that magic summer would have anything to do with it.

I still don't care. I was in love with the 1980 Mets. They weren't the first Mets team I was ever hung up on, but I think, given where I was in life, that they were my first love. I didn't date or anything like that in high school, so that description may be apt, as apt as it is sad. When I was ten, I learned that You Gotta Believe! At seventeen, I was infatuated beyond belief.

Once that summer got going, I don't think it ever occurred to me that this team wasn't a contender. I don't think I ever saw a reason it couldn't win. Manager Joe Torre was a genius. Doug Flynn was a Gold Glove second baseman in the making. Tom Hausman was my candidate for Cy Young.

Cy Young? *I* was young. I was old enough to know better but chose not to. I had already learned far too much in the previous three years that I was dying to forget. 1980 and its mere hint of success would cleanse me and it would consign me. It would shove me up to the next level of fandom, just as Mike Vail teasing me with that hitting streak in '75 did, just as Jerry Koosman making my wish come true in '70 did. It was like every five years something happened to me.

It was like magic.

ELEVEN

WIRED

No way could it have been as much fun to have been in on the most successful period in Mets history without having persevered to the very bottom of the pit that preceded it. How anybody could relish 1984 to 1990 without having experienced every single indignity that transpired between 1977 and 1983 eludes me. Maybe some people prefer shortcuts. But the seven years of veritable feast wouldn't have been as filling if it weren't making up for all that famine.

It is a badge of honor for fans to claim they are "long suffering." Few actually want to engage in the heavy lifting the suffering entails. My shoulders still act up from hauling 1977–1983 around. But the delight I feel elsewhere on my person from the seasons that emerged from their morass wouldn't be nearly as tangible without it.

Here's to the losers. Here's to them leaving.

* * *

My alma mater, the University of South Florida, in Tampa, required one summer semester out of every student. It paid for the air conditioning, I guess. I chose May, June, and half of July between my junior and senior years to get it done. The Mets chose that precise interval to stop being losers and start being contenders. They were welcome to start doing that at their convenience, natch, but I wish they had told me in advance so I could have arranged my academic calendar a little better. I sure would have liked to have seen the birth of what appeared to be a shining new era.

I had hung in with the Mets from a distance every September and every April during the denouement of their lengthy fallow period. I got the summers in New York to fully comprehend how they had not improved. And I had my spring cameos in nearby St. Petersburg. In March 1984, that meant a sneak peek at a local youngster named Dwight Gooden. Word had it the kid from Tampa threw very hard and rather precisely. What I saw at Al Lang Stadium one Sunday afternoon convinced me he could make our rotation. The new manager, Davey Johnson, agreed. Gooden, along with Ron Darling and Walt Terrell (heretofore, the Texas strangers we had received for trading Lee Mazzilli), anchored a newly constructed pitching staff. Tom Seaver's triumphant 1983 homecoming had been erased by a clerical blunder that sent him to the White Sox for no apparent reason, but Keith Hernandez was installed at first. Darryl Strawberry, a Rookie of the Year award in his enormous back pocket, manned right. Mookie Wilson was a fixture in center, Hubie Brooks at third, Wally Backman was getting a shot at second, Jose Oquendo—the first Met born after me—at short . . . even George Foster had begun to look alive.

How bad could we be?

I wasn't a good manager of time then. I'd at last joined the school's daily paper, the *Oracle*, in May and was put to work as Board of Regents correspondent. There were road trips to Tallahassee, several hours each way. There was an American Lit class that met four times weekly. There were four classic novels that had to be read by mid-June—and I really detested having to read fiction when there were authentic box scores demanding my attention. There were term papers due in the blink of an eye. There was a lot going on. There wasn't much sleep. And there were the Mets climbing through the National League East, challenging the old order, the Phillies; and the *nouveau riche*, the Cubs who had restocked on the fly, for first place.

Something had to give and it wasn't going to be the Mets, winning more than they were losing for the first time since I was starting eighth grade.

Instead, it would be sleep.

* * *

The requirement was for nine (9) hours of academic credit. So why was I up for fifty-four (54) of fifty-seven (57) consecutive hours on June 19, June 20, and June 21? Blame it on a near-lethal cocktail of chronic dishevelment, youthful hubris, and *Winesburg, Ohio*, the book for which I owed a term paper of the big-ass variety but hadn't, as of June 18, actually gone to the library to research. I also had to read *The Great Gatsby*, cover to cover, before I could sleep. There seemed to be a final that demanded it. I also had to tend to my job at the college daily, where I could have written the headline on my own obit:

AS JUNIOR EXPIRES FROM EXHAUSTION,
STRAW CLOCKS CARLTON FOR 3-RUN HR

It's how I would have wanted to have gone out.

At twenty-one, I wasn't as young as I used to be (the previous November, I pulled off 68 hours awake in a 75-hour span, but I was only twenty back then), so I needed a little somethin'-somethin' to stay up. My booster of choice was NoDoz, something I was using only once—I swear!—not to gain an edge, but to recover from sleepiness. Even that little foray into perfectly legal over-the-counter drug use made me feel like a dirtbag. I skulked into a 24-hour Eckerd Drug in the middle of the night Tuesday—or was it Wednesday?—to buy my first fix. I had to ask a kindly old pharmacist out of central casting where he kept it. I felt like such a lowlife purchasing it, but I swallowed however many I needed to properly analyze Sherwood Anderson.

NoDoz turned my insides into a giant piece of cardboard, the kind you might get with your shirts if your dry cleaner boxes them. Forget about NoDoz being habit-forming. I couldn't stand it. Nevertheless, I remained awake . . . widely so.

Fueled by performance-enhancing substances, I got the book read, got the research done, got the paper written, and got to the Arts & Letters building in time for the final. I even managed to stagger into the elevator and out onto the third floor. Just before the test, I stopped in the ladies room.

That's not a typo. I had to go to the bathroom, so I went into the first one I saw, the one closest to the elevator. At the very moment I wondered who let the urinals out, a woman in the hall barked at me: "Hey! You can't go in there!" Hey, I just figured that out. My brain snapped out of its seven-second delay and back into real time. I did a U-turn, put my head down, found the right facility and, feeling relieved, went to class. Apparently I passed the final. I'm pretty sure I avoided that third floor my entire senior year, lest I see that barking lady again.

* * *

You'd think after being up for almost two-and-a-half straight days that all I'd want to do was drop into bed. And that's all I did want to do. Except that on this Thursday afternoon, at whatever time it was, I had one piece of business remaining.

I had to find out how the Mets were doing.

They were at Shea, without me, trying to attain first place. I may have been delirious from lack of sleep, but I was clearheaded enough to lunge not for my bed, but for my phone. For Sports Phone. (516) 976-1313. The Mets had entered the day a half-game behind Philadelphia. It was too dreamlike to imagine where they'd be if they won.

Sports Phone sent my head into the clouds. Within sixty seconds, the voice on the other end was telling me it had been 7–7 in the seventh when Rusty Staub, our beloved Rusty Staub who was the Met right fielder the night the Mets went into first for the first time in 1973, lashed a pinch-single to plate Hubie Brooks. George Foster then scored on an infield out. *9–7 Mets.* One inning later, Ron Hodges—the hero of that very same nearly first first-place night in '73 when he clutched the ball that had struck the top of the wall in the top of the thirteenth and drove another ball into the outfield for the win in the bottom of the thirteenth—walked with the bases loaded. *10–7 Mets.* Three reliable Doug Sisk outs later, the score was a final. Like Sports Phone, the Mets were fast and first. *First-place Mets.*

FIRST-PLACE METS!
FIRST-PLACE METS!
FIRST-PLACE METS!

On the afternoon of June 21, the last day of American Lit and the first day of summer, the New York Mets, last-place team last year and five of the last seven years, moved into first place.

The Mets were in first place! The Mets were in first place! It was really happening. It wasn't just a rumor. I wasn't just rooting for a lousy team for the rest of my life. I didn't need NoDoz to stay up a few more hours into the evening to enjoy the sensation. My roommate, also named Greg, also from Long Island, and, yes, also a Mets fan (whoever made the housing assignments must have thought it would cut down on confusion) came back from wherever he'd been and I told him. Joyousness swept the room from the window to the door.

And then—if you'll excuse the latter-day colloquialism—I collapsed.

* * *

Refreshed on Friday morning, I went to Home Town News and bought the thin but essential national edition of the *Daily News*. There was a back page headline blaring METS MOVE INTO 1ST. This was no first-place 1–0 after Opening Day gag where the papers would run a ha-ha METS IN FIRST headline either. This was 36–27, the real thing. I clipped the headline and taped it to my dorm room wall (just as I used to clip and save those early April versions that mocked me but were better than nothing). I ran back to Home Town News on Saturday for Friday's *Post*, two pre-Internet days after the fact, so I could read Dick Young write about how the Mets, Cubs, and Phillies were "playing footsie with first place." Percentage points might be needed to clarify the standings, but for the balance of the next week, our toes rested on top of theirs.

It was true. We were in a pennant race. The genuine article. The Real McGraw. On the first day of summer, the whole world knew our name.

I just had to get out of Tampa and back to Shea Stadium. I just had to.

* * *

When I returned to Shea on a Tuesday night in July 1984, everything was different. It was still Shea, and there were my high school buddies Joel and Larry with me. The Mets were there. But it was way different from what I'd remembered.

First, there were people, loads of them. We had to stand in a long ticket line and we could purchase only Upper Deck accommodations. Quite a departure from Bob Murphy's news flash that plenty of good seats were still available, come on by if you're in the area.

There was also lots of offense. The Mets kept scoring, and so did the Cardinals. But there was something else on the premises that had been missing as long as I had been a Mets fan: supreme confidence. It did not discourage us when the Cardinals briefly pulled ahead. We were so giddy with the rarefied air of first place that we even got sucked into doing the wave.

It took ten innings. It took Keith Hernandez stepping up for the fourth time in the game with a runner in scoring position and, for the fourth time, driving him home. Keith (or Mex, as we had begun calling him) singled off his trade partner Neil Allen and Mookie scored and the Mets did something they had never done with me in attendance.

They increased their first-place lead.

Something else was new and different: elation. Pure, unbridled, unconditional elation. Not qualified hope, not divining some good from mostly bad, not thinking that we were a couple of players away. We had Keith Hernandez. He was the player away that other teams now were. We were in first place and there was elation on the Shea Stadium ramps as Joel and Larry and I descended. First everybody chanted "WE'RE NUMBER ONE! WE'RE NUMBER ONE!" to reiterate the obvious as regarded our standing in the National League East. Then, as if throwing off the shackles of seven years of obscurity and oppression, the chant switched to "STEINBRENNER SUCKS! STEINBRENNER SUCKS!" Interleague play didn't exist in 1984, nor, as far the eye could see, did Yankees fans. This was a Mets night. This was a Mets town.

Twelve

ADULT EDUCATION

My mother the card. She could tell some real gut-busters. Like the time I gave blood in high school without her prior knowledge. I was eighteen and didn't need parental consent. She accused me, quite loudly, of "selling my blood" to some minority group or another. When I pointed out there are benefits to the families of blood donors in case of an emergency, she added I was trying to kill her.

What a comedian!

Oh, and then there was college. I mentioned I'd be going to class on Rosh Hashanah, which was not widely observed where I was (and something I didn't observe for myself). Although this information was delivered by phone and not shiv, Mom told me a month later, "My back has hurt ever since you said you weren't going to *shul*." My words could cause back pain?

She was hilarious!

One more. I met my first girlfriend during my freshman year and was fairly enthused about it. When my mother saw a picture and divined her ethnicity . . . what was that phrase she used? I'd rather not repeat it here in presumably polite company, but it was some of her best material.

The original funnywoman, my mother!

You can keep your Totie Fields, your Phyllis Diller, your Roseanne Barr. I had my mother. And my mother was a scream.

I heard the word "insane" thrown around quite a bit when I was little. It was years before I discovered there was a corresponding word. "Sane" didn't come up a lot around our house.

"Your mother has free-floating anxieties that tend to put everybody on the edge of hysteria," my father once (and only once) acknowledged after another of her sky-is-falling, you're-killing-me tantrums.

My mother made it difficult for me to ride out the normal contours of a first relationship. When I was diagnosed with mononucleosis and attendant hepatitis over Christmas break of my sophomore year at my parents' condo near Fort Lauderdale, my girlfriend of apparently offending descent offered to come over and visit from Miami. *Uh, that's not such a good idea*, I uncomfortably mumbled, feeling not just jaundiced but like a jerk. Though my mother was always concerned for my physical well-being—after giving me hell about the blood, she brought me home some cookies to help replenish my insides—she seemed to take delight in noting the hepatitis made me ineligible for future blood donations.

Boy, did those anxieties float in some strange directions.

* * *

That's whose roof I was strongly invited to live under starting in May 1985. I was moving back home to Long Beach with my parents after college. I could have been a lot more proactive about building a sustainable career, about being on my own, but that would have taken effort, and my efforts were clearly directed against one goal: watching the Mets.

So I decided to take both the easy and hard way. Easy enough to go home, hard enough to live with my mother . . . except for one detail that kind of snuck up on me. Sometime during the renaissance of 1984, my parents had become Mets fans.

They had never been Mets fans! They had never been baseball fans! Maybe when they were kids, for the Dodgers, but not as far as I could see. I was the outcast, the oddball, even in my own family. It was one against three, my sister unable to tell third base from first (she once took pictures of the grounds crew thinking they were the players) and my parents, who avoided almost all contact with the game I loved.

We didn't speak the same language where baseball was concerned. For example, I wasn't in the habit of lying to my mother, but I was left with no choice in April of 1976. We were in the car (its radio reception not quite what it was before the antenna was screwed with in the Roosevelt Avenue parking lot) en route to some afterschool shopping trip at good ol' TSS when she asked me to promise that until school was out in late June that I wouldn't be distracted by the Mets, my grades already falling far from their elementary school standard of excellence to their new junior high marks of indifference. The level of distraction available to me was essentially watching games on TV and reading about them the next day and maybe calling Sports Phone to fill the void. Oh no, I swore, it won't be a problem. The season doesn't really get going until summer anyway.

A bald-faced lie, but I was left with no choice.

My father, though quiet and outwardly sane, was pretty good with more subtle putdowns of what I was into. On a September Sunday in my beloved 1980 season, when the U.S. Open was finishing and the football season was starting and the Yankees were closing in on another division title, I was at the kitchen table, wrapped up in the fading Mets.

"All those other sports on," my dad asked, "and you're watching this?" He shook his head and walked away.

* * *

In 1985, however, they were engaging me in baseball talk. It was more than a passing fancy. They knew what time the game was gong to be on. They knew who was pitching (even if my mother asked every night "who's backing him up?" as if Davey designated a particular reliever the way he did a starter). My mother named a stuffed dog I gave her Ralphie in honor of shortstop Rafael Santana. My father bemoaned bad at-bats by Darryl Strawberry.

It was so strange!

Maybe they were bandwagon fans. I'm not instinctively against bandwagon fans. What's the fun in rooting all alone? Besides, if there was ever a team to whose bandwagon was worth jumping on board and holding tight, it was that of the mid–'80s Mets. If you wanted to be introduced or reintroduced to baseball, who better to show you the diamond than a welcoming committee of Mex and Mookie and Doc and Straw and Kid and HoJo? Who wouldn't want to hang out with those guys?

Perhaps my constant rooting since the age of six had rubbed off on my mom and dad. Or it could be they were bored. I never asked where this blast of baseball came from. After a childhood feeling very lonely in my Met-loving ways around the house, I returned as a college graduate to find I was not alone. Mom and Dad were crazy about the Mets. They were crazy about cable because it included SportsChannel. My mother began to imitate the way Ralph Kiner and Tim McCarver pronounced things. Dad did too. They thought it strange how Ralph said "lihg" for "league" and "Duhwight" for "Dwight."

But they were into it. They read the same sports sections I did. They turned on the game in the car like it was their idea in the first place. We watched the Mets together on many nights, the three of us. We had something to talk about together, the three of us. We were Mets fans together, the three of us.

Go team?

* * *

Not that it was all sac flies and high fives. My mother was still my mother. She could snap back into form without warning. Lenny Dykstra, a sparkplug center fielder called up when Mookie got hurt, could be on third, Backman could be on first, Hernandez could be up, and the next voice I'd hear wouldn't be Ralph Kiner's, Tim McCarver's or even Steve Zabriskie's. It would be Sandy Prince.

"Why aren't you going to Jewish singles nights?"

That was always big with her, these Jewish singles nights she'd apparently heard more about than I did. In college it was, "Why aren't you going to Hillel?" Shoot, the only singles that interested me that summer were those generated by Lenny and Wally at the top of the order so they could be converted into runs by Keith, Gary, and Darryl. I wasn't particularly concerned with where any of them went to temple.

Though I had actually embarked on a serious letter-writing/ stalking campaign of a young lady who was still living in the Tampa Bay area (it didn't take), I'm pretty sure my mother decided I was gay my first summer out of college based on the choice I made to sit home evenings, watching ball instead of chasing tail. My mother decided at one time or another that every one of my friends, most of my college roommates, and a random sample of total strangers were gay, so I didn't get too defensive about it.

"I'm not going to Jewish singles night. I'm trying to watch the Mets."

Still, getting to know my parents on an adult-to-adult basis was an education unto itself. The most fascinating thing I learned about these people who had always looked off in disinterest as I babbled on about the Mets when I was a kid was, in 1985, that they were diehard Mets fans. Anything I picked up beyond baseball was a bonus. Anything I had to ward off between innings was the cost of doing business.

* * *

My professional and residential instincts may have been off—my sporadic freelance writing endeavors weren't going to get me out of the house anytime soon—but I knew a good baseball season when I saw it. 1985 was everything it appeared to be from the time it started when I was back in school, when Gary Carter was homering to beat Neil Allen on Opening Day, when 41-year-old Rusty Staub was dragging his old body into the right field corner to make an age-defying catch on the day I graduated. It was worth putting a life on hold for as they persevered through the summer, particularly one endless nineteen-inning night in Atlanta (game won at 3:55 A.M.—even my night owl mother was asleep). The Mets and Cardinals went at it nip and tuck, hammer and tong, cliché and platitude all summer long. Then came September, when everything was kicked up the proverbial notch. After a riveting California trip (Keith, Gary, Mookie, and Doc all doing Amazin' things), the Mets returned home to play three games against the Cardinals. They were tied for first, with 82 wins, 53 losses apiece. It is no exaggeration and there is no irony intended when I say it felt as if my whole life was leading up to this moment, to this series, to this pennant race, to this season, to these Mets, and to that week.

You know how you look forward to certain things and they inevitably disappoint you? This wasn't one of those things. This was every bit as good as I imagined it would be. The scores of the three games were 5–4, 1–0, and 7–6.

For the first one, I wore "lucky glasses" (an old prescription) and watched with my parents. Danny Cox had the nerve to hit George Foster with a pitch and there was a bit of tension, but HoJo defused it with a grand slam. Keith Hernandez, who had been called to testify in a drug trial in Pittsburgh in the middle of the West Coast trip, returned to a standing ovation. Dick Young had conniptions over this latest affront to His America. We had our Mex. The Mets won.

For the second one, Joel and I decided we would go. This was very presumptuous of us because the pitching matchup was Gooden vs. John Tudor, a 21-game winner that year. But neither of us had ever witnessed a pennant race in person, so we decided that even if the game was sold out, it was worth buying from a scalper. This, too, was a little haughty because this was a race every other Mets fan in New York—and there were millions of us now—wanted in on. I rushed home from one of my Manhattan assignments (I worked briefly at an ad agency writing movie descriptions for the boxes home videos came in; get a copy of Sylvester Stallone's *Paradise Alley* on VHS sometime to see my handiwork) and was late in picking up Joel. We drove to Shea but found no parking except under an overpass. And then we found no scalpers. It turned out the scalpers wanted to see Gooden and Tudor as much as we did. Denied entry, we wound up in the same Rockville Centre bar where we watched the Mets and Braves play most of their nineteen innings on the Fourth and Fifth of July. Much different game, much different result. Gooden was brilliant. Tudor was that much more so. It was scoreless in the tenth when Orosco relieved Gooden and Cesar Cedeño homered. *Cesar Cedeño?* I thought he was retired.

Tudor protected his own lead. The Cardinals won.

For the third one, an afternoon affair, everybody was abuzz. Everybody. It was dubbed Baseball Thursday in New York—the Mets and Cardinals in a fight for first at Shea and then, at night, the Yankees and Blue Jays in the Bronx for something similar. The Yankees had a good team that year but could never quite overtake Toronto. They certainly had their followers but they were never the story in 1985 that the Mets were. Still, for the first time ever, it was thought the two New York teams, who were almost never good at the same time, could play in an old-fashioned Subway Series. I wasn't necessarily looking to share the spotlight. Not that we couldn't beat them if we had to, but why even start? Either way, we were doing our part, jumping on irascible Joaquin Andujar for six early runs. We would cruise. How could anybody blow a six-run lead? You'd have to ask Ed Lynch, who did (his arm was never the same after he was attacked on the Dodger Stadium mound by Mariano Duncan in his previous start). What Lynch didn't give back, Orosco did. It was 6–6 in the ninth after Willie McGee, the National League's leading hitter and MVP that season, homered off Jesse. We should never have let it get this far and now we had no right to expect what happened next: Mookie singled, Wally moved him over, and Keith—MEX!—singled to left. Mookie, who used to score from second on ground balls for bad Mets teams, wasn't going to be denied a chance to put his speed to good use. Vince Coleman fumbled the ball and Mookie scored. The Mets won.

* * *

The Mets' one-game lead in mid-September had transformed into a three-game deficit by early October, the last week of the season. We turned stagnant while the Cardinals turned it on. Luck would send us to St. Louis with a simple mission: win three games against the Cardinals and be tied for first with three to play. Then it would be anybody's race, and we'd have home-field for a one-game playoff.

The first game of the series matched Tudor vs. Ron Darling. Not Gooden, Darling. Mets fans actually sent telegrams to Davey Johnson and told him, no, you're doing this all wrong. Warm up Darling in the pen and make Whitey *think* you're going to start him. Then, out of nowhere, Doc enters the game. It was as crazy as it sounded, but not without some sanity to it. Doc was 23–4 and the best pitcher in the world at the time. This was the biggest game the Mets were playing in more than a decade. But Davey avoided the temptation to take his cues from Western

Union. Darling did not let down his manager. Nor did Tudor, the second-best pitcher in the world. It was another scoreless duel. Ronnie went nine—Davey wasn't pushing his young starters in any game to do anything superhuman; these pitchers had futures. Tudor again pitched ten shutout innings against the Mets. In the eleventh, Ken Dayley entered for the Cards. And Darryl Strawberry, whose May–June absence with a thumb injury was probably what made this a race to begin with, took him deep. How deep? Very deep. How deep? Clock deep. It was 10:44 Central Daylight Time when Darryl put the Mets up 1–0 in the top of the eleventh inning, smashing one off a clock on the facing of the grandstand in right field at Busch Stadium. Orosco was right on time to save it and the Mets were within two games of first place.

In the second game, the Mets sent Gooden to the mound. The opposing pitcher didn't matter. It was Gooden. It was 1985. There were some balls hard-hit against him, but in the end Gooden won his final game of the year. The numbers would be entered into the ledger for the ages: 24–4, 268 K's, 1.53 ERA. That was Dwight Gooden in 1985 at the tender age of twenty. That was the lowest ERA in baseball since 1969, the year the pitcher's mound had been lowered to encourage more hitting. That was a pitcher who was only in his second year and, it followed, could only get better. That kid, two years my junior, was the human being I thought most highly of in the world. The Mets were within one game of first place.

I watched the third game, as I had the previous two, with my parents and the entire Metropolitan Area. Channel 9 reported record ratings for each night of this series. I, again, wore my lucky glasses. But I didn't like what I was seeing. The Mets nicked Cox for a run in the first but Foster, who had the opportunity to prove every doubting Mets fan wrong, only confirmed our worst suspicions about him. With the bases loaded, he bounced out and the Mets came away practically empty-handed. Rick

Aguilera, in the biggest start of his (or almost anybody's) life, let the Cards tie it in the second. Then the home team, spurred on by their obnoxious fans who dumped beer on Lenny Dykstra and referred to the Mets as "pond scum" (a David Lettermanism), pulled ahead. St. Louis was up 4–2 after six. And after seven. In the eighth, the Mets got a run back, HoJo singling home Straw. There could've been more but Davey was reduced to using Ray Knight and Ron Gardenhire, and in 1985, they were not keys to success. The Mets entered the top of the ninth down one run and one game. This was it. This was the season. This was what my whole life was leading up to.

Two outs came and went. Then Keith Hernandez, formerly of the St. Louis Cardinals, came up. He was booed. He was hated. He was reviled for being a big, bad New York Met and, not incidentally, for testifying with immunity at that big, bad baseball drug trial in Pittsburgh that, while a member of the St. Louis Cardinals, he was a user of cocaine. He was a forgiven hero at Shea. Not at Busch. Whatever punishment he'd be meted by the commissioner, it wasn't coming now, so he'd have to take his medicine this way. Keith Hernandez had come to town to try to steal a division title from his old team. He had been a user. The fans kept booing. Keith kept hitting. Keith had already, in this game, the one my whole life had led up to, collected four hits.

Hernandez singled off of Ricky Horton. He was 5-for-5. My mother was thrilled. My father was thrilled. I was thrilled. New York was thrilled.

Whitey Herzog, the sneering Rat, made a pitching change. Horton out, Jeff Lahti in, Gary Carter up.

This was it. This was truly it. Our best player; the National League's Player of the Month for September three days into October; the guy who started 1985 in December 1984 while I was still in college by being traded to us; the guy who shooed away Neil Allen on Opening Day; the guy on the Norman Rockwell–style posters WOR-TV sold to raise money to fight muscular dystrophy; in the Ivory Soap commercial; in all the commercials; our very own superstar catcher; our cleanup hitter; our future Hall of Famer, the only one—it would turn out—from this team.

Gary Carter came up with two out and one on, the Mets down by a run. If Carter could take Lahti over the Busch Stadium wall, the Mets would lead 5–4. They'd be three outs from being tied for first place with three games remaining in the 1985 season, the best season of my life, the best season of everybody's life.

Gary Carter hit a fly ball to right field. Andy Van Slyke caught it.

Cardinals 4, Mets 3. The Mets were two games out of first place.

It was over. Having seen enough, I threw my lucky glasses on the floor.

"Don't do that to your glasses!" Mom and Dad admonished in unison. Great. At the moment I needed to be in the company of Mets fans, they reverted back to being parents.

I went upstairs and found a Whitey Herzog card. I brought it downstairs with a thumbtack and began defacing it in the kitchen. I handed the tack to my mother and she joined in.

Eight years earlier, when she had decided to surprise me with the little change bank shaped like a miniature Mets batting helmet that wasn't a miniature Mets batting helmet, I was just old enough to twist my words into a pretzel so as not raise her ire. I tried to seem grateful for the gift but she realized she had screwed up. Nobody won.

Now I was grown up. And she was grown up. And we had just stood together for the first time hating the Mets' mortal enemy as if he were one of the neighbors we couldn't stand. We took turns, my mother and I, destroying Whitey Herzog.

So 1985 wasn't a total loss.

THIRTEEN

WE DID IT, THAT'S IT

When was it settled? When did we know 1986 was going to be the definitive inverse of 1977 or 1979? When did we know there was no way we were going to lose the same way we knew seven and nine years earlier there was no way we were going to win? Some would say it was when 1985 ended close but cigarless. Others might point to the crafty offseason acquisitions of lefty starter Bobby Ojeda and righty platoon second baseman Tim Teufel. Perhaps it was the moment grandstanding commissioner Peter Ueberroth gave Keith Hernandez a community service out from an otherwise mandatory suspension for his previous admission of drug use, and Mex, grudgingly placing principles aside, took it so he wouldn't let the team down—it's hard to fathom the Mets as unbeatable with Mex's projected understudy, Tim Corcoran, batting third and playing first. A most satisfying myth is that Davey Johnson told reporters, "We're going to dominate" and, having spoken the unspeakable (Busch Stadium bulletin boards be damned), the Mets followed his orders.

Confidence wasn't a problem for the Mets or Mets fans when '86 started. Nor was winning. The Mets more or less had it clinched by May. They played the rest of the schedule for entertainment value.

* * *

Every summer for a few years, my July birthday present to my
mother was tickets to a future Mets game. Having forgotten the
firemen and the mustard dispenser from 1975, she decided one
game a year would be festive. I was going to argue? My annual
parental game in '86 was in early September, a Monday night
when my father would have rather been watching the Giants and
Cowboys but this was 1986, so even football could wait. It was
actually a terrible game, the Expos jumping all over Ojeda, but
it didn't much matter to my mother. She kept chanting "Let's
Go Mets Go!" à la the chorus from the just-released and already
ubiquitous New York Dream Team single and video in which
we were assured the Mets had the teamwork to make the dream
work. Getting the age-old chant of "Let's Go Mets!" wrong was
like her conviction that Davey Johnson had a reliever designated
in advance to work behind the starter. It was a little off. But it was
harmless. I liked that she cared enough to chant at all.

We did leave a little early in deference to the score and the
Giants and Cowboys, but we stopped on the way home at Lenny's
Clam Bar in Rockville Centre and talked about the game and the
season and the team. If I didn't know any better, I would have
sworn I was out with friends.

* * *

The Mets foreshadowed October by making us just an eensy
bit nervous about clinching. It had been a foregone conclusion.
The *Daily News* ran a magic number graphic every day since June,
a cartoon of Davey preparing to pull a rabbit out of a hat (a sly
reference, I wanted to believe, to The Magic Is Back). Whitey
Herzog, such a hardass in 1985, surrendered in June. If he were

Davey, he told reporters, he'd be drinking champagne every night. I made an unprecedented trip to our neighborhood liquor store to buy a bottle of bubbly with which we would toast our first division championship in thirteen years, my mother, my father, and me.

The champagne chilled but good in the fridge. The Mets went to Philadelphia to get it over with on September 12. The magic number was two, which was fine because the Phillies had overtaken the Expos for second place. Beat them and we win the East. Mike Schmidt, however, made some proclamation about not letting the Mets celebrate on that awful Veterans Stadium carpet and played hard. The Mets had a bad weekend and got swept. It was frustrating for those who drove down, but no worries. The lead was still impregnable. The Phillies won another game while the Mets flew to St. Louis and lost again. The champagne was still very, very cold.

There were, to repeat, no worries. But the experienced Mets fan grew a tad uneasy that if winning a division that had been essentially won by May was going to be work, what would the playoffs against Houston and all their pitching be? The experienced Mets fan put aside those creeping doubts the next night when the Mets broke their season-high four-game losing streak and cut the number to one. The '86 Mets being the '86 Mets, it almost appeared preordained that they'd lose just enough games on the road in order to clinch at home.

And they did. Doc, down from the mountain of 1985 but still quite effective, threw a complete game and the Mets beat the Cubs 4–2. The Mets were champions of something. A generation that had grown up watching 1969 and 1973 highlight films during rain delays did what it assumed was expected of it, and rushed the field. Thirteen years had passed since there was a reason to jump the railings and play on the grass. This generation of Mets fans, those at Shea the night of September 17, anyway, apparently had been waiting too long and had too much aggression stored up for this moment. They rushed everything in sight and tore the field to bits . . . with a day game scheduled for the next afternoon, no less. Head groundskeeper Pete Flynn grumbled that fans like these didn't deserve a champion. The celebration played on television as kind of mean-spirited. The Mets would start lining up mounted police to prevent such a demonstration of enthusiasm from ever happening again.

The instant Backman fielded Chico Walker's grounder and threw it to Hernandez for the final out, things got weird back in Long Beach. I yelled "WE DID IT!" and ran to my mother to give her an enormous hug. This was far weirder than thousands of fans ripping up sod. I had been in a cold war with my mother at least since she snapped, "Don't go bringing home any other races!" at me in college, when she learned my girlfriend was Asian.

I didn't trust her. I didn't say more than I had to. I didn't like getting trapped in conversations with her. But this season and the season before it, we had the Mets. The Mets transcended all that familial nonsense. Yes, I was certain as the champagne finally emerged from the fridge, we did it.

* * *

The Mets stopped being inevitable in the first inning of the first game of the playoffs. Mike Scott's split-finger fastball to Gary Carter took care of that. It wasn't that Scott threw it for a strike. It was that Carter couldn't believe it was legal. There had been lots of talk heading into the National League Championship Series that Scott was scuffing his way to success. Carter asked home plate ump Doug Harvey to inspect a ball that crossed the plate funny. Harvey ("God" was his nickname) said it was fine. Carter struck out. The Astrodome turned into the Thunderdome.

The Mets were in trouble.

Mike Scott passed time as a Met the same as dozens of his contemporaries did from 1979 to 1982: without distinction.

I attended his one shining moment at Shea, the night he provided the opposition to Fernando Valenzuela at the height of Fernandomania in '81. Scott was his equal on the hill. Nobody cared. Almost 40,000 showed up to breathe in the fumes of some other team's phenomenon. We lost 1–0 to the Dodgers. I felt bad for Mike Scott.

For the last time.

Under the tutelage of Roger Craig, an Original Met for crimney's sake, Scott learned to throw that split-fingered pitch. Word leaked out to us civilians that he got it to dart and dive by scuffing the ball. Sandpaper, probably. It made more sense to believe a washed-up Met, discarded for fourth outfielder Danny Heep, cut a few corners rather than blossomed away from Shea. Everything else Frank Cashen had done worked beautifully. It defied 1986 Met logic to believe a trade would come back to bite him. Heep was moderately useful—even if my mother never stopped calling him "a dunner," as in slow-witted. Scott was about to be Cy Young. And in Game One of the 1986 NLCS, the man who doctored the ball was more effective than Doctor K himself. Scott beat Gooden 1–0, same score he lost to Valenzuela by.

It was just one game, but it was one game too many. Four years after we figured we were done with him, we'd have to keep an eye on Mike Scott.

* * *

The flagship ghost of Mets trades gone bad, Nolan Ryan, pitched next for Houston. It had been fifteen years since he'd been swapped for Jim Fregosi. Fregosi wasn't playing anymore. Ryan sure as hell was pitching. Fast after all those years. Fast and ornery. He knocked down Lenny Dykstra. Lenny, however, was one you could knock down but he'd get up again. Lenny was the original tubthumper. He singled after being dusted, keeping alive a rally that supported Bobby Ojeda's complete game ten-hit victory. The back pages called Bobby O THE EQUALIZER, after a detective show on CBS whose lead character carried a card that asked "Got a problem? Odds against you? Need help?" We weren't supposed to need an equalizer. Good thing we had one.

* * *

Game Three was Saturday afternoon at Shea. The odds should have been with us. Ron Darling, 15–6 in the regular season, turned them right around with a dreadful first two innings. We were buried 4-0. Hundreds of times in my Met life I assumed that meant the end of the game. There was almost never a Steve Henderson around when you needed one.

But this was 1986. It was different. The Mets were playing on October 11 for a reason. Darling settled down and allowed nothing else through five. Rick Aguilera, a fifth starter on a team that was using only four in the postseason, pitched a scoreless sixth. Lefty Bob Knepper, the third Astro starter and traditionally the toughest on the Mets, had given up nothing. If it had been some other year, he might have continued to do just that. But this was, as previously reported, 1986.

An Astro error allowed one run. Then Darryl Strawberry willed three more. He pulled a Knepper pitch down the line, fair enough, one Loge above the fence. He hit more majestic moon shots normally. This was one was relatively earthbound but had the requisite gravity behind it to tie the game at four. It, like I, was plenty high.

There was much happiness in the house among my parents and me, immediately followed by much consternation when, in the top of the seventh, Ray Knight threw a ball past Hernandez and the Astros edged ahead. I was nervously fingering my father's plastic Miami Beach backscratcher, a souvenir from a family trip in the early '70s. When the Astros scored, I snapped it in half. (Whoops.)

The Astros led 5–4. At Shea, which wasn't supposed to happen. Their setup guy, a rather repulsive chap named Charlie Kerfeld, put the Mets down with ease in the eighth. Gary, slumping (thinking too much about those scuffed pitches?), bounced one to the mound. Kerfeld grabbed the ball, waved it at Carter—we're "the bad guys"?—and threw him out.

The tension was such that I scratched and scratched away on the fabric of the ancient not-so-easy chair in my parents' bedroom until I had scratched a swath of it off one of the arms. (Whoops again.) When I noted what I had done, my mother informed me to leave her furniture alone. I remembered I shouldn't reveal any information that could be used against me.

We could very well be screwed here. Three outs from being down 2–1 in games, three outs from having to face Mike Scuff Sunday night, the entire extraordinary season on the precipice of morphing into a trivia question. *What team posted a record of 108–54 and won its division by twenty-one-and-a-half games only to slink away pathetically in the playoffs?*

It was a question Lenny Dykstra would never allow to be asked. Wally Backman, who like Lenny hadn't started but somehow was up to lead off in the ninth, bunted his way past Astro closer Dave Smith, then advanced to second on a wild pitch. Heep, the alleged dunner, flied out. Dykstra stepped up. "The man they call Nails," as Murph identified him. Lenny nailed Smith all right. It was a high fly to right. It hung in the clouds for seconds . . . *one thousand one, one thousand two* . . . Keith Jackson on ABC didn't much react to it. I could swear it was a home run. Its trajectory indicated it wouldn't be caught. The only place it could land was in the Mets' bullpen, like Steve Henderson's six years earlier in this very same room. We won then, 7–6.

We won now, 6–5. Lenny Dykstra, the man they call Nails, hit a game-winning homer that flipped the score, the series, that nebulous quantity known as momentum. The process by which the Mets trumped the Astros ruined a backscratcher (which I eventually replaced) and damaged a chair (forgotten about in the euphoria), but no one should have ever believed winning a pennant would be as easy as winning 108 games.

As if to prove that point, Scott again diminished the Mets in Game Four, a three-hitter to go with his five-hitter from Game One.

* * *

After Game Five was rained out—maybe Somebody decided scheduling games on Yom Kippur wasn't kosher—we went to Suzan's house to break the fast. I was informed that her neighbors would be joining us, including a daughter roughly my age. I groaned. No, no, I'd like her. She's a Mets fan!

It was October 1986. Who wasn't?

The neighbors came over. We were introduced. My mother cleverly steered the conversation to, "How about those Mets?"

"Oh, the Mets," said the neighbor's daughter. "I'm so sick of hearing about the Mets."

That ended that.

* * *

The closest 1986 ever came to facing 1969 was Game Five. Nolan Ryan, thirty-nine, started for Houston, Doc Gooden, twenty-one, for us. For an afternoon at Shea, they were both young fireballers. Ryan could have been mistaken for the hotter prospect: twelve K's, two hits, one walk, almost completely untouchable across nine innings. Only a fence-grazer (not majestic, just real effective) by Strawberry got the Mets on the board. Gooden pitched like the wily veteran he never really got to be: nine hits, two walks, only four strikeouts over *ten* innings. He, too, gave up but a run. It was the most phenomenal pitchers' duel Shea ever saw with so much on the line.

Neither legend would seal the deal, however. The bottom of the twelfth rolled around, the game still tied at one. Backman, as on Saturday, sparked the Mets on a ball that never left the infield. He again found his way to second, this time on an errant pickoff throw. Hernandez, always dangerous, was walked to make way for ice-cold Carter. Pitching was Kerfeld, the bespectacled lout intent on making a name for himself with a little New York–bashing. "I'm ready to get away from this zoo," he told reporters. "I'm ready to get back to where some real people are and get away from these animals." He was not popular at Shea.

Nor would he be successful. Carter, batting a frightening .048 in the series, avenged the ball-showing episode from Game Three by singling up the middle, scoring Backman. The Mets won 2–1 and took a 3–2 series lead. It was a breath-holding classic all the way.

By the next afternoon, it would be largely forgotten.

* * *

When people speak of Game Six of the 1986 National League Championship Series, the conversation inevitably rolls around to how the action from the Astrodome stopped New Yorkers and their commuter trains in their tracks. With an unusual start time of 3:00 P.M. Eastern, its ending was likely to bleed into rush hour. It almost didn't, actually. Bob Knepper was so tidy in dispatching the Mets that when I flipped over to *Live At Five* on Channel 4 during the commercial break preceding the ninth inning, it was reported glumly that this was about over and the Mets would almost certainly be staring down the barrel of Mike Scott if they wanted to see the World Series.

I wonder if Channel 4 ever aired a retraction.

As a freelancer, I may not have had much of an income in 1986, but I was able to fix myself in front of a television. I kept staring at some work I had to do, some calls I had to make. So I wouldn't feel terribly guilty about giving myself so completely over to the Mets, I made one call to somebody I didn't think would be in at about 2:55. Let the phone ring three times and hung up. *Well, I tried.* With that, I closed up shop for the day and sat in the room I used for my office (my sister's old bedroom) and watched the Mets go after their first pennant in thirteen years.

The Astros jumped on Ojeda for three runs in the first. They tried to squeeze for a fourth but it backfired and Kevin Bass was a dead duck at the plate. That fourth run would have come in mighty handy for Houston down the line.

Ojeda settled in for some good pitching in the second. Sadly, Knepper was on top of things immediately. While Bobby O kept us in the game, Bobby K kept us off the board altogether. Through eight innings, the Mets had garnered just three baserunners. No scoring on either side, but what did the home team need to worry about? Channel 4 was already projecting an Astro victory.

However, Channel 7 was still counting the returns. This election to the World Series was far from settled.

Sitting, standing, squirming, I certainly believed in my Mets. Every Met who came up was going to get a hit, was going to break this drought, and was going to get this thing won. And if they didn't, well, screw Mike Scott. We're due to get to him.

I don't know if I really bought it, but sometimes a fan does know certain things about his team. Sometimes his gut, churning acid as it does, is onto something. Thus, when Lenny Dykstra, pinch-hitting, lofted a fly ball that eluded a shallow Billy Hatcher in center and Lenny sped it into a triple, I knew something. I knew, down 3–0 in the ninth, we were going to win this game. Sometimes a fan just knows.

Scott may have been invincible, but Knepper was human. Mookie got to him next with a single. It was 3–1. We were going to win. After Kevin Mitchell's grounder moved Mookie to second, Mex doubled him home. It was 3–2.

We were going to win. We would have life beyond the Thunderdome.

Knepper was done. Smith, the mopey closer who surrendered Dykstra's homer three games earlier, came on. He walked Carter. He walked Strawberry. The bases were loaded with one out. Knight hit a fly ball to right. It was deep enough. Mex scored, the others moved up.

We were tied! We were going to win!

Backman would pinch-hit for Tim Teufel. Astro manager Hal Lanier ordered him walked to load 'em up again. He needed Smith to get one more out at any base, otherwise their season would be all but over. Smith's entire series had been a disaster: the ninth in New York on Saturday, now this. The only batter he had retired without consequence of the seven he'd faced was Danny Heep, between Wally's bunt and Lenny's homer the other day.

Luck would have it that Heep was up next. Seeing as how Smith had walked three batters in this inning and had just come off throwing four balls on purpose to Backman, it then stood to reason that Heep wouldn't have to do very much to drive in the winning run. His bat on his shoulder might do the trick nicely.

I wasn't a big Danny Heep fan—I thought most fans gave him too much credit for simply not being George Foster—but I always tried to convince my mother he wasn't so bad, and he was a professional hitter (whatever that meant). But in the ninth inning of Game Six in Houston, I had to admit I could learn something from my mother when it came to baseball. Dave Smith threw Danny Heep one ball after another. He threw him ball four, maybe ball six, on three-and-two. Heep swung and missed it.

My mother was right. Danny Heep was a dunner.

* * *

Rick Aguilera had picked up for Ojeda in the sixth and kept the Astros off the board. Aggie handed it off to Roger McDowell, another '86 Met others liked a lot more than I did, in the ninth. I thought the "crazy relief pitcher" comparisons to Tug McGraw were lazy—Tug was a tortured soul and genuine flake; Roger wore silly masks and lit hotfoots in the dugout. But my reluctance to embrace his persona notwithstanding, McDowell was no dunner on the mound. He threw five fantastic innings. The Astros remained shut out. So, unfortunately, did the Mets after Heep's unnecessary strikeout.

While Roger was working very seriously, my phone kept ringing. Various friends, none of whom you'd label Mets fans, were calling, each watching because it was the kind of game you couldn't take your eyes off. I was the biggest Mets fan they knew. They wanted to see how I was holding up.

As long as we were alive, I was fine. My parents downstairs were doing the same. Sure was exciting, one and all agreed. If it were any more exciting, we would have needed trained emergency medical technicians as skilled as McDowell.

It took extra innings in the Astrodome to make me realize EMTs is an anagram of Mets.

* * *

There was a breakthrough in the top of the fourteenth. Even as it occurred, it was a blur. Somebody hit the ball, and somebody in a gray uniform scored. That's all I needed to know. That and Jesse Orosco was coming in for McDowell. I liked Jesse a lot more than most fans did. He had been a Met in '79 when the Mets were so cheap they eschewed veteran pitching help and kept three raw rookies around on Opening Day: Neil Allen, Mike Scott, and Jesse Orosco. None of them was ready. One of them was traded for Keith Hernandez. One of them loomed over the horizon if we didn't win this game now. One was going to save it for us. I mean, there has to be a rule that says you don't take a lead in the top of the fourteenth only to give it back.

Billy Hatcher didn't read that rule. With one out, Hatcher launched a long fly ball down the left field line that wasn't left enough. It hit the foul pole. The game was tied at four.

The phone rang some more.

* * *

If I, guy answering phone and running between upstairs and downstairs TVs was exhausted, imagine what the players in Houston felt like. They dragged themselves through a fifteenth inning and into a sixteenth. The Mets were going to outlast the Astros. A bigger blur of runs presented itself at home plate. The Mets went up 7–4. Orosco was going to go out and finish this up once and for all.

Except it wouldn't be that easy. There was an out, a walk, two singles, another out, and a single. The Astros' ups were a blur, too, but theirs came wrapped in rainbow stripes. The impossible on top of the already unbelievable was at hand. Denny Walling was on second, the Astros were down only one run, and Kevin Bass, universally concurred as Houston's best hitter, was at the plate. Carter and Hernandez converged on Orosco. Jesse was barely standing erect. Keith, it would be said, threatened Gary with physical harm if he called for a fastball from the nearly dead reliever. Kid didn't need Mex to tell him that.

The count went to three and two. Jesse Orosco threw a slider. Kevin Bass swung and missed it. The Mets were National League champions. That was not a blur. Nor was this.

The moment it ended, I did by instinct what I did when the division was clinched. I flew into my mother's arms again. "THAT'S IT!" I yelled this time. The words weren't out of my mouth when I noticed my declaration was far different from September's. Then "we" won. Now I could take no credit for four hours and forty-two minutes of what Bob Murphy called "heart-stopping" baseball.

That was it.

Bring on the World Series.

* * *

Not so fast. Boston, AL champ, leapt out ahead of us 2–0 at Shea. We tied it at Fenway. Then we fell behind. But big deal, I thought. We're the '86 Mets. With the Houston precedent on our side, who could take this backs-against-the-wall jazz all that seriously after the NLCS? The Mets would return to Shea and think of something. I knew my team. I was sure of it.

FOURTEEN

SURE

I was sure the Mets would win Game Six of the 1986 World Series as it began on Saturday night, October 25.

I was sure of it when some dude named Michael Sergio parachuted into Shea Stadium, wielding a "Let's Go Mets" banner. He got arrested.

I was sure of it when Roger Clemens began mowing down Mets batters, not giving up a hit for four innings. When it came to generating offense, they couldn't get arrested.

I was sure of it when the Red Sox bolted to a 2–0 lead off Ojeda. Ojeda, quick deficits, and Game Sixes were already a proven combination.

I was sure of it when the Mets broke through in the fifth, beginning with a Strawberry walk and steal, followed by a Knight single to score Darryl and a Mookie single that, combined with a Dwight Evans error in right, put Ray on third.

I was sure of it when Danny Heep ground into a double play, scoring Knight to tie it at two. It wasn't the most optimal at-bat, but he wasn't a dunner anymore.

I was sure of it when Knight threw a ball out of Hernandez's reach on a grounder, setting up the lead run in the seventh. These things happen.

I was sure of it when Mookie threw out Jim Rice at home from left for the third out of the seventh. Mookie wasn't a left fielder by trade. And he didn't have that great an arm.

I was sure of it when erstwhile Met Calvin Schiraldi, part of the package that brought us Ojeda, replaced Clemens. Clemens was done in more by a blister than the Mets. Schiraldi had emerged as Boston's closer late in the season. A whiny talk show caller had weeks earlier predicted the Series would end with Calvin Schiraldi striking out Gary Carter. Nonsense.

I was sure of it when erstwhile ex-Met Lee Mazzilli led off the bottom of the eighth with a pinch single. Mazz returned to Shea in August, reborn from 1979 and all those rancid, empty years, scooped up from the scrap heap after the last-place Pirates released him. George Foster, who was supposed to usher in a post-Mazzilli era of success, got on management's last nerve when he charged them with racism for sitting him down (never mind his color-blind .227 average). Mazz, like Seaver in '83, like Rusty in '81, returned to where he belonged. Mazz had better timing.

I was sure of it when the bases were loaded with one out and Gary Carter took a mighty swing against Schiraldi and it was enough to score Mazz from third on a sac fly. We were tied 3–3.

I was sure of it when Knight and Mookie got on to start the bottom of the ninth . . . maybe less so when HoJo—whom Davey didn't order to bunt more than once—struck out and Mazz, then Dykstra each flied out. One of those fly balls would have scored Knight, theoretically, but who's to say those fly balls would have been hit had HoJo gotten a bunt down? Or that Mazzilli, still in the game in a double-switch that famously annoyed Darryl because he was the one who got switched out, wouldn't have been walked to set up a double play and Lenny would have come through? On the other hand, I watched a Spring Training game that March in which HoJo laid down the most beautiful bunt I've ever seen to this day. Still, I was sure the Mets would win Game Six and stay alive to win in Game Seven even if it was going to take extra innings.

* * *

My father didn't seem to have free-floating anxieties that tended to put everybody on the edge of hysteria. His demons rarely came out to play the way my mother's did. He was the quiet one, every friend who ever came over to the house testified. He watched sports with interest and insight and enthusiasm but except for pounding a low ceiling tile out of its socket at the Garden during a Knicks-Celtics playoff game in 1973, I'd never seen him react wildly to a game of any kind.

But I had never seen him watch the 1986 Mets on the brink of elimination before. I had never seen his superstitious side. I had never seen anybody do what he decided to for the tenth inning of Game Six. He got up from the bedroom where he was watching with my mother and went into the kitchen. He plucked a *Wall Street Journal* from his tower of unread papers and sat down at the kitchen table to leaf through it. The kitchen TV was on, but he decided that if he acted as if he didn't care what happened, nothing bad would befall the Mets.

As he pored over stock tables and I, who had been shuttling between upstairs and downstairs all night, preoccupied my antsy hands with a bowl of Grape-Nuts Flakes, Dave Henderson stepped in to lead off against Rick Aguilera, the pitcher who was part of the Mazz-Straw double switch. Aggie had pitched a scoreless ninth. He was, albeit once it barely mattered, the Mets' most effective starter for much of the regular season's second-half runaway. I was sure he'd do his part here against the Sox in the tenth, just before midnight.

Henderson homered off Aguilera.

Midnight struck. I was no longer so sure.

* * *

My father berated himself for letting the little man inside the TV know he was paying attention. My mother groaned. I discarded my Grape-Nuts Flakes and have yet to come near another bowl of the stuff since. It was bad luck. Everything was bad luck. Dave Henderson was suddenly the inverse of Steve Henderson. He had hit the most horrifying home run in the history of Shea Stadium.

All at once, 1986 was falling apart. Henderson was the big hero from the Red Sox's ALCS comeback over the Angels. Now he was doing it again. Aguilera was now the fifth starter from the first half of the season when he couldn't get the key outs. It wasn't just Henderson now. Wade Boggs came up and doubled. Marty Barrett, who'd been killing us the whole Series, singled him home. It's 5–3 instead of 4–3. It's two runs instead of one run. It's that much less surmountable now.

Bill Buckner gets hit by a pitch and goes to first. A Jim Rice flyout guarantees he's left there. But the damage is done.

* * *

Down two with three outs separating us from defeat, I decided that I needed to take in the bottom of the tenth upstairs, by myself. I headed back to my office, my sister's old bedroom. It's where I watched Ron Swoboda double home Cleon Jones on October 16, 1969, and Swoboda score on an error thereafter and the Mets win the World Series that day. It's where a duckling was reborn a swan and where I signed on for a lifetime hitch of monitoring every Met action and reaction that followed Cleon catching that last out from Davey Johnson. It's where a little plaque that read "World Champions 1969" hung behind the TV (the Panasonic I inherited from my parents when they upgraded, the Panasonic on which I watched Steve Henderson go deep on

Allen Ripley, June 14, 1980). Mark gave it to me the previous Chanukah, a consolation prize for the Mets not becoming the World Champions of 1985. Joel saw it and pronounced it sad. Not sad the Mets won in 1969. Sad the Mets hadn't won since.

I was by no means sure the Mets could come back, but I wasn't completely forlorn. We were still the '86 Mets. 108–54. Houston. Wally, Keith, and Gary due up. Who the hell was Calvin Schiraldi anyway?

* * *

I turned on the stereo in my bedroom and cranked up Bob Murphy. Back in my office down the hall, I lowered the volume on Vin Scully and Joe Garagiola. They were already spewing about how the Red Sox were on the verge of ending a sixty-eight-year drought between World Series titles and how Marty Barrett was the Miller Lite player of the game.

Shut up Vin and Joe. If I'm going down, I'm going down with Murph.

* * *

C'mon Mets! C'mon! You've got to have two runs in you. You definitely have the right guy coming up.

Wally Backman. I love Wally Backman. There's nobody I'd rather have come up in this spot than Wally Backman. Wally Backman never lets me down. He's the most dependable guy on this team. Who got on base in Game Three against Houston to set up Dykstra? Wally, that's who. Wally is not going to allow the Mets to go down. He's going to get on. We can still do this.

WALLY! A lousy fly ball to leftfield. Jim Rice catches it. One out.

Shit.

That's OK. It's just one out. We're not dead yet. Keith Hernandez is up. Keith is only the most clutch hitter in all of baseball. We've seen it all of this year and last year and the year before. Keith is the reason we're any good at all. God, I love Keith Hernandez. There is nobody I'd rather have up with everything on the line. Keith can get on. There's only one out. We can still do this.

Home run swing! Deep! But it's dying. Of course it is, it's Shea. That annoying Dave Henderson catches it in center. I hate that guy. Two out.

Shit.

* * *

I was sure we were doomed. I was sure the 108 wins no longer mattered. I was sure defeating Houston in Game Six was for naught. That was Game Six then. This was Game Six now. The Mets who couldn't be stopped were, in fact, one out from total stoppage. The 1986 Mets, so destined to put another plaque on the wall behind the TV, would do no more than wave a National League pennant. They did that in '73. That was fine then. You had to believe it wasn't enough now.

* * *

Schiraldi's unhittable. Didn't do jack for the Mets in his '84 and '85 cups of coffee, but now he's going to win the World Series for the Red Sox. Him and Dave Henderson. That fucker who called WFUV and said it would be Schiraldi on the mound to finish off Game Seven, striking out Gary Carter, he was off by one day.

The last out *is* gonna be Gary Carter.

Shit.

* * *

Fucking Carter. He's the last guy I want up there. Who made the last out last year against the Cardinals? Carter. Who hit .255 this year? Carter. Who is not going to come through in a situation like this? Carter. Can you picture him actually getting a hit here?

Carter got a hit.

Oh, why bother? Stop teasing me. I've lived through this too much as a Mets fan, all these false rallies, all this false hope in ninth innings and extra innings all my life. So Carter gets a hit. Big deal. We're still losing by two and look who's coming up.

Kevin Mitchell. Damn it, I don't want him up there.

Mitchell had a nice start this year when he made the team out of St. Petersburg and was playing all those positions, but has he done a damn thing since they went to Wrigley and he decided he was going to hit it onto Waveland Avenue every time up? I read his father was there and he wanted to impress him. Seems all he did was go into a season-long slump. Wasn't he hitting like .349 and what did he wind up at? .277, I think. Geez, he's a rookie who swings at everything now. This is no time for Kevin Mitchell.

Mitchell got a hit! Carter's on second!

Oh, goddamn it. Now I have to take this seriously. Why can't they just get this over with? It's as good as done anyway, probably. I hope we win, but I can't believe we will.

Look who's up. Knight.

Fantastic. Ray Knight. Perfect ending to a perfect year. Ray Knight was the *worst* player on the 1985 Mets. If he had been any good at all, or if Davey had benched him and put HoJo in like he should've, we would've beaten the fucking Cardinals last year. Instead he batted .218. I'd never booed a Met before but I couldn't help myself. Ray Knight was just so fucking awful! It was nothing personal. It was more directed at Davey for sticking with this stiff.

So this year Ray Knight makes us think everything is fine. He hits six homers in April and he hits that game-winner against the Astros on Fireworks Night and suddenly Ray Knight is a good player again. But y'know what? I don't believe it. This is all a setup. Ray Knight is going to revert to form right now. He's going to pop up or ground out or swing through one of Schiraldi's fastballs. We are so fucked and now it's worse because they're getting our fucking hopes up.

KNIGHT SINGLED! CARTER SCORED! 5–4! MITCHELL'S ON THIRD!

WE'RE ALIVE!

I can barely breathe.

* * *

It was official. 1986 no longer had to worry about being ho-hum. It took 162 regular-season games, six NLCS games, five World Series games, and nearly ten innings of this, but we were now on a par with 1985 for what we can loosely call excitement. We also reached the point where the Mets could start being the Mets for real, start being the Mets as we had always known them. It was quite gratifying to have that joyride through the National League, the mammoth lead, the whole universe anointing us favorites, and opponents seething at our greatness. But that wasn't us. Down to a final out with nobody on and reaching into the depths of our being to salvage three consecutive singles to remain extant . . . to get within one run and ninety feet of tying it and ensuring we'd continue . . . yeah, *that* was us.

I had given up. I had honestly given up. I never gave up (not counting, like, 1978) but here I had. Wally was a great chance. Keith was a great chance. They didn't happen. When they didn't, I gave up. I stopped believing.

Maybe I had to, just once, to remember what it meant to believe.

* * *

John McNamara was changing pitchers. Out went Schiraldi. In came Bob Stanley, the old Red Sox closer, the one their fans no longer liked. Kind of like us and Orosco.

Mookie Wilson's up.

Oh, this sucks.

Mookie. Of all fucking people, Mookie. Has Mookie *ever* gotten a big hit for us?

OK, I know he has. He won a game off Bruce Sutter when I was sitting in my dorm room calling Sports Phone my first semester. I thought it would propel us toward the split-season title in 1981. It didn't. And Mookie did score from second on ground balls in 1983. But Mookie *now*?

Mookie has been nothing but unfulfilled promise for us since 1980. Tim Raines became the player Mookie was supposed to become but didn't. Mookie has never been a good leadoff hitter or a good clutch hitter. Mookie doesn't know how to take a pitch. Mookie strikes out all the time. This is how it's gonna end, isn't it?

C'mon Mookie! Don't swing at everything.

Y'know what would be great right now? A wild pitch. I'm always saying that and it never happens. But man, a wild pitch would score Mitchell and tie the game.

Oh shit! Mookie's gonna get hit! Wait! He jumped out of the way!

IT'S A WILD PITCH! OH MY GOD, THAT'S NEVER HAPPENED BEFORE! I ASKED FOR IT AND IT CAME!

WHERE'S MITCHELL? SCORE! SCORE!!!

He scored! He scored! Game tied! 5–5! We're not gonna lose! We're not gonna lose! Mitchell scored! And Knight's on second!

COME ON MOOKIE! COME ON!

* * *

If I heard what happened next from outside my own head, it sounded like this from my room, from the stereo, from Bob Murphy, over WHN:

And a ground ball trickling . . . it's a fair ball. It gets by Buckner!

* * *

This is what I know I heard, because this is what I screamed:
IT WENT THROUGH HIS LEGS!
IT WENT THROUGH HIS LEGS!
AAAGGGHHH!!!
AAAGGGHHH!!!
I DON'T FUCKING BELIEVE IT!
I DON'T FUCKING BELIEVE IT!
AAAGGGHHH!!!
AAAGGGHHH!!!

* * *

Rounding third is Knight. The Mets win the ballgame! They win! They win!

* * *

If it was worth screaming twice, it was worth screaming more.
AAAGGGHHH!!!
IT WENT THROUGH HIS LEGS!!!
I DON'T FUCKING BELIEVE IT!!!

* * *

Gary Thorne chimed in:
Unbelievable, the Red Sox in stunned disbelief!
They weren't the only ones.

* * *

There were fourteen steps that separated upstairs from downstairs in our house, from where I was watching to where my parents were watching. While I was in the midst of my fifth (of fiftieth) AAAGGGHHH!!!, I leaped them in one furious bound. Well, not really, but it felt like it. I was downstairs in an instant. Dad couldn't believe it. Mom couldn't believe it. She believed enough in advance to videotape it, in case the Series should end in the tenth—though why we'd want to see it end in the tenth considering that would mean the Mets would have lost . . . oh, never mind—and kept telling me, "I taped it! I got it on tape!" Larry called. Larry, barely a fan most nights, was at a wedding and had to leave and listen in the car. He was calling me from his new "portable phone." I didn't know you could make calls from cars (Larry and his silly gadgets). He was heading over to ask me to explain how all this happened. My mother taped it, I said. You can see for yourself.

Because how the hell could *anyone* explain it?

FIFTEEN

ASCENT TO ASCENDANCY

As Shea Stadium neared its end in 2008, the team ran a survey in which fans were invited to vote for the most memorable moments in the history of the ballpark. It was no surprise that the tenth inning of Game Six of the 1986 World Series—the Buckner game—was voted No. 1. It was voted the No. 1 moment in team history during a similar promotion in 2000. Certainly through the night of October 25, 1986 (technically the morning of October 26, 1986), I voted it the No. 1 moment of my life.

And the Mets winning Game Seven, and thus the World Series? It finished fifth in the 2008 poll.

Fifth? Even when taking all the variables into account—online voting, younger skew to the voters, more recent events fresher in the mind's eye—that's shocking. Do the Mets win a lot of World Series? As of September 28, 2008, the day Shea Stadium emptied out for good, October 27, 1986 was still the last time they had won one.

* * *

That aspect of the vote was shocking. Yet it was kind of understandable. When you're following the No. 1 act of all-time, you're going to look almost insignificant by comparison, no matter what you pull off. Even if it's winning the World Series in a seventh game for your second and most recent world championship.

But it wasn't insignificant. It wasn't inevitable either. It's very easy to say it was, that after Mookie tapped that grounder through Buckner's legs the Red Sox were done for. They weren't. They were tied, just like us. They were good, just like us. They got a break, even. It rained Sunday so they could rearrange their rotation and send Bruce Hurst out to the hill Monday night. While Barrett reigned as Saturday's Miller Lite Player of the Game (NBC never revoked that particular honor), Hurst was already World Series MVP. It wasn't official, because it's never official until it's over, but word had leaked out that he'd be receiving the award for his Game One and Game Five wins, assuming the Red Sox held on in Game Six. And who wouldn't have assumed that?

* * *

We can say now that the Red Sox' early 3–0 lead off Darling was no biggie, that when a ball ticked off Darryl's glove and landed in the right field bullpen, it didn't matter. But for several innings the Mets were not touching Hurst—one hit through five—and Darling didn't make it through the fourth. The World Series was not a done deal. Nothing was helping until Davey sent El Sid in from the bullpen. That turned everything around.

Sid Fernandez was one of the most maddening pitchers the Mets ever had. No-hit stuff, it could have said on his business card, but forget about poise and concentration. He may as well have been Pete Falcone when things started to slip away. Yet on the night it all could have slipped away from the Mets, Sid of all people put everything right. He entered with a runner on second and two out. He walked Wade Boggs and then allowed nothing. Seven batters, seven outs, four by strikeout. Sid Fernandez preserved the season just long enough for the offense to wake up and rescue it.

One out into the bottom of the sixth, Lee Mazzilli stepped to the plate as a pinch-hitter. For the second straight game, he singled. Mookie Wilson, Lee's successor in center in the early '80s, followed with a single of his own. Tim Teufel hung in with Hurst and worked out a walk. We were one hit from getting back in this thing. The same guy I put my trust in on Saturday night/ Sunday morning was up: Keith Hernandez.

This time Mex came through, lacing a single to center that scored Mazz and Mook, narrowing Boston's lead to 3–2. Gary Carter sent a fly ball to right that Dwight Evans trapped, and Backman, pinch-running for Teufel, scored to tie it. Mex should have been on second, but umpire Dale Ford made a slow call on the trap and Keith was forced out.

Now, however, I would say it was inevitable. McNamara sent Schiraldi, shell-shocked from Saturday, to start the last of the seventh. Ray Knight greeted him with line-drive homer to left that gave the Mets their first lead. Larry, no master of timing, had called just as the seventh commenced, mildly distracting me. But when Knight's bolt cleared the fence and I screamed with delight, Larry acknowledged "that's what I wanted to hear" and left me alone for the rest of the night.

There wasn't much more screaming from there on out. It was methodical how the Mets dismantled the Red Sox bullpen. Boston just kept trotting guys out there and the Mets just kept hitting. We led 6–3 going to the eighth. McDowell lapsed and let them get close in the top of the eighth, but I can honestly say it didn't occur to me the Red Sox could come back. Well, maybe an ounce of doubt crept in when it got to be 6–5 and Roger hadn't retired anybody, but Jesse came in and, in one of my favorite baseball clichés, restored order. In the bottom of the inning, Darryl took one of his long swings and sent the ball a long way and he took a long time circling the bases. Jesse Orosco himself knocked in a run with a base hit to center.

Jesse would pitch clear to 2003, yet he never did that again.

* * *

Top of the ninth. Mets up 8–5. Orosco still pitching. Ed Romero popped out foul. Wade Boggs grounded to Backman. Marty Barrett, after thirteen hits off Mets pitching in the series, was in no position to deliver a fourteenth.

Murph?

Now the pitch on the way . . . he struck him out! Struck him out! The Mets have won the World Series! And they're jamming and crowding all over Jesse Orosco . . . the dream has come true, the Mets have won the World Series, coming from behind to win the seventh ballgame.

* * *

I stood in front of the television in my parents' bedroom when Barrett swung and Orosco was jammed and crowded. I threw my cap at the ceiling. I have no recollection of what I said or screamed. I rushed over to hug my mother just as I had when the Mets beat the Cubs for the division and the Astros for the pennant. It lacked the spontaneity of the first two, but this hug was no less sincere. Years of tension, mistrust, suspicion, and brooding dissipated when Orosco struck out Barrett. Without qualification, I hugged my mother.

Mom would live clear to 1990, yet I never did that again.

* * *

The ball getting by/through Buckner may have been transcendent, but the fifth-greatest moment in the history of Shea Stadium had longer legs. The second the Mets became world champions, everything changed. Maybe not forever, but for hours and days and weeks and months. The Mets were champions.

Not seventeen years ago, but right now. They had ascended to the throne. They were on it. The stuff about being defending world champions, that would be for 1987. By then it would be a different team and a different season. By then they'd be 0–0 and they'd be in a twenty-six-team tie with the rest of baseball. By then everybody would be trying to knock off their crown. Here, from October 27, 1986 until the next game, there was nothing anybody could do about them. The Mets had ascended, and now we could all enjoy their ascendancy.

The Mets ruled. There was nothing like it.

* * *

The highlight films always end with the parade, which is too bad, because the entire offseason following your team winning a world championship is one long parade. Not that the parade itself was bad. Well, actually, it was frightening to attend, but having missed the last one (when I was six), I was going to throw myself into whatever crowd there was, no matter how massive.

And it was massive. All of downtown was jammed. I didn't need my feet. I was just carried along. I saw some vehicles that may have carried some Mets. I couldn't tell. I was enveloped in Mets fans. Or maybe it was just an angry mob. There was ticker-tape, shredded computer paper, whatever it was. A tiny dot of it wedged itself between the frame and lens of my glasses. I did not remove it for about two weeks.

I went back to the offices of the magazine where I had a recurring gig in 1986, wearing my satin Starter Mets jacket, a jacket I was given for my eighteenth birthday in the months between finishing fifth in 1980 and fifth in the first half of 1981. Somebody in the elevator asked me if I had just run out and bought it that morning.

Like Knight against Schiraldi, I teed off pretty good on that one.

* * *

I bought a couple of T-shirts. I bought a couple of pennants. I bought Royal Crown Cola cans that detailed all the Mets' accomplishments, including the 108 wins. I saved every newspaper that featured the Mets on the front page, including one that indicated the team's trip to the White House was delayed because Reagan administration officials feared the damage they'd cause (the Mets, after all, had wailed on the National League pretty badly all season). I wore my good old Mets jacket everywhere. I wasn't alone. If there was ever an offseason to be a Mets fan, this was it. Mets fans were everywhere. The Mets were everywhere. They'd been invited to toss ceremonial jump balls at the Nets opener, then the Knicks opener. Their good karma extended to the Giants, who won their first Super Bowl that January. The Giants began a long winning streak the night the Mets won the World Series. Snap counts and such were disrupted that Monday night at the Meadowlands because football fans were following a baseball game at Shea.

A shirt was produced: CITY OF CHAMPIONS, Mets logo, Giants logo, 1986. I bought that, too. I saw a Christmas tree ornament with the Mets logo and the World Series emblem. I didn't buy that. I should have.

The World Champion Mets were everywhere. Cars had bumper stickers. Stores had signs. I had letters. Letters from friends in college I'd lost touch with. They saw the Mets won. They thought of me and reached out. Congratulations, they said.

Thank you, I replied.

Sixteen

THE BRIDGE

There was some bitching among Mets fans when it was announced Billy Joel would have the honor of playing the last standalone concert at Shea Stadium (not counting the merengue and salsa shows on Hispanic heritage nights). Billy was known to have had Yankee sympathies. Unpure, the critics carped.

Having loved Billy Joel's music in high school almost as much I had loved Steve Henderson's home run, I was more forgiving. Billy showed up at Shea for a press conference, slapped on a Mets cap, and paid homage to Casey Stengel and Vinegar Bend Mizell. I'm easy. I give celebrity dispensations. They're too busy becoming stars to be fans.

Besides, there was enough Met pedigree to Billy Joel's career to make him legit. He sang the national anthem before Game Two of the '86 Series, the Doc vs. Clemens matchup. "New York State Of Mind" was the tune to which we wandered down the ramps as a matter of course in the 21st century. While the Mets were battling the Astros in Houston, he was playing the Garden and it was there that some 20,000 New Yorkers learned the pennant had been won. Billy Joel may not have bled orange and blue, but he brushed up against enough of it.

One other thing he had going for him was a hit he had in the summer of 1986. Actually, it was one of my least favorite Billy Joel hits, "Modern Woman" from the *Ruthless People* soundtrack. Too forced, too peppy, but it's the only song I know of that actually mentions the year in question in the form of a question:

"After 1986," the Piano Man queries, "what else could be new?"

It would turn out to be a most salient question for the next two decades at least.

* * *

Rick Aguilera, skipped over as a starter in the postseason of '86, was not making the most of his opportunity the night of May 11, 1987. Staked to a 2–0 lead at Cincinnati, he gave it back in the bottom of the third. It was 2–2 when I turned off my radio that Monday night. Aggie and the struggling Mets would go on to lose 12–2. But that's not why I stopped listening. I would have liked to have continued, but I didn't want to be rude.

That day I had been working in the city at one of my freelance assignments. Usually I'd go home afterwards. That Monday night, I was meeting a friend from college who was still more or less attending school. He was in town for a "summer in New York" semester. He had just broken up with his fiancée and decided to ditch Tampa for a while. He found out about this New York thing and thought it would be a nice change of pace. We could hang out, he said.

So I agreed to meet him after work, even though the Mets were playing. My social life was still essentially the Mets. If Aguilera was showing signs of going down in flames, I guess I could stand a change of pace for one night.

My friend and I had planned to go out somewhere. Maybe we'd wind up at a bar where the Mets game would be on. But my friend had this way of attracting strangers and foisting them on me. He found these two girls who were also from my alma mater, also doing the summer semester thing. So as I stood in the lobby of the residential Parc Lincoln Hotel on the Upper West

I'm ready to meet my destiny—or
at least my destination.
(Courtesy of David G. Whitham)

Now if only that darn
train would get here.
*(Courtesy of David G.
Whitham)*

2008: Two ballparks, no playoffs. (*Courtesy of David G. Whitham*)

Future home of Citi Field parking lot. (*Courtesy of David G. Whitham*)

This used to be my playground. (*Author's collection*)

My first Shea Stadium purchase, rendered instantly obsolete by sale of
All-Star Jim Fregosi to Texas. *(Author's collection)*

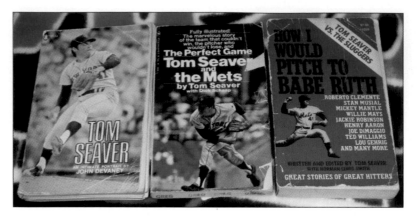

I read a lot as a kid, albeit mostly about the same thing.
(Author's collection)

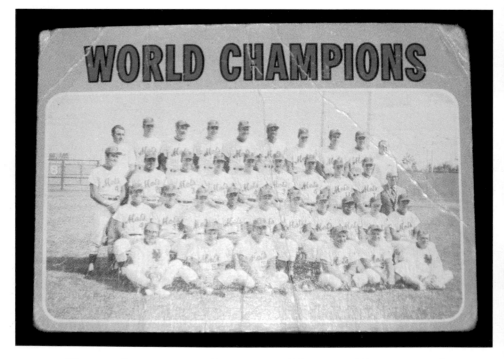

Those early memories of 1969 never fade, even if this 1970 card
commemorating them does. *(Courtesy of the Topps Company, Inc.)*

To get my mind off disastrous December 1975 trade of Rusty Staub for
Mickey Lolich, my family treats me to cake. Or was this my January 1976
Bar Mitzvah? *(Author's collection)*

What's stranger: that the Shea vendor who sold this batting helmet to me in 1977 would materialize in our living room six months later as my sister's future husband, or that I still have the batting helmet? *(Author's collection)*

I spent a weekend in the Catskills with these guys. I don't think I made much of an impression on either of them. *(Courtesy of the Topps Company, Inc.)*

My wife and me, 1989, just after we got engaged. I bought her
the jacket for the occasion. There's a ring down there, too.
(Author's collection)

Everything I touch eventually turns to orange and blue.
(Author's collection)

Sweet nectar of playoff
clinching, 1999.
(*Author's collection*)

What was wrong with Shea? Nothing one more coat of paint couldn't
cover up. (*Courtesy of David G. Whitham*)

A marker for Shea's longest fair ball . . . and a de facto warning track to keep you from falling over the edge of Section 48. (*Courtesy of David G. Whitham*)

Seven postseason appearances make seven good reasons to love the Mets, but mostly I love the Mets because I love the Mets. (*Courtesy of David G. Whitham*)

Full house gathers on September 28, 2008 to Shea goodbye, Shea farewell and Shea amen. (*Courtesy of David G. Whitham*)

Daniel Murphy became the latest Met to learn that old adage,
"Don't look back, the Phillies and Brewers are probably
gaining on you." *(Courtesy of David G. Whitham)*

Ryan Church takes the last cut before the demolition crews start hacking away.
(Courtesy of David G. Whitham)

Say good night, Gate E.
(*Courtesy of David G. Whitham*)

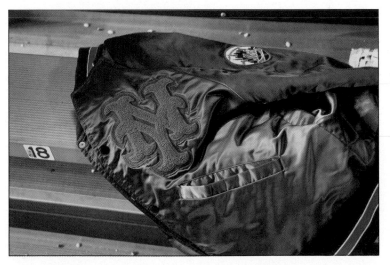

In what's left of the Picnic Area,
I lay down my shield.
(*Courtesy of David G. Whitham*)

Side of Manhattan waiting to meet him and saw he was bringing company, I switched off Aguilera. I didn't want to, but I figured I should be polite.

Ten minutes later, I discovered after 1986 what else could be new.

* * *

Ten minutes of walking a few blocks down Broadway was all it took to realize the girl I met in the lobby was who I was going to be with forever or for as long as could be arranged. It was like meeting the Mets in 1969. It was not just love but total commitment at first sight.

Her name was (and still is) Stephanie. It was just one of those things where you hit it off inside of twenty minutes. I'd had only one semi-serious relationship prior, to the girl whose background didn't meet with my mother's approval. My first date with that young lady was an exhibition game in St. Petersburg. She, an art major, called it "the baseball exhibition." It was at Al Lang Stadium, down the block from the Dali museum. That was Spring Training. That was practice.

This was going to count.

All four of us—me, Stephanie, my friend, and Stephanie's roommate (whom my friend had his eye on before we all hooked up in the lobby)—went to see the Mets take on the Giants that Friday night, May 15. El Sid had a no-hitter going for five innings and tripled in the fourth. Such activity did not mesh with Sid's delicate and substantial frame and he left in deference to his knees. Doug Sisk, on unfriendly terms with most of Shea (everybody but me) since the middle of 1984, came in, gave up some hits and some runs, but it was no biggie. Darryl, Dykstra, and HoJo all homered. Mets won 8–3. It was hardly the headline.

This was. We sat in our Upper Deck box, Section 8, and Stephanie took in the twinkling vista of the ballpark and the

Whitestone beyond it. "My first baseball game," she declared. "Neat!"

Neat. Yes it was.

While the Mets slipped and slid and drug-rehabbed through the first third of 1987, Stephanie and I spent as much time as possible together. I found myself shutting off games for innings at a time. It was worth it. It was 1987. I daresay that even if it had been 1986 it would have been worth it.

We were in my car when it was announced Tom Seaver, left unsigned after his stint with the Red Sox, was coming back for one more (ultimately aborted) try as a Met. The Mets were rather desperate for starters and this wasn't just any forty-two-year-old righty who'd been out of action for nine months. He was Tom Seaver. As I exulted over the news, Stephanie asked why Seaver was ever traded in the first place.

My girlfriend—all of nineteen, holed up in Florida for a half-dozen years, originally from Kansas but with a couple of small stretches of her childhood spent north of the city—knew who Tom Seaver was.

You bet I was in love.

There was a midweek afternoon when we couldn't be together. She asked on the phone how my day had been. Doc, in his second post-rehab start, pitched well and the Mets won, I said. Ask me how my day was and I'll tell you how the Mets did. Realizing this was not a universal answer for "how was your day?" I added oh, you probably don't care about that.

"If it's important to you," she said, "it's important to me."

Stephanie had just printed me a license to go on and on about the Mets for the rest of our natural lives.

Repeat: You bet I was in love.

We had known each other for three weeks when it was acknowledged between us we'd eventually get married. The accent was on eventually because she had only finished her first year of college and I was still proceeding as if I had just graduated.

She would need three years to obtain her degree. I'd need just as long to get my act together. But it was a no-drama done deal. We would get married. The voids wouldn't be fun. In fact, after she and her roommate got on their Amtrak back to Florida in mid–June, I fell into what felt like an endless funk. It was short-term, however. Stephanie and I were engaged to be engaged.

Why couldn't everything about 1987 be that easy?

SEVENTEEN

DON'T BLAME SCIOSCIA

If I say "Terry Pendleton" to you, you know what to do. You throw something, quite possibly at me for even bringing his name up. When Terry Pendleton hit the home run that is universally identified as the death knell for the 1987 Mets, I threw a shoe. There is a wall in the house where I grew up that may very well still be Terry-fied.

I could bring up plenty of other discouraging episodes from the 1987 season, everything from Doc Gooden testing positive for cocaine on April Fool's Day to Jesse Orosco surrendering an anvil of a homer to Luis Aguayo in Philadelphia almost exactly six months later. That was the least fun 92-win season I could imagine. I did so want 1987 to be the icing on '86, to be the great comeback to top all great comebacks, to certify us as a dynasty. It wasn't going to happen.

Didn't make it any more pleasant to accept, but when there's nothing left to believe, You Gotta Accept.

Likewise for 1988, the least loved playoff year in Mets history. The Mets, their 100 wins, their division title, and their return to something close to '86 form have been swept under the carpet of Mike Scioscia's imitation of Terry Pendleton. It was another top of the ninth inning, it was another 4–2 lead, it was another two-run bomb, it was another extra-inning loss, it was another prelude to ultimate defeat.

I accept that. What I don't accept is Mike Scioscia's assigned role in Mets history. Mike Scioscia (meaning Mike Scioscia's home run, 'cause, quite frankly, who cares about the guy?) was a telling blow in the context of a 4–2 lead becoming a 4–4 tie, but he didn't end it all for the Mets. Not in that game, not in that series, not in that era, not forever after.

* * *

The Dodgers were going to be easy pickings in the National League Championship Series. They had already been easy pickings. We beat them ten of eleven in the regular season. Orel Hershiser had racked up 59 consecutive scoreless innings, the greatest such streak in baseball history, but they had no punch and not much pitching behind him. The closer you looked at the Dodgers, the less you saw. Steve Winwood's most recent hit, "Roll With It," was parodied quite accurately, I thought, on WPLJ: the Mets were gonna roll over L.A.

In 1988, nothing I cared about would be so simple. We won the first game at Dodger Stadium in our last at-bat and the news coverage afterwards struck an "of course, the Mets always come back in the postseason," chord, precisely the kind of presumptuousness that raised my trouble antenna. I'd been growing more and more superstitious since the night in 1985 I decided watching the Mets in the kitchen was bad luck. No sense screwing with the gods by presuming we'd always come back late.

A column appeared in the *Daily News* under David Cone's byline the next day declaring the Dodgers were no match for the Mets, and that their pitchers after Hershiser were a bunch of "high school" stiffs. David Cone went 20–3 in 1988, but he was no contender for the Pulitzer. The Dodgers rocked Cone in Game Two.

He shouldn't have said that, or let it be ghosted in his name.

The series shifted to New York. Modell's was selling K Kloths, our answer, apparently, to the Homer Hankies that blanketed the Metrodome in the World Series the year before. I thought they were silly. I also ran out and bought several. It was '86 all over again, at least a little. When the Mets kept playing, there was more stuff to buy. It was the price of admission to the postseason. I'd have to start making some postseason money.

Game Three was rained out Friday. Saturday found Shea a field of muck, but they played anyway. Tommy Lasorda brought back Hershiser on short rest. He wasn't sharp. The tableau wasn't pretty, muddy as it was, but the Mets slapped around three Dodger relievers in the eighth and won going away, 8–4. We were up in the series 2–1. Sunday night we'd have Gooden. They'd have John Tudor, no longer the invincible robo-pitcher who tortured us in '85 as a Cardinal.

It was a long wait Sunday afternoon. The ALCS finale provided a bit of a distraction, with the powerful A's sweeping the Red Sox out of the playoffs. I had a friend from high school who was living in Boston and became a Sox fan. One of the rewards out of 1986 was teasing him lightly. When his series was over, I gave him a call. I got his machine and left my condolences, adding that with the Red Sox done, at least he'd have no conflict of interest when the Mets played Oakland in the World Series.

I can't believe I was that presumptuous.

* * *

Sometimes you just feel the worst coming on. Sometimes one moment encapsulates all your fear and dread. Sometimes the Mets get a runner on third with nobody out and they strand him there. Such was the case in the sixth inning of Game Four. Kevin McReynolds doubled to lead off. Fine. Carter, bad knees and all, tripled him home. Fantastic. It put the Mets up 4–2. Wonderful.

It would be simple stuff to drive in Kid from third, to increase the lead, to give Doc (who had given up only one hit since the first) a greater cushion. Gary had chased Tudor from the mound. Brian Holton entered. How could Brian Holton keep the Mets from delivering a runner from third with nobody out?

He could and he did. Tim Teufel struck out. Kevin Elster walked. Doc, pitching too well to be removed, grounded into a double play.

How did we not score Carter? You don't extract a triple from those legs and leave him on third. You just don't.

You just don't.

There's nothing inherently mortifying about holding a 4–2 lead, just as there is nothing decisive about leaving a haughty telephone message. These were still the 100–60 Mets, those were still the Dodgers who lost to us ten of eleven times. But something wasn't right. I was in my twentieth season as a Mets fan. I could feel it.

Uneasily I watched with my parents, as in '86. Doc pitched on, as in '86. He didn't win any of his postseason starts then. He didn't win Game One of this series even though the Mets did. It would sure be nice to get Doc a win. He pitched through the seventh, giving up only a walk to our old pal Danny Heep. He pitched through the eighth, setting down L.A. in order. The Mets didn't score either. We got to the ninth still up 4–2, Doc still pitching.

Uneasy. Just uneasy.

Sending a reliever into start the ninth even when the starter had been very effective for eight innings was becoming an accepted practice in baseball by 1988. Tony La Russa was in the process of turning Dennis Eckersley into a Hall of Famer by doing just that in Oakland. The Mets had Randy Myers as their closer. Myers threw harder than any fireman they'd ever had to that point. He was probably the only closer, other than Tug at his peak, who never made me exceedingly nervous. Randall K. Myers, as Tim

McCarver liked to call him, wasn't a sure thing, but he had blown only three saves in the regular season, none since July.

On the other hand, Doc was Doc. He was pitching like Doc. If he'd never again pitch quite like he did in 1985, he had put drug rehab and all that disappointment behind him, behind us. I liked to see Doc complete games. He'd done it ten times in 1988. It wasn't really that much a variation from the norm to leave him out there. Since the first inning, he'd given the Dodgers no runs and exactly two hits.

Uneasy anyway. Uneasier when John Shelby walked to lead off the top of the ninth. Nobody ever wants to see a leadoff baserunner via the walk. Six seasons of McCarver had pounded that into my head. It was a warning sign. Myers should be warming up, should be coming in.

Or not. Doc was Doc. That's what I told myself.

Mike Scioscia was up next. He was a respected catcher, but when it came to hitting, he was more Luis Aguayo than Terry Pendleton. In more than 400 at-bats in 1988, Scioscia had homered only three times.

Naturally, Scioscia homered and tied the game in the ninth. If they wanted to go up three games to one and near the World Series, the Mets would have to beat the Dodgers in extra innings. Boy would they have their chances. The Mets would put one on in the tenth, two on in the eleventh, and three on in the twelfth. They would not score in any of those frames. The twelfth was the real killer because in the top of the inning, with two outs, Kirk Gibson drove a ball over the center field wall to make it 5–4. Lasorda had to use three relievers in the twelfth, two of them Met apparitions and the other an angel of Met death.

Tim Leary started the inning. Leary was briefly, four years after Seaver went to Cincinnati and three years before Gooden came out of the minors, the most highly regarded pitcher the Mets had. In early 1981, he looked golden in Spring Training, made the team despite Frank Cashen's objections, and blew his arm out in his first start in the cold of Wrigley Field. He would work his way back to the Mets, but never evoke Seaver or Gooden again. After giving up hits to Mackey Sasser and Mazzilli, he induced a flyout from Gregg Jefferies, a prospect as highly touted in 1988 as Leary had been in 1981.

Jesse Orosco was called on for the two lefties who followed. He walked Hernandez but got Strawberry to pop up. Orosco had thrown the last pitch in the last World Series at Shea and exulted mightily. Tonight he left the mound with his glove firmly attached to his right hand. We wouldn't see him at Shea again until 1998, when he visited as an Oriole. By then he'd be greeted warmly. He'd be remembered for 1986. We would want to forget about 1988.

Orel Hershiser came out next to get McReynolds. Surely this was desperation on Lasorda's part. The day before, the Dodgers' closer Jay Howell got himself suspended for pitching with pine tar on his glove. In his absence, it was all hands on deck, even your ace starter from the day before. Hershiser was Lasorda's seventh pitcher of the night. He had pitched into the ninth Tuesday and logged seven more innings on Saturday. Lasorda was insane.

Yet it worked. Hershiser—who made for a deceptively friendly ghoul (we'd see him hum hymns with Johnny Carson that fall)—teased a short fly ball to center out of McReynolds. Shelby had to hustle in to catch it, but the Dodgers were good at hustling. They had just hustled the Mets out of Game Four.

* * *

As with Pendleton in 1987, Scioscia in 1988 is blamed for everything. His hitting that homer has even been fingered as a turning point for the franchise. If Gooden doesn't give it up or if Myers comes in, the Mets almost surely lead that series 3–1 and a second world championship is within tantalizing reach. Instead the Mets lose Game Four, lose Game Five, win Game Six but lose

Game Seven, and it is the Dodgers who move on and beat the Athletics in five games and become champs for 1988.

I don't buy it.

It was stranding Carter on third that killed us.

It was loading the bases in the twelfth without scoring that killed us.

It was me making that phone call to Boston that killed us.

It was Cone's ghostwriter, Bob Klapisch, typing that high school crack that killed us.

It was El Sid having little the next day that killed us.

It was Gregg Jefferies getting hit by a batted ball while running the bases in Game Five that killed us.

It was Kevin McReynolds not being Kevin Mitchell that killed us.

It was the unhyped Tim Belcher shutting us down twice that killed us.

It was Ojeda's finger nearly coming off in a hedge-clipping incident that put him out of action for the series that killed us.

It was Darling showing up with nothing, absolutely nothing, in Game Seven that killed us.

It was Hershiser's excellence in Game Seven on top of his grit in Game Four that killed us.

It was Lasorda's guts that killed us.

It was the K Kloths and the lack of noise you get from waving as opposed to clapping that killed us.

It was Kirk Gibson's almost unsung twelfth-inning homer that killed us.

It was the karma-irking cheering from the Shea throng when Gibson couldn't immediately stand up after sliding into second in the fifth game that killed us.

It was the recurring appearances of John Shelby that killed us.

It was making an unnecessarily big deal out of Howell's pine tar that killed us.

It was Scioscia's homer, Doc not being pulled and Myers not coming in that killed us, too, but they didn't act alone. They had accomplices.

Everything that could make a difference went against us in the 1988 NLCS. It just did. We didn't roll over L.A. We just kind of rolled over. We truly lost that series in seven games, not on one pitch or one decision or false presumptive move.

Scioscia wasn't *the* turning point, not by my reckoning. The Mets had the bottom of the ninth, three extra innings and three games after that to salvage the pennant. They had 1989 to attempt to make up for it. They had 1990 for that matter. They had plenty of chances. Sooner or later, you've got to take advantage of one and not sit around and blame Mike Scioscia for all your problems.

* * *

I wish I had given myself this kind of pep talk in 1988. Instead I moped just like a Mets fan might after losing a distressing seven-game series in October, just like a son whose mother was diagnosed with cancer in August, just like a writer who lost his two biggest clients in June. Why would have I expected the Mets to have overcome adversity when all I did was let it overcome me?

It, like me approaching my 26th birthday, was getting old fast.

EIGHTEEN

COMEBACK PLAYER
OF THE DECADE

Except for the Mets maintaining their grip on first place, and one trip to Tampa to make the most of Stephanie's sophomore spring break, 1988 was a disaster for me personally. My freelancing career, which had veered from sporadic to steady since 1985, was dwindling to nothing. Some clients just didn't require my services anymore. My two biggest, who were direct competitors (I was so not into what I was doing that I didn't realize it), discovered I was writing for each of them and they both disassociated themselves from me. The clock was ticking toward spring 1990, Stephanie's eventual graduation, and I had done nothing but watch the Mets and write stories for low-paying trade magazines like *Truckstop World*. Before I could truly survey the scope of my professional wreckage that summer, I was distracted from the yowls downstairs. My mother was in pain.

My mother was always complaining of a bad back or a bad something. I'd say it was usually bad vibes. After the elation of 1986, we kept watching the Mets together, but that was the respite from the rest of our relationship. Things grew tense again once I had a new girlfriend who, no, wasn't Jewish. Mom met Stephanie one time during our early courtship phase and couldn't have been more polite, but I was warned within a week of those pleasantries that she—my mother—had no intention of "supporting any *shkutz* babies," which is a pretty nasty sentiment to let loose. If I had learned anything from my college romance, it was to have my back up for when I inevitably met another girl who my mother wouldn't like for whatever reason.

I didn't make a big deal of it, but I dug in with my mother where Stephanie was concerned. In college, she could bully me a little. In what was now real life, I wasn't going to put up with it. I held my ground every time she revived the old chestnut about meeting Jewish girls. No, I said, I've met all the girl—singular—I plan on meeting.

One Thursday night in February of '88, just before ten o'clock, I was sitting down to do what I did every Thursday night at ten. I was going to watch *L.A. Law*. My mother picked that moment to call me to the stairs to discuss something that's been eating away at her. It would make her feel better, she said, if Stephanie and I, if we are going to get married, were married by a rabbi. I'm descended from a long line of rabbis, I was reminded.

Oh yeah, absolutely, I vamped. We discussed it and we decided that's the way we're gonna go. Married by a rabbi, you betcha. I'm gonna go watch *L.A. Law* now, OK?

Stephanie and I had never discussed clergy. We were both quite agnostic. But she did say if it's important to me, it was important to her. It was important at that moment to concoct a conversation and conclusion. I had TV to watch and a mother to get off my back.

* * *

My mother kept resisting my father's insistences about seeing a doctor in July of '88. Even as she took to bed, even as she insisted on a commode for next to the bed. She feared finding out why she was in such pain. But the pain overcame her irrationality, so we took her to South Nassau Hospital in Oceanside on the first Sunday in August when the Mets were at Three Rivers holding off the Pirates 6–2.

She'd be in there Monday when Pittsburgh called up an unheralded minor leaguer named Rick Reed and he beat Bobby Ojeda 1–0 on ABC.

She'd be in there Tuesday when the Mets traveled to Chicago for the first official night game in Wrigley Field history and lost.

She'd be in there Thursday when Gary Carter finally got a monkey off his back and hit his 300th home run against the Cubs.

She'd be there Friday when a doctor told my father and my sister that my mother had cancer. I was told second-hand and urged to not say anything to her just yet. It would only worry her more and she was already plenty panicky.

* * *

She was there Saturday while the Mets were home playing the Expos. I had tickets to that game but couldn't find anybody to go with me and it didn't seem such a priority to rush to Shea. So I went to the hospital and sat with my mother and listened to the game on her radio (South Nassau didn't get SportsChannel.)

There wasn't much concentration on Montreal winning 7–4. Somebody must have let her in on her condition because it was urgent to her that we discuss Stephanie. She was sure this girl is very nice, but I was Jewish and there was this long line of rabbis . . .

I didn't anger. I stayed very calm. Somebody had to be calm. I put it as plainly as I could.

"Mom, you know how you always said that when you met Dad you knew within ten minutes that it was *beshert*?" (That's Yiddish for destined to be; I sure did pick up a ton of Yiddish growing up.)

"Yes."

"Well, that's how it was for Stephanie and me."

"Really?"

"Yes."

Somehow it had never come up before. All her free-floating anxieties that tended to put everybody on the edge of hysteria had obscured the simple matter of whether this relationship was the right thing. It was, I said. Of course it was. This wasn't *L.A. Law* talking. This was the truth.

"I'm so relieved," she said.

I was relieved, too. Yes, a little that we could drop once and for all this subject, but more that in her hour of need, fighting the pain and this horrible ailment (she had to know more than what anybody had told her) she could find relief in my long-term happiness.

That didn't mean she wasn't crazy. She was, after all, my mother. But she did, through her filter of crazy, care about me.

* * *

The Mets made one notable change in advance of the 1989 season. They traded Wally Backman, in many way their most vital organ from 1986 (combination heart, spine, guts, *cojones,* and filth-covered epidermis), to assure Gregg Jefferies of a position to call his own. Jefferies had lit up Shea late in '88. He'd never come close to doing so again. I'm not sure if anybody's replaced Wally Backman yet.

I also made one notable change in advance of the 1989 season. I got a full-time job. Couldn't put it off any longer. I'm not sure why I was so intent on avoiding people in a professional setting for so long. I guess I saw my sister (often my role model) making a go of freelancing and, indulging certain antisocial tendencies, wanted to try it. It wasn't my bag. In the winter of '89, I found a magazine on Long Island that covered the beverage business. I'd always had a love affair with soda. I was allergic to milk as a kid. I started collecting soda cans when I was thirteen. *You mean there's a magazine that covers this stuff?*

Why not? There was a magazine that covered truckstops.

I called on spec and was told there was a sudden opening for associate editor. A lot of writing would be involved. My interview went swimmingly. I explained to the editor that I might require a little flexibility because of my mother's health. He was very sympathetic, said no problem. She's going into Roosevelt Hospital in the city for chemo in a few weeks, I said, but I'm not too worried. Roosevelt is where they reattached Bobby Ojeda's fingertip from the hedge-clipping accident.

The editor stared at me blankly. Five years of immersion in the Mets hadn't prepared me for the existence of New Yorkers who weren't immersed in them as well. But I got the job.

* * *

I had to set myself up at a Great Neck lunch counter with a Walkman to follow Opening Day. I couldn't be in front of a television for nine innings as I had when I freelanced, but it was still Opening Day. It was still an event. Backman was gone. Jefferies was entrenched. Don Aase, a journeyman reliever, was the only new face. He pitched the eighth and ninth and saved the win over the Cardinals for Doc. Mike Scioscia hadn't ruined everything. The Mets were 1–0. My mother asked that night what was this new pitcher's name again . . . Assman?

* * *

Chemotherapy was everything it was cracked up to be for my mother: gruesome. She stayed overnight at Roosevelt, my father sitting up with her, me coming in after work. There were wastebaskets by the bed. They weren't for tissues. But the treatment was apparently working, nausea notwithstanding. My mother was usually well enough to turn her attention from telling me how to conduct my love life to telling me how to conduct myself in my new job. Yes, she was back.

* * *

Beverage World allowed me to see the world. Well, it gave me excuses to travel "on business" to Florida so I could see Stephanie on somebody else's time. I became a whiz at discovering trade shows and conferences that absolutely needed our attention. They mostly happened to be where my girlfriend was. I also discovered that some events took place in cities with major league ballclubs. The first time I had to go to Chicago, I weaseled out of a NutraSweet cocktail party, jumped into a cab, and asked the driver to take me to Comiskey Park, the original one. I loved Comiskey Park. If I hadn't loved it, I would have loved that I was suddenly going to it anyway. This job was working out pretty well.

There was no business excuse for my trip to Florida in mid-June. My friend who introduced me to Stephanie was getting married . . . to Stephanie's roommate from that trip. They kind of had to get married on the fly, if you get my drift. My mother did when I kind of slipped in to the conversation that I'd be away this weekend down in the Boca Raton area. My friend, I said, was getting married and I'm the best man.

"He knock her up?" she asked.

"Yeah, something like that," I said.

When I flew back to New York that Sunday, I discovered something was missing: Lenny Dykstra. The Mets had traded him and Roger McDowell to the Phillies for Juan Samuel.

First no Wally, now no Lenny. The best part of the '80s had been them getting on and running wild. Still, Juan Samuel was pretty good. An All-Star. The Mets were in a tight race with the Cubs, Expos, and Cardinals. Maybe Samuel would be a big help.

* * *

Juan Samuel was not a big help. He was, in fact, a disaster. A Fregosi. He used to be good. He wasn't anymore. He used to be a second baseman. The Mets stuck him in center. The Mets were still in a race, but they didn't look all that much like frontrunners.

* * *

Doc was pitching some of his best ball since 1985. He was up to 9–2 right after the Dykstra trade. He got his hundredth win. All the potholes notwithstanding, Doc was still Hall of Fame bound. He was 100–37 lifetime, and only twenty-four years old. Then Doc felt something in his shoulder. He lost a couple of decisions, falling to 9–4. Then it was announced he was going on the disabled list. The Mets would need a pitcher to replace him. After dabbling with their own callups, they made a bold move at the deadline.

They traded for Frank Viola, the best pitcher in the American League the year before, the World Series MVP the year before that and a Long Island native, even. The Twins didn't want to pay him any longer and accepted five inexpensive pitchers in his stead: four prospects plus Rick Aguilera, who had become a pretty decent late-inning reliever for us. Aggie was the winning pitcher in Game Six, the Buckner game. It was the worst win in the best game in team history. He won because he was taken off the hook. But he was an '86 Met. Now he was an ex–'86 Met. It was a growing club.

At the very same trading deadline, the Mets cleaned house a little more. They waived Lee Mazzilli, who was claimed by the Blue Jays. Mazz had already had a second life as a Met, first discarded in spring '82, later reclaimed for the stretch run in '86. He had those two pinch-hits against Boston. He had succeeded Rusty Staub and Ed Kranepool in the time-honored role of pinch-hitter deluxe. Lee Mazzilli was a Toronto Blue Jay now.

So was Mookie Wilson. Juan Samuel had made Mookie obsolete in management's eyes. Mookie Wilson, you may recall, sent a ground ball trickling until it got by Bill Buckner. That was 1986. This was 1989. This was the year we traded Mookie Wilson for Jeff Musselman, a relief pitcher of no known talents. To paraphrase what Jackie Mason had said of Ronald Reagan and the presidency, Jeff Musselman was a *wonderful* pitcher, a *terrific* pitcher, a *marvelous* pitcher . . . it's just that pitching wasn't his field.

Mookie Wilson and Lee Mazzilli helped the Toronto Blue Jays win the American League East in 1989.

* * *

My mother persevered through a couple of more chemo stayovers. I was a hit in my job. When I told the powers that be that it was necessary for me to attend a conference in Tulsa and interview a consulting firm outside Kansas City in August, I went with everybody's blessing. It was just a coincidence that Stephanie was visiting her grandma in Wichita at the very same time . . . and that the Royals were home.

Upon changing planes in St. Louis, I picked up the *Post-Dispatch*. Their big sports columnist, Bernie Miklasz, railed against the Mets who were playing the Cardinals at Shea that weekend. They were the big bad New Yorkers, he wrote. They lost Gooden, so they grabbed Viola. They were ruining it for everybody else in the NL East, he grumbled.

* * *

It took a while but the Mets would begin to live up to the paranoid Midwestern columnist's delusions. Viola struggled a bit, but surely it was temporary. The Expos had made a similar bold move, trading young Randy Johnson to Seattle to secure Mark Langston, but it was the Cubs who latched onto first place.

Nevertheless, the Mets got hot post-Mookie and won fifteen of nineteen to pull within two-and-a-half of first. On Sunday August 20, however, as the Mets led the Dodgers 3–1 in the ninth at Shea, Don Aase, after getting two outs (the second of them Mike Scioscia), gave up two singles and then a home run to L.A. second baseman Willie Randolph. It was Randolph's first homer of the year. (What an Assman.) The Mets would lose 5–4 and, despite hanging close enough to call it a pennant race for most of September, were widely acknowledged as screwed. Pendleton . . . Scioscia . . . Randolph . . . every year a home run everybody could point to as blowing the season.

This was becoming quite the annual ritual.

* * *

I invited Stephanie up for a long weekend in September. As I was still living at home, I reserved us a room at the Diplomat Motor Inn of Rockville Centre. My mother was feeling a little achy again and, really, I preferred a little privacy besides. She flew up on a Friday and we went over to the house for dinner. We ate in my parents' bedroom, around the TV, around the Mets game. My mother wasn't really up for the kitchen.

Saturday we had theater tickets. It was unseasonably chilly (the aftereffects of Hurricane Hugo), so I presented Stephanie with something I'd been planning on giving her for a long time: her very own Mets Starter jacket. It was white, the trainer's model, but otherwise it was a perfect complement to mine, the blue one. Both had the big spongy NY and the Mets skyline logo patch.

I also gave her an engagement ring that day. She accepted it with just a touch more gusto than the jacket. But just a touch.

At Shea that afternoon, Long Island's own Frank Viola beat Mark Langston, but neither ace helped his new team in the long run as much as the youngsters for whom they were traded, Rick Aguilera and Randy Johnson.

* * *

We had our evening out Saturday and the next day went over to the house. "Meet your official future daughter-in-law," I said to my parents. They were a little slow on the uptake but when the hand with the ring was put forward, everybody got it. We were engaged.

This was taken as good news (with no talk of rabbis). Mom called Suzan, whom I had also kept in the dark. She and Mark raced over with some cake. The six of us celebrated the occasion like, I thought for the very first time in my life, a normal family.

* * *

We couldn't stay normal for long, though. At least my mother couldn't. We swung by Monday morning again. Mom said the ring looked kind of big on Stephanie's finger. Yes, I said, I thought I knew the size, but had it wrong. You should take it to Roosevelt Field right now and have it resized, she said. No, I said, we're going to drop by the office to share our news with my coworkers and then we're going to the Mets game tonight. Stephanie said the same chain jeweler where I bought it had a branch near school and she'd take care of it once back in Tampa.

The Mets were eliminated by the Phillies that night at a surprisingly empty Shea Stadium. I sat and brooded for a few minutes at the end, causing us to almost miss our train. There'd be no postseason again and my fiancée was flying away in the morning. I had reason to brood.

After dropping Stephanie at LaGuardia on Tuesday, I went back to work in Great Neck. My phone rang. It was my mother calling to berate me for not taking Stephanie to the jewelers immediately. She could see how disappointed she was, how "her little face" just sagged with sadness—a characterization Stephanie laughed at quite a bit. I was, naturally, annoyed that my mother was getting all up in my business but couldn't help but think it was all right. Mom used to attack me for getting serious with a *shiksa*. Now she was taking her side, albeit in an imaginary dispute.

Could I deal with two Mrs. Princes? I would never know.

* * *

The three of us—Mom, Dad, and me—watched the final home game of the 1989 season, versus Philadelphia, in the kitchen. Keith Hernandez in the eighth and Gary Carter in the ninth received standing ovations. It was clearly their final at-bats as Mets. Dating back to the previous December and the trade of Backman, this brought the 1986 casualty count to eight. The last batter Shea would see in the 1980s would be Gregg Jefferies, allegedly the franchise player of the future. Jefferies was not only disliked by his veteran teammates, his *ex*-teammates still had it in for him. After Roger McDowell retired him on a groundout, the pitcher came after him. A fight broke out on the last play of the home season. It didn't seem like too many Mets were taking Jefferies's side against their old crony.

The '86 Mets were no more, but at least a few of their remnants were going out in style.

* * *

Right after the season ended, my mother went back into the hospital, Roosevelt, not for chemo but for another operation. The cancer was making the most portentous comeback of 1989. It occurred to me I didn't mind the Mets finishing second to the Cubs. This wasn't the time for playoffs. Mom would be in Roosevelt into mid-November. The last baseball game we watched together was the Giants and A's in the World Series, Game Three, post-earthquake. She found it amusing that I was rooting for San Francisco because they used to play in New York.

Cancer and the attendant anxieties overtook her after a few weeks at home. She threw a horrible, pain-driven fit on a bone-chilling Sunday and it was back to South Nassau. It was starting all over again. It was never going to end until it ended. Mom was only in South Nassau for a few days, but long enough to call me at work from her room. Loaded on morphine, she wanted to know what she was doing there. Said she'd asked Suzan where her own mother was. Suzan had to tell her her mother was no longer with us. This came as surprising news to her. I rushed to the hospital to tell her the Mets had just sent that stiff Juan Samuel to the Dodgers. I figured any news that wasn't about her dead mother was good news.

* * *

She was back at Roosevelt just before Christmas. On break from USF, Stephanie came up to spend the week surrounding my birthday with me. We were going to Larry's place in Jersey City for New Year's Eve but stopped by the hospital before visiting hours ended. The whole family was there. My mother was doing much better from the morphine drip. She urged us all to stay. It was New Year's Eve—they're bringing in a band . . . there's going to be dancing!

Either the morphine was so effective or I was so used to listening to my mother that I actually believed it for a minute.

* * *

That, give or take a couple of hours, is how the 1980s ended for me, in a hospital room in Manhattan, a sixty-year-old woman who had held us all under her sway hallucinating about Guy Lombardo. She'd be there until late February, no longer lucid. My father was beaten down from the experience. So was my sister. I kept going to work, trying to ignore how much like death the house smelled. My mother was set up in the back room where we usually stored whatever we didn't know what to do with. My father paid for round-the-clock health aides, a nonreimbursable benefit. They were nice ladies. I saw more of them than I did my mother. I didn't like going into that back room.

The '90s were upon us. I finally found an apartment for Stephanie and me, in the same town Suzan and Mark lived in. I put off moving because it seemed crass to abandon ship with my mother in the back room, but a week before Stephanie's graduation, I had to act. As my friend Chuck and I struggled with shifting furniture around a tight spot onto the staircase that led from the kitchen to the basement and eventually out the door, my father sat at the table reading a *Wall Street Journal* with the Mets on in the background. He wasn't paying any attention to the Mets, just as he feigned doing on October 25, 1986. Except now he wasn't feigning ignoring the Mets. He was feigning ignoring me and Chuck.

I didn't blame him. It was all too much.

* * *

I flew down to Tampa for Stephanie's graduation and to help her pack, and we came up together to our new home. My father picked us up at Kennedy, took us to breakfast, and then over to what was about to be my old house. He asked gently if we would like to see Mom and of course we said yes.

This was the end of April. Mom was physically decimated and hadn't said anything coherent for three months. It wasn't just the smell that kept me out of that room. It was everything. That wasn't my mother anymore, I reasoned. That was somebody I didn't recognize.

But I'll be damned, she recognized Stephanie. For maybe two or three minutes, she perked up. Complimented her beautiful blonde hair, asked about specific classes she had taken that semester, even asked how Stephanie's mother's part-time job was going. She barely knew her but she remembered.

* * *

On Sunday, June 17, 1990, Dwight Gooden faced the first-place Pirates in Pittsburgh. He was throwing exceptionally hard. The Three Rivers radar gun was notoriously fast, but so was Doc. For the first time in his career, he threw a pitch that reached a hundred miles per hour.

A few hours after her favorite pitcher raised his record for the season to 5–5, Sandra Prince passed away. It was a nearly two-year battle with cancer. Cancer won in a blowout. We went into the back room and saw a body. That wasn't my mother either. It was just a body. I didn't stay long.

* * *

The funeral was Tuesday. Suzan was arranging the wardrobe for the guest of honor. In my parents' bedroom was that stuffed dog I gave my mother in 1985, the one named for Rafael Santana. I had embellished it the following year with a 1986 WORLD CHAMPIONS button. I slipped it off the dog and handed it to Suzan. As long as you're giving the clothes to whoever's doing the dressing, I asked, would you mind including this?

Call it our final championship hug.

Nineteen

WHAT KIND OF PERSON?

O n April 30, 1990, less than twenty-four hours after we had officially moved in together, Stephanie West found out what she had signed up for. She heard a noise in the bedroom and came rushing in from the living room. It was me, having a fit. I was yelling at the radio because David Cone, ball firmly in hand, was yelling at the first base umpire in Atlanta while two Braves baserunners crossed home plate unmolested. Coney forgot to call time. I didn't forget to tell Stephanie this is the sort of thing that might get me riled, but she sort of had to see it to believe it.

It was important to me, so it was important to her. Then again, she was important to me. A pennant race with the woman I loved along for the ride would be, if the Mets cooperated, the best pennant race ever.

* * *

What kind of person agrees to live with the biggest Mets fan anybody knows? Good question. So far all I've really told you about Stephanie is she went to a game with me in 1987, accepted a Starter jacket and engagement ring from me in 1989, and once recognized the name Tom Seaver. That would be good enough for me, but it would give short shrift to the woman I love (though I have to confess I've never heard of anyone being given long shrift).

Very funny. Very dry. Very patient. Very placid. Very loving. Very supportive. Very sharp. Very real. Very much everything I could have ever hoped for when I was mostly hoping Aguilera wouldn't give up too many runs that fateful Monday night in Cincinnati three years earlier. Aguilera lost. I won. My winning streak continued into 1990 (and beyond).

By osmosis, Stephanie became a Mets fan. By osmosis, Stephanie became a more knowledgeable Mets fan than a lot of Mets fans I knew. She labeled Kevin Elster "the cute one." She made intermediate backup catcher Orlando Mercado memorable by rolling out the r's *(Mer-r-r-r-rcado)* on the occasion of his rare at-bats. She teased me out of the habit of calling every enemy pitcher, hitter, or manager a moron by lightly observing, "You sure think a lot of people are morons." She came to recognize the fierce urgency of listening to *Mets Extra* with Howie Rose and learned to avoid, for her own climatological concerns, night games before June without gloves.

Stephanie was no competition for the Mets just as the Mets were no competition for Stephanie. My team, my fiancée, and I made for an isosceles love triangle.

* * *

All things considered in the wake of June 17, 1990—the day my mother died was also the day the Mets began an eleven-game winning streak—I couldn't have been happier that I had one more pennant race that resembled those we had in the '80s. But perhaps all the celebratory high-fiving took its toll on me. Lots of writing/typing at the beverage magazine didn't help. Tendinitis made my right wrist its summer resort. I was in unusual amounts of pain. My publisher said I could type with one hand if need be.

I wore all manner of strap and splint on that wrist for months. One looked like the thing bowlers wear. Another inspired some dirty jokes around the office. I went to an orthopedist who injected me with cortisone and told me to "go home, relax, and watch the Mets." I hadn't said a word to him about baseball. Guess he could see it in my eyes.

* * *

The Pirates were young and hungry, with Barry Bonds and Bobby Bonilla leading the way. The Mets began to lose what Bob Murphy might have called some damn things. Things became more damned when Elster, our shortstop and matinee idol, went down with a torn labrum in his right shoulder. They tried to treat him by shooting him full of Indocin, the same anti-inflammatory steroid prescribed for my wrist. "Hey!" I thought in empathetic excitement. "That's my medicine!" But he couldn't play with one shoulder anymore than I could type with one hand. And without your starting shortstop, you lose a lot of damn things.

It had been ten years since the Magic Is Back summer of 1980. This was a far better team than that, but the bell curve of 1990 wasn't all that dissimilar from a decade prior. In the middle of the season, the '90 Mets won 26 of 31. They may have played as well as I'd ever seen them. Every cylinder was cooking. But after the engine cooled, they were a team that gave every indication that an era, the one with 1986 at its center, was ending. It had temporarily withstood a change in managers—Buddy Harrelson in for Davey Johnson—and myriad personnel shifts, but after a fashion, excellence again and again, the Mets' self-saluting slogan, runs out of agains.

No Elster. Catcher Mackey Sasser slumped badly after a home plate collision rocked his world. Almost everybody, save for Dave Magadan, cooled off. Frank Viola and John Franco weren't sure things either. The Pirates kept up the pressure. They had replaced the Cardinals as the team that wouldn't get out of our way.

More new Mets were brought on board. Another catcher (we used seven that year), Charlie O'Brien. An old enemy, former St. Louisian Tommy Herr. He'd play second, Jefferies would go to third, HoJo would take short. Nobody but Herr was playing his best position. In need of more consistent starting pitching, Buddy moved Ron Darling out of the rotation in favor of Julio Valera.

Progress. Valera was hot stuff in Tidewater. Darling was yesterday's news: '85, '86, the no-hit bid ruined by Vince Coleman on Pendleton Night. The era wasn't over, but it wasn't long for this world.

The Mets hung and clung despite all their problems. They held a half-game lead early in September. Every game was, as it had been in '85 and '87, crucial. Every loss hurt worse than my wrist. Every shriek carried overtones of agony.

* * *

Stephanie, who had settled into Long Island life pretty nicely (finding a social work job in the city fairly quickly and adapting to the LIRR), was drawn into my baseball rhythms. She discovered what a pennant race was, what falling out of first in September meant. The horrible noise I let out at the end of April when Cone didn't throw home found a bookend when Lee Smith fanned Howard Johnson in St. Louis.

"What's the matter?" she asked, this time rushing into the living room from the bedroom.

"HoJo. Struck out. We lost. DAMN!"

Stephanie got used to my noises.

* * *

This was also my first pennant race without my mother, at least in the modern era. She was gone but my dad was still in

Long Beach. Just because the three of us couldn't watch games together anymore didn't mean two of us couldn't.

Or so I thought. Still popping Indocin in early September, I drove over to his house to watch a crucial showdown between the Mets and the Pirates. When the season began, I would've called it my house and I wouldn't have felt so strange watching this game. Mom and Dad and I watched all the big ones together in '85 and '86 and '87 and '88 and what few big ones there were to watch in '89.

In '90, I needn't have bothered. When my mother died, so did my dad's interest in baseball, practically all at once. He barely looked up from his *Wall Street Journal* or at the game from Pittsburgh. I didn't go over to his house for baseball after that.

I got used to Dad's baseball obliviousness. My mom's absence, too, though the fact that she was missing a pennant race bugged me. One morning before work I found myself dropping off a video at Blockbuster. My mind was on the Mets, as usual, and it wandered to John Franco, the new closer. Mom would've recognized him as the guy who was always getting us out when he was with the Reds. She didn't much care for him then. Neither did I. I still didn't have much use for his suddenly erratic ways (while Randy Myers became a Nasty Boy for first-place Cincinnati), but there was something about him I couldn't help but root for. Probably that he was from Brooklyn, like my mother. Sitting in the Blockbuster parking lot, I was struck by one thought: Mom would've liked John Franco on the Mets.

I cried for a minute and then drove off to the beverage magazine.

* * *

The Mets played just well enough to stick near the Pirates so that they still had a reasonable chance when Pittsburgh came to Shea in mid–September for two must-win games. This was this

year's version of the Mets-Cardinal showdowns with St. Louis in
'85 and '87. Actually, since those didn't go so well, I hoped they
were something better.

They were. For a pair of nights in the middle of September,
Shea was bursting at the seams and delirious. So was David
Cone. He was far removed from his blunder in Atlanta our first
night in the apartment. This was September, and David Cone
was a September pitcher. He struck out Bobby Bonilla to end the
first and bullrushed the home dugout. He high-fived everybody
in sight. In the bottom of the inning, Magadan (.328 that year,
best Met average since Cleon Jones; knowing that won me a *Mets
Extra* trivia quiz) doubled home Jefferies and Keith Miller. Two
runs were all our nutjob with the Laredo motion needed. David
Cone pitched a three-hit complete game with eight strikeouts.
The Mets won 2–1 and closed in on the Pirates.

The next night, I didn't get home in time to watch from the
beginning. So it was in my 1981 burnt-orange Toyota Corolla,
barreling west on Atlantic Avenue in Freeport, that Gary Cohen
let me know Darryl Strawberry had sent one soaring off Doug
Drabek, the National League's Cy Young Award winner that
season, and over the rightfield fence. *Outta here!* Three-run homer!
A two-zip deficit was now a 3–2 lead in the fourth. Bedlam filled
my tinny speakers. I honked my horn and high-fived my steering
wheel the way Cone had slapped his teammates' hands the night
before. (All at once, my wrist felt fine.)

It was confirmation, as if we needed any, that Darryl was
worth the Jose Canseco–type money he'd been demanding all
summer, that Frank Cashen would look quite the fool to let a
twenty-eight-year-old, left-handed slugger (37 HR, 108 RBI)
who runs well, drips charisma, and comes through in games like
this take a free-agent hike.

The Mets added another run and handed Doc Gooden a
4–2 lead. He wasn't as dominant as Cone, but Gooden was—
as every other back-page headline since 1984 had blared with

or without irony—good enough. In the eighth, Doc gave way to Franco, who didn't blow it. The Mets won 6–3. We were now only a game-and-a-half back with 19 to play, including three to finish the season in Pittsburgh. It's the Pirates who would be chasing us by then, I reckoned.

* * *

Instead, the era ended. We got that one wonderful series against Pittsburgh, that final burst of Darryl and Doc together as one, and then we got next to nothing. Doc kept winning. His final record was 19–7, phenomenal when you consider it began 3–5. Viola and Franco couldn't quite nail down wins and the offense couldn't do anything in one particularly abominable doubleheader versus Montreal non-studs Brian Barnes and Chris Nabholz. There was no Pendleton, Scioscia, or Randolph home run to spell doom. There was just not enough to the Mets anymore. The seventh year of plenty dating back to 1984 was plenty good in a lot of ways, but it wasn't good enough.

It was over.

* * *

The MVP of 1990 wasn't Doc. It wasn't Darryl. It wasn't Magadan. It was Stephanie. She clinched it twice.

First, there was the game when the Mets were mathematically eliminated. I couldn't watch it. I had to fly to San Francisco on beverage business. Never did I bolt from the plane more purposefully after the captain turned off my FASTEN SEATBELT sign. Marched to a pay phone and called my fiancée for the word on the crucial Mets-Cubs score.

Before I could ask the question, I got the answer. "They lost," delivered in properly mournful tones. As a bonus, she had taped

Mets Extra for me so I could dwell on my disappointment as she knew I would want to do in the offseason.

Second, there was the Friday morning in November when she nudged me awake so I could hear it from her before I had to hear it on the street. Darryl Strawberry, she said, had signed with Los Angeles.

After the East was not won, Stephanie had given me this little toy to lift my spirits, a tiny baseball with a face and legs and a Mets cap. Wind it up and it walked deliberately, not altogether unlike Dave Magadan. As it sunk in that Frank Cashen had confirmed the era's end by allowing the best slugger the farm system had ever produced to become a Dodger, I did the only thing I could think of. I got up, I walked to the flat surface where the tiny toy baseball with a face and legs and a Mets cap sat, and wound it up. It walked on its flat surface until it came to the ledge. Then it fell to the floor. Then I trudged back to bed to sulk.

Stephanie didn't think this reaction silly at all.

What kind of person chooses to live with the biggest Mets fan anybody knows? My favorite person in the world, that's who.

TWENTY

WELCOME HOME

After the 77–84 letdown of 1991, Stephanie and I got married (by a rabbi). After the 72–90 debacle of 1992, we adopted our first cat, Bernie. With 1993 becoming an obvious disaster from the word go, we adopted Bernie an older brother, Casey, in late April. It was good to have distractions from the Mets. But the Mets were coming to get me nonetheless, and who should unleash them on me but my loving family?

For my thirtieth birthday, New Year's Eve 1992, my family threw me a surprise party. I was genuinely surprised . . . surprised and touched. They rounded up a bunch of my high school friends and some coworkers and lured me to Suzan's house under false pretenses and, just like on TV, jumped out of the shadows and yelled "SURPRISE!" It worked.

There was no theme beyond the obvious, but the subtext was clear. I had been alive thirty years; I had spent most of them rooting for the Mets. I fed the perception myself when Larry handed me the largest bottle of champagne I had ever seen. On December 31, 1992, I told him I would save this very special bottle for the next time the Mets won the World Series.

Stephanie and I opened it on our next wedding anniversary. I'd gotten a great hint in the intervening months that I'd be waiting an incredibly long time to drink it otherwise.

The ultimate gift that night was a silver box with a Mets logo taped to the top. I opened it and within was an envelope filled with tickets. Mets tickets. Mark, former begrudging vendor, put aside his venom for Shea Stadium and visited the advance ticket window and created for my benefit a customized mini-plan for 1993: Fifteen pair of tickets (15 X 2 = 30).

It was a sweet, sweet gesture on the part of my brother-in-law, my sister, and my father, all of whom chipped in to make it happen. It was exactly what they could rightly figure I would want.

Who wouldn't want fifteen opportunities to spend quality time with your 59–103 1993 New York Mets?

* * *

What Bernie was to kittens, 1993 was to horror-show baseball seasons. It was state-of-the-art. And it darn near turned Shea Stadium into a litter box.

Two dismal fifth-place finishes—hard to believe as recently as 1990 we considered coming in a close second an indignity—had come and gone and we hadn't any idea how much worse it was going to get. The '93 Mets weren't some run-of-the-mill losing team. They were a classic of the genre: epic in their awfulness, sultans of cellar.

They weren't very good and they made no bones about it. Any team can lose 25 of their first 37 (after a misleading 2–0 start), 52 of their first 73, 103 of their first 156 (before a cosmetic 6–0 finish). There's usually at least one team in baseball every year that loses a hundred games. It's never pretty but it's not necessarily astounding.

This was. And I got to see loads of it up close, from right inside the cat box.

Much of the carnage took place far away, in the clubhouse

or on the road, out of public view. I didn't see bullying Bobby Bonilla threaten Bob Klapisch, the coauthor who detailed the '92 Mets' shortcomings in the immediately obsolete book *The Worst Team Money Could Buy* with a vague invitation to show him the Bronx. I didn't see cranky Vince Coleman punch his ticket out of town by tossing firecrackers in the Dodger Stadium parking lot and injuring a little girl in the process. I didn't see miscast Bret Saberhagen spray bleach on reporters (playfully, it was said). I didn't see uptight manager Jeff Torborg and then overmatched GM Al Harazin given their walking papers—though I cheered the news both times. I didn't see this year's savior, used-to-be All-Star shortstop Tony Fernandez, diagnosed with kidney stones nor did I see the guy he was traded for, Darrin Jackson, be told he suffered from Graves' Disease, the ailment that befell Barbara Bush. Are your outfielders supposed to encounter the same health issues as former first ladies?

* * *

Opening Day (my first) was swell. It was the Colorado Rockies' debut in the National League and the sun shone and Doc pitched a shutout and for a couple of hours I could buy the business about the Mets regrouping from '91 and '92; they were actually the consensus pick to finish first in the division. I had, independently of the fifteen-pack, bought tickets for the second game against the Rockies as well. It was my holiday gift to the rest of our editorial staff. We sat in the sun again and watched the Mets outclass the Rockies again.

Fourteen more games followed. The Mets lost ten of them. And it wasn't just the numbers that gnawed at me. It was the grinding effect of witnessing a team that was determined to lose lose. The Mets did something they had never done before: they finished seventh. The last time you could do that in the National League, in the pre-divisional ten-team National League, the Mets weren't good enough to finish seventh. Now, in the expansion year of 1993, the Mets were bad enough to finish behind the Florida Marlins.

I saw the Mets lose to the recently invented Marlins on consecutive days in May. I saw the Mets lose in front of many if not all of the '73 Champs on Old Timers' Night (no Tom, no Willie, no Yogi) in June. I saw the Mets lose on the twentieth anniversary of my very first game at Shea, July 11, this time to the Dodgers and a dazzling rookie reliever named Pedro Martinez. But I didn't throw up afterwards.

* * *

I saw the Mets lose with Anthony Young on the mound. It was as historic as the Rockies' opener. When Anthony Young, better known as A.Y.—a rather lazy year for nicknames—started the June 27 game against the Cardinals, his record was 0–9. In 1992, he had lost his final fourteen. Anthony Young was chalking up a worse mark than I was. If he lost one more time before winning, he'd own the record for consecutive losses by a pitcher. Mets fans were snapping up programs the way they had on Opening Day because they figured they might be worth something (ghouls).

On June 27, I sat in Loge and watched Anthony Young no-hit the Cardinals for three innings. What a way to break a losing streak—the first no-hitter in Mets history! Now that program would *really* be worth something!

The Cardinals scored three runs in the fourth. In the seventh, Young left, trailing 5–3. That was the final score. Joe Magrane got the win for St. Louis. A.Y. had his 24th consecutive L for the Mets, 24th of an eventual 27. As usual, he didn't look bad, but strictly speaking, from a relentless bottom line perspective, he was now the worst pitcher ever.

And I saw it.

* * *

This six-month birthday present wasn't necessarily getting me any closer to that jumbo bottle of champagne and the games were yielding some pretty bitter results, but 1993 became a pivotal year for me at Shea Stadium. Familiarity bred the desire for more familiarity. Busy with my magazine, busy with my wife, busy with our cats, when the '90s commenced I was barely going to any more games than I did in the '70s. Only two games in '91, a big four in '92. Sixteen games was a revelation. Sixteen games made Shea Stadium feel like home, and not just as the home park for my favorite team. I no longer felt I was just visiting. I felt like I belonged there. I started going a lot in 1993 and I'd keep going a lot until there was no more Shea Stadium.

Banner Day sealed it. Banner Day was the one tradition (besides falling apart after seven or so years of competence) that was pure Mets. It began in the Polo Grounds in 1963, co-opted by management when the fans painted up bedsheets and displayed them from every rafter. M. Donald Grant didn't care for the freedom of expression, but realized it was better to join the mob then fight it. Banner Day followed the Mets to Shea. It was an annual highlight of the promotional schedule. It used to take place between games of doubleheaders when there were doubleheaders. In '93, it was scheduled for early afternoon prior to a three o'clock start against the Rockies in late August.

It had been a long time since Opening Day. The Rockies weren't very good, but they were better than us. Everybody was better than us. But Banner Day was special. It was my first Banner Day. I didn't participate. I was just happy to be there watching the procession. There were hundreds of fans showing off their love for the worst team in baseball. I don't remember what any of the sheets said, but they were supportive. If I had designed one, it would have said I KENT STAND THIS TEAM ANYMORE.

But I was having a very banner day. It was a Sunday. Stephanie was with me. I had promised not to make her my default +1 for every game when I couldn't find anybody else, but she was into Banner Day. She was charmed by the whole thing, delighted to sit behind home plate in Loge, in the shade, not adversely affected by Frank Tanana's terminally crummy pitching, the 6–1 loss, or the Mets' 45–85 record, putting them a mere 36 games in back of the Phillies. I felt the same. I was with the woman I loved at the place I loved. Even with the 1993 Mets completely unraveled in our midst, I couldn't have been more at home.

TWENTY-ONE

VIRTUAL REALITY AND RICO BROGNA

The quietest decent year the Mets ever experienced was 1994. Any year would seem good after 1993, but the Mets actually played well. Before the strike, they flirted with .500. Better yet, they unveiled a new favorite player for me, a first baseman obtained from the Tigers in a minor league deal, Rico Brogna. The kid could hit and field and do all kinds of unMetlike things (like not spray bleach on people, not threaten reporters, and not explode firecrackers in the general direction of children). When the strike came, it was visions of Rico going 5-for-5 in St. Louis that kept me going until whenever there'd be baseball again.

I needed a new favorite player. My old one was out the door.

The end of Dwight Gooden's Mets career came in June of '94, and with it there went the last '86 Met. He tested positive again for cocaine. It meant a suspension that outlasted the length of his Met contract. Nobody here was ready to give him another chance. Maybe if he'd been the Doc of '85, but the Doc of '94, despite a few vintage efforts, was just some pitcher named Dwight when his time expired. His ERA after his final, atrocious start against the Pirates was 6.31. In 1985, it had been 1.53. In 1985, there had been K's hanging from the left field Upper Deck and clapping every time there were two strikes on a batter. In 1985, every Doc Gooden start was a happening. In 1994, Dwight Gooden left Shea Stadium quietly.

* * *

At *Beverage World* we had America Online installed on one computer, our art director's. When he went home, I could log on, wait ten minutes for everything to load, and search for beverage headlines. I was very focused on the task at hand until one April night in 1994 when I noticed the other buttons on the AOL screen. There was more than business news. There was sports news. In fact, there was an entire sports section. Within it was an area devoted to baseball: bulletin boards for every team. I clicked on the one for New York Mets.

Whoa! There were Mets fans from everywhere there. Probably more Mets fans on AOL than there were in the Upper Deck on any given night in 1994. There were discussions going on regarding dozens of topics. When would Jason Jacome be called up? Why won't Dallas Green give Kelly Stinnett more starts over Todd Hundley? What's wrong with John Franco? Will we ever warm to Jeff Kent?

This is pretty cool, I thought. So I wrote something and clicked. It appeared where others could see it and read it. Somebody did and acknowledged it.

After a lifetime of writing for teachers, writing for editors, writing for truckstop operators, and writing for soft-drink bottlers, I was writing for Mets fans.

* * *

Virtual reality merged with actual for the first time on June 17, 1995. Bill Pulsipher, one of those minor league phenoms over whom Mets fans with a modem obsessed, was making his first major league start, at Shea. The Mets were floundering since rematerializing at strike's end, hence there was no harm in letting a twenty-one-year-old pitch to the Astros. Pulse (he already had a nickname) would lose handily, get hurt the next spring, and never succeed Koosman and Matlack among lefthanded Met legends as we who showed up at Shea for his debut had hoped, but Bill Pulsipher's first major league start was a milestone event nonetheless.

Joining me for Pulse's coming out was the first Mets fan I ever got to know online, first from the board, then from this other new thing called e-mail. His name was Jason. He had just moved to New York from Washington, D.C., having lived in a few places since a childhood in Suffolk County. Or part of a childhood. To be honest, I've never gotten the story straight. It's never really mattered. Meeting Jason online and then out in front of Gate D at Shea Stadium changed how I perceived life's possibilities.

There were more Mets fans out there. You didn't have to wait for them pop up next to you at work. That's how I met the only Mets fans I had gotten to know in the early '90s. This was pretty standard procedure pre-AOL. There was no Hillel for Mets fans, no "singles nights," if you will. You lucked into the people who liked the same things you did or you didn't, just like you did when you were in elementary school and junior high and high school and college. You could meet some good people that way, and I had, but you could only meet so many.

This was different. People who signed onto AOL and sought out the Mets bulletin board amid the thousands of boards and forums and whatnot this futuristic world contained . . . they were like me. They came looking to talk about the Mets and read about the Mets and dwell on the Mets as if there was nothing unusual about it. This wasn't weirdo-driven sports talk radio. Not that there weren't weirdos, but this was interactive. It wasn't callers to WFAN being hung up on. It was a sense that we were all in this together, Mets fans who cared enough to find other Mets fans.

First I wrote about the Mets and somebody read it. Then somebody wrote back about the Mets. And now I was at a game watching the Mets with him. Would wonders ever cease?

* * *

It was wrenching to have Tom Seaver torn from the team in his eleventh season. It was painful to watch Dwight Gooden cast out in his eleventh season. Rico Brogna was a Met for only three years. Came up in June '94 and went down with an injury in June '96, so he didn't really play all that much. But goodness I loved watching him. He was smooth all around, polite as hell in interviews—no slight consideration in the wake of Bonilla, Coleman, and the similarly departed Saberhagen. I went out of my way one afternoon in the city to show up at an autograph signing of his. I never did that. Being that it was 1995, the line wasn't very long. He couldn't have been nicer to everybody.

Right before Thanksgiving in '96, the Mets traded Rico. It wasn't the kick in the head that the Seaver trade was. More like the shins. But it hurt. I'd stuck through this new terrible era, found a player to call my own from the rubble, and they were sending him away to Philadelphia for two relievers of no renown (Toby Borland and Ricardo Jordan). Rico was still on my mind at Thanksgiving. To one of those "what's new?" questions when you should respond, "Nothing much," I went on about the anger and sadness I experienced about losing Rico Brogna, one of the few players who really shone (when healthy) those last few years.

The reply, from my non-fan inquisitor: "Well, I don't want to be mean, but if they're not very good, maybe they were right to trade him, you know?"

No, I didn't know that. But as the day went on, this response, not mean so much as uninformed, gnawed at me. Talking about the Mets with non-fans when they were winning was never particularly rewarding. Now that they weren't very good (and another local team was), it struck all the wrong chords. I'm spending 365 days—366 in '96—obsessing about the Mets. I'd been doing it since I was six. I was thirty-three. It hadn't killed me.

In some way it had made me stronger, or at least more fulfilled than I'd feel otherwise. I'd just come through my sixth lousy season in a row. It began to dawn on me that if I were going to talk about the Mets, I should probably talk about them to other Mets fans. I should probably limit my contact with non–Mets fans since, really, all I wanted to talk about was the Mets. I should also probably continue the Mets fan outreach program I had begun via AOL. I met a virtual stranger and we became friends with nothing but the Mets in common. I liked that more than I was enjoying many of those I knew in allegedly real life.

Finally, I concluded, I should squirm out of any Thanksgiving obligations that don't include Lee Mazzilli.

Twenty-Two

PRIDE
(IN THE NAME OF METS)

The first hint that the Mets wouldn't be terrible forever post-1990 came on little cat feet. No wonder I liked it so much.

It was May 3, 1997, an inauspicious Saturday, with enough A.M. rain to convince me and anybody else supposed to go to Shea that there would be no game. It was wet and I was tired. I didn't really want to go. At times like those when I thought foolish thoughts, I asked myself a question: who am *I* to *not* go to a Mets game? I grabbed an umbrella and I went.

I had been invited by my second-ever virtual AOL friend, Laurie. Laurie and I connected in a boardwide debate over booing. She was against it. So was I, but I thought John Franco deserved it every now and again. We became pals anyway. For this Saturday, she had an extra ticket she would leave me at Will Call. Just bring ID, she said.

I donned my green golf jacket, took my train to Jamaica, changed for a train to Woodside, and then, instead of automatically climbing toward the 7, spied a Port Washington–bound Long Island locomotive coming my way. Great, I'll just get on here and take it the six minutes east. They didn't always stop at Shea Stadium, but they did when there was a game.

I'm standing by an exit when a conductor comes by for my ticket. Where'd you get on? he asked. "Woodside," I said. "For Shea." "Shea?" he asked. "We don't stop at Shea unless there's a game." "There's a game today," I told him.

"There is?"

"Yeah, there's a game."

It was news to him. It was news to the entire crew that had planned to blow right by Shea en route to Main Street, Flushing. He notified the engineer or the motorman or whoever actually drives a Long Island Rail Road train that we would be making an unplanned stop. There's apparently a Met game today.

We slowed. An announcement blared:

"YANKEE STADIUM."

Ha-ha. I got off.

I was alone. Utterly alone. The Mets were taking the field at this very moment and not a single soul besides me was disembarking. On a Saturday afternoon in New York, nobody else from Long Island had joined me on public transportation for this affair. Maybe they hopped the 7 at Woodside except I didn't see anybody else get off the railroad there either.

I walked up the LIRR steps alone. I walked across the LIRR boardwalk alone. I cut through the Roosevelt Avenue overpass subway station alone.

Alone. Alone. So alone. When I came down the steps and crossed Roosevelt and headed left toward Will Call, I could hear the PA inside Shea. The game had started. Everybody who was going to be there for it was there for it already. There was nobody . . . I mean *nobody* else in Casey Stengel Plaza. You know that standard shot they would show during the first innings of Mets telecasts of fans ambling off the 7 extension staircase, rushing, as Terry Cashman put it, to the stadium in Flushing?

There was none of that. A Major League Baseball game was just underway over a big blue wall, an event whose score would be repeated on newscasts and recorded in newspapers and researchable in archives for all time and there was nobody making a late dash for it.

Nobody but me. And it hadn't rained a drop since I left the house.

I went to Will Call, between Gates D and C. There was a woman behind a window. I told her my name as I fished out my driver's license to prove that I was indeed the person for whom a ticket to a Mets game had been left.

She put up her hand as if to say "don't bother" and handed me an envelope with one ticket. Mine, from Laurie. Gate E.

I passed through the turnstile, was handed a Dunkin' Donuts travel mug that celebrated the 1996 accomplishments of four "RECORD BREAKERS" (Todd Hundley and Lance Johnson to the left of the Mets and Dunkin' logos, John Franco, and Bernard Gilkey to their right), and I escalatored up to Field Level.

Laurie was waiting for me in the right field corner, also alone. I don't mean she didn't come with anybody else. I mean nobody else was sitting in the right field corner. Hardly anybody else was sitting on the first base side of Field Level. Or the third base side. Or any side of any level.

When you examine the boxscore for the Mets-Cardinals game of May 3, 1997, you will read there was a paid attendance of 16,248. Good fiction can be amusing. The next day in the *News*, Mets officials conceded threatening weather had kept the crowd down to a turnstile count of about 4,500. "About" was charitable. I'm pretty good at counting the house. If I'd been ambitious enough, I could have literally counted the house. There were no more than 2,500 people in the stands, vendors included.

Yes, it had rained. Yes, Ed Coleman had been on WFAN in the morning hedging, hemming, and hawing on whether there would be a game and whether it would start on time. He sounded surprised when it was given a go. Nevertheless, the Mets couldn't round up 3,000 witnesses on a Saturday afternoon to watch them play baseball? Professional baseball?

But there they were: Rick Reed pitching and not giving up a hit 'til the fifth; Todd Hundley and John Olerud each homering; Carlos Baerga going 4-for-4; Carl Everett, Rey Ordoñez, Steve "The Beez" Bieser, all building a run; Takashi Kashiwada closing out a 5–1 victory. It pulled the Mets to within a game of .500.

And nobody saw it. Almost nobody. As close to "literally nobody" as I'd ever been a part of. Attendance was so sparse that I had a hunch that Laurie and I might show up on television. In those days, SportsChannel repeated a condensed version of the game late at night. "SportsChannel Light," they called it. Stephanie set our VCR to tape SCL and sure enough, as Olerud rounded first on his homer, the camera picked us up in the distance: a speck and a blob clapping away.

I was the blob in the green golf jacket.

I was something else as well. I was excited. Sure, a Mets win is always exciting, but geez . . . I don't know. This was different. The Mets had been playing pretty well coming into this soggy Saturday. They had won six of seven. I suppose they had won six of seven a few times between 1991 and 1996, but here they were, a month into the season and they had won almost as many as they had lost. After six years of famine, it was manna from heaven. And this game, with however many hundreds of Mets fans who had joined us, was like a private heaven.

We were in on the ground floor. The Mets were about to get good. Only a few of us knew about it. I did. Laurie did. Nobody else cared. Almost nobody, that is. I accompanied Laurie back into Manhattan and then got out of the subway to do a little CD shopping at the Virgin Megastore in Times Square. Among the throngs of consumers—more than were at Shea Stadium an hour earlier—was another person carrying a RECORD BREAKERS travel mug. Somebody else in the world was at the Mets game.

The sun had come out, too.

* * *

A few years later, Bobby Valentine opened a restaurant across the Grand Central from Shea. Stephanie and I went there for lunch on the Saturday before the Super Bowl. It was just before Spring Training kicked off so I guessed the owner might be around. And he was. It was as quiet in Bobby V's as it was for his team that Saturday in 1997, so it gave us a chance to exploit his hosting. Bobby posed for photos with each of us and autographed a pocket schedule with his picture on it. Meeting the manager of the Mets, to me, was a bigger deal than meeting the president of the United States, no matter who the president was at any given moment. Bobby V was my commander-in-chief, the way Gil Hodges had been, the way Davey Johnson had been. Of course we were dressed in Mets sweatshirts and such, a detail the attentive manager noted.

"Thanks for wearing your Mets stuff," he said.

"Thanks for making us proud to wear it," I told him.

I was fawning but I meant it. Bobby Valentine can do no wrong by me after 1997. Bobby Valentine piloted a Mets team from nowhere into a playoff race. You can't call it a pennant race because it was for a Wild Card. We came up short by four games to the Florida Marlins, but I almost didn't mind. Bobby V and the Rick Reed, Steve Bieser, Matt Franco, Luis Lopez Mets of 1997 gave me back the baseball season. They gave me back validation for why I was such a fan. Six years of rooting for a team that veered from bad to worse and worse to atrocious had taken it out of me. I wasn't going anywhere—where was I going to go?—but the thrill was dripping out of the bottle. How many more years of sub-.500 finishes and Generation K flameouts and Dallas Green huffs and all-around dismay would I have to endure?

None! None at all from 1997 into the next century. Bobby Valentine and his minions did that. They weren't all dead-end kids. Olerud was a legitimate hitter. Edgardo Alfonzo, inserted at third to play every day by Valentine, was as clutch as they came. Whatever was fueling his power, Hundley could hit homers. There was some talent. But there was no expectation any of it would mesh. And *that's* what made 1997 quite possibly the most fun year I ever had as a fan.

The Mets went 88–74 in 1997. They beat the Braves in huge series in June and July. They beat the Yankees in the first-ever regular-season game between the neighbors (all hail Dave Mlicki!). They found ways to prevail over Curt Schilling and Pedro Martinez. They had a knack for eighth-inning lightning and ninth-inning rallies. They briefly floated into a Wild Card lead in late July. If the season ended today, I told my baseball-challenged sister, the Mets would be in the playoffs. All my sister knew about baseball was the Yankee version preempted her favorite radio talk shows.

"I wish the season would end today," she said, kind of supportively.

* * *

The 1997 season never needed to end. It was a dream. Only a Mets fan would dream of a third-place finish, but what can I tell ya? There was a Bubbling Under the Hot 100, cult classic feel to the season: sneaking back into the competitive conversation; stealthily re-entering the fray; the Mets never quite good enough to make the playoffs but never going away.

The crown jewel of 1997 came on September 13 at Shea, a game I witnessed from my living room. The Mets are down 6–0 to the Expos. They lose this one and the dream probably dies sooner than it has to. The Mets are being one-hit going to the ninth. I'm as mopey as can be. But we get a couple on, we get a couple in. It's 6–2. Still it's rather hopeless. Amazingly, we load the bases with two outs. Carl Everett, kind of an unsavory character by then, steps up. All I can do is hope and secularly pray for a grand slam off Montreal closer Uggie Urbina. It's too far-fetched to work.

Everett rips one to right . . . foul for strike two.

Oh, that's it, I said to Stephanie. You don't get more than one of those swings. You don't hit a foul home run and then hit one fair.

Then, with innocence and sincerity and heart, she delivered the three little words I needed to hear:

"You gotta believe!"

Two pitches later, Carl Everett hit a grand slam. The game was tied at six. In the eleventh, Bernard Gilkey would hit a three-run homer to win it.

I believed.

TWENTY-THREE

THE FUN POLICE

Based on my interactions with the other breed during their Chernobyl-like contamination of New York's baseball atmosphere, Yankees fans are:

Often clueless. In 1995, as hubris was clearing its throat, a new coworker tagged along on an office outing to Shea. It was a doubleheader against Cincinnati. After a couple of weeks when he let it be known with regularity that he was from the Bronx and the team from the Bronx *ruled*, baby, he asked a pertinent question during the first game: "Hey Greg, do the Mets play the Reds in the second game, too?"

Lacking values. Prior to Opening Day 1996, when we were going to be back and be better behind the Generation K–armed forces of Jason Isringhausen and Paul Wilson (Pulsipher was already on the DL), a Yankees fan at work asked who I thought would have a better record this year, us or them? Us, I said. "Care to make it interesting?" he dared me. What, baseball isn't already interesting? Baseball is the most interesting game ever invented! (FYI, I lost $21.62 in a bet I didn't want to place—the $1.62 portion was my idea. I thought *that* made it interesting.)

Unclever tools. Observing the Mets shirt I was wearing one day in 1996, an executive of the company that published my magazine, a stuttering Yankees fan, informed me, "Th-th-that shirt would've been more appropriate to w-w-wear in 1969." Civility and a desire to maintain employment restrained me from responding, "F-F-Fuck you."

Reflexively dismissive. Nothing like an afternoon game, right? The Mets were playing in Houston, the last week of the 1996 season. It was baseball until there'd be no baseball, so I happily flicked it on in my office. Play-by-play filled the air. One of our ad salesmen wandered by and heard the joyful noise. "Who's playing?" he asked. "Mets and Astros," I said. "Oh, *that's* not important," he responded as he walked away. As if there's such a thing as an unimportant baseball game.

Easily duped. Manhattan was flooded with suburban Yankees fans after the 1996 World Series. Something about a parade. I was continually pestered for directions downtown. I sent every inquirer up to 57th Street.

Oddly intrusive. One fine June evening in 1998, Rick Reed carried a perfect game into the seventh inning against the Devil Rays en route to a 3–0, three-hit shutout. Entering the turnstiles to the 7, I saw a teen who decided this would be a good night to stand with a sign reading REAL BASEBALL IS PLAYED IN THE BRONX!

Unwelcome visitors. Interleague play . . . what a joy. The Mets crafted six-packs of tickets in 1998 that were generally five whatever games plus one Subway Series contest. Mets fans gobbled them up. But so did Yankees fans. Thus, although Real Baseball was apparently played elsewhere, they swarmed Shea throughout the season, not just during NY-NY games. This is how the "Yankees Suck!" chants were born. They didn't materialize from thin air. They were provoked in self-defense . . . in defense of sanity. Typical unsolicited Yankees fan remark at Shea Stadium, circa 1998, "I'm coming to all three games and I'M BRINGING A BROOM!" At which time you can shove it up your . . .

Exhibitionist asses. Some Yankee would do something helpful for his team and the reaction of Yankees fans always involved pointing at the cap. LOOK! IT'S AN "NY!" And we were supposed to do what? Trade ours in? Genuflect? Check our holsters and see if we remembered to pack heat? Also, one of their fans once gave two middle fingers to our section for an entire half-inning. I'm not kidding.

Fun police. For sheer entertainment and uplift, I attended no game greater than the Matt Franco game, the 9–8 victory over the Yankees on July 10, 1999. The Yankees hit six homers. Mike Piazza hit one that was longer than all of them combined. Mike put us up 7–6 in the seventh. For the only time in my life, I just spouted every bit of venom I could think of at another fan in retaliation for all the toxic, obnoxious behavior I had to endure all afternoon (sure showed her). After realizing "oh crap, they can still come back," sure enough, they came back and led 8–7 going to the bottom of the ninth. But Rickey Henderson gets on, Alfonzo gets on and, bless his never-gonna-hafta-pay-for-another-drink-in-the-borough-of-Queens soul, Matt Franco singles them both in against Mariano fucking Rivera and we win 9–8 and it's V-Y day in Row T of Upper Deck Section 36. There are hugs and Hallelujahs and prayers of thanksgiving and the sweet, sweet rasp of victory (neither I nor my friend Richie could speak clearly for two weeks). Within about two minutes: *Big deal, you're still in second place. . . . The Mets are so bush, acting like they won the World Series. . . . Seriously, fellas, who's got the rings?* Who empowered them to monitor our euphoria?

Ubiquitous twits. It's a great night to be a Mets fan, October 8, 1999. We've just enjoyed our first playoff home game in eleven years, an uncharacteristically easy win over the Diamondbacks, taking a 2–1 lead in the NLDS with the potential clincher tomorrow. On the 7 into the city, there is much positive chatter, until one voice is raised in protest. It's some jerk wearing a Yankees cap, demanding to know why Mets fans are always talking when they haven't won anything yet. I'll answer that after you tell me why a Yankees fan is on a subway train from Shea Stadium after a National League playoff game . . . and can craft such an ill-timed inquiry.

Raised poorly. I'm out and about in the early afternoon of October 17, 1999, hours before Game Five of the about-to-be epic NLCS. I'm trying to get away from reading or thinking about another do-or-die versus the Braves; it's gotten so bad that I need a distraction from my alleged diversion, baseball. Anyway, I'm at a shopping center somewhere on Long Island, wearing a Mets T-shirt, when I pass a mother and two sons, the oldest of whom is, at most, twelve. He's wearing a Yankees cap. I say nothing. He says, "Mets. Ha!" and begins to chortle. The mother doesn't slap him or admonish him. She joins in the laughter. Child abuse is a serious crime. Parent abuse, in this case, could be excused.

Graceless clods. LIRR, the morning before Game Three of the 2000 World Series. I'm wearing one of my many Mets jackets to work. We pull into Penn Station. A woman sees this and says, "Good luck." Before I can respond in the affirmative, she adds, "but the Yankees are going to win tonight." Joliet Jake in *The Blues Brothers* hated Illinois Nazis. I have it in for Long Island Yankees fans.

Sadistic bastards. "Who Let The Dogs Out?" made for an unlikely if catchy anthem as we captured our first pennant since

1986. Alas, the day after the 2000 World Series ended, there were drawings of tortured canines taped to every fax machine in our offices. "DEAD PUPPIES!" was the caption. What did the Baha Men ever do to you?

Occasionally prescient. I visited Yankee Stadium five times, four times when the tickets were free. One of those occasions was a regular-season game featuring the Mets. From the left field boxes I watched Bobby Jones give up a 5–3 lead. In a blink, the Mets were down by six. Those of us there to support the Mets sat quietly while the game got further and further away from us and the majority in attendance roared. Somebody standing behind me bellowed at the Mets' rookie leftfielder, "HEY TYNER! IT'S TIME FOR YOU TO MAKE AN ERROR!" And in that very same at-bat Jason Tyner made an error.

TWENTY-FOUR

199.9 WAYS TO THE
1999 PLAYOFFS

1. The best month ever to be a Mets fan was the thirty days encompassing September 21 to October 20, 1999, particularly if you're not picky about including a world championship in the package.

2. You can't have everything.

3. 1999 had everything but a pennant and a Series and a parade.

4. From a decade beyond, that seems almost like a technicality.

5. What a season, what a crescendo, what a climax.

6. We join 1999 in progress, after 150 games, when the Mets were 92–58, within a game of the Braves, and heading down to Turner Field, their bête noire, for a three-game series that could determine the division title.

7. Oh it did . . . dammit.

8. First game was the Chipper Jones festival of pain, with a homer from the left side (off Rick Reed) and a homer from the right side (off Dennis Cook), leading to a 2–1 loss.

9. Second game saw Bobby Valentine do a ton of managing— batting Melvin Mora for Benny Agbayani; batting Shawon Dunston for Darryl Hamilton; batting Matt Franco for Shawon Dunston; batting Bobby Bonilla for Rey Ordoñez; running Jay Payton for Matt Franco, and batting Todd Pratt for Orel Hershiser in the course of three consecutive plate appearances in an effort to outfox Bobby Cox—but to no avail as the Mets lost 5–2.

10. The finale was a weekday afternoon game during which I disappeared from the office for a very long walk with my Walkman.

11. Down 6–3, the Mets got two on in the ninth against John Rocker and brought up Edgardo Alfonzo with two out.

12. As I listened, I decided I'd better keep walking, lest the rally expire on my head.

13. Fonzie flied out, bringing to mind Ellen DeGeneres's recollection that, "My grandmother started to walk five miles a day when she was seventy years old—she is ninety-seven today, but we don't know where the hell she is."

14. The Mets, now four back of the Braves, trudged to Philadelphia where on a Friday night Masato Yoshii was beaten 3–2 by Joe Grahe, who had been out of the major leagues since 1995 and who would never win another game for the rest of his career.

15. On Saturday, I needed to buy a new set of headphones for my Walkman, which had become every bit as worn out as my nerves by the recent downturn in Mets fortunes.

16. When I plugged them in, I got to listen to a description of Phillies' second baseman David Doster diving through the air to nab a line drive, start a double play, and quash an eighth-inning rally that kept the score 4–2, the eventual final.

17. David Doster, like Joe Grahe, hadn't been in the bigs since the mid-'90s and would not play a single inning in the major leagues in the 21st century.

18. Sunday was when I'd be taking matters into my own hands, as my friend Richie would be driving us down to the Vet for what he fancied as a fortieth birthday present to himself.

19. Richie knew somebody who somehow upgraded us into one of the Vet's luxury boxes which, to be honest, wasn't the least bit luxurious—we had to crane our necks to watch the unkind out-of-town scoreboard and see how the Braves were continuing to win.

20. The Braves hadn't lost since they started playing us the previous Tuesday and we hadn't won, our losing streak reaching six when, trailing 3–2, Rickey Henderson tapped a slow grounder to second with one out and the bases loaded and he jogged his way into a game-ending double play.

21. Faced with the reality that we had been swept by the going-nowhere Phillies with a week remaining, I was the saddest person inside a Veterans Stadium Super Box.

22. Until I looked down and found Richie the birthday boy splattered on a slab of Super Box concrete and Astroturf, giving him saddest-person honors for September 26, 1999.

23. On the drive back up the New Jersey Turnpike, we heard Pokey Reese had hit a three-run homer to lead the Reds to a twelve-inning win over the Cardinals, meaning not only had the Braves clinched the division that Sunday, but now we trailed in the Wild Card race.

24. We pulled over at a rest stop and it was Sunday of the living dead, one northbound zombielike Mets fan after another having heard the news on WFAN that our postseason fallback position was now disintegrating, each of us staring wordlessly at one another.

25. The next day in the papers, John Franco was insisting the Mets would still make the playoffs, which made me dislike John Franco more than ever.

26. I wrote and e-mailed a poem to every Mets fan I knew that day, the final verse ending with *Pack up the gear and get on the bus/Playoffs this year?/The choke is on us.*

27. The night after that, as I met Jason outside Gate E for the opener of the Braves-Mets three-game series that now meant nothing to Atlanta and everything to us, he noticed that for the first time he could remember that I wasn't wearing a Mets shirt or a Mets jacket or a Mets cap to a Mets game.

28. "Trying to fool the gods by a lack of regalia?" he asked, to which I simply nodded.

29. The silliest Mets regalia of the night was on sale at the concession stands where you could buy a T-shirt with the Mets logo, the Braves logo, and the banner BATTLE FOR THE EAST, which had obviously been printed up more than a week earlier.

30. Nobody's regalia worked except that of the Atlanta Braves, who won 9–3, shoving us a game-and-a-half behind the Astros, who had been overtaken by the fiery Reds in the Central.

31. We were back at Shea the next night, me and Jason, his wife Emily, and her father, whom I hadn't seen in just about exactly a year.

32. "You two will remember each other from collapses of seasons past," Jason reintroduced us.

33. The 1998 Mets lost their final five games, causing me to swear off baseball forever, a pledge I rescinded before too long.

34. Now the Mets had lost seven in a row and were pulling an even more odious *el foldo* and I was, once more, at the precipice of saying goodbye to the game I loved for thirty years, seeing as how it was in the habit of killing me late every September.

35. Yet, with Greg Maddux on the mound for Atlanta and the Braves leading by a run, the fourth inning unfolded as such: Hamilton singled; Roger Cedeño singled; Ordoñez singled; Al Leiter (!) singled; Henderson singled; Fonzie singled . . . and John Olerud hit a GRAND SLAM!

36. Holy mackerel, the Mets drip-drip-dripped on the great Maddux until Olerud blew him up, allowing the Mets to cruise

home with a 9–2 win, break the losing streak, pick up ground on at least one of the Central teams we were chasing, and returning me to my avocation as a baseball fan.

37. Both Maddux (pitching) and I (attending) entered the night with 19 wins in 1999—only one Greg left Shea a 20-game winner that night.

38. For the first time, I'd be attending an entire series, Laurie and I guests of a former colleague from *Beverage World* who now worked for a beverage company that held season tickets (my concept of conflict of interest completely in dry dock if it got me into Shea).

39. We sat in the right field corner of Field Level, trying to see over some kid who insisted on holding aloft a sign that read THANK YOU MR. GREEN, a good seven years before Shawn Green became our rightfielder (we never did figure out what it meant and we never bothered to ask).

40. We were able to see fine when Fonzie tied the game at three in the bottom of the eighth with a line drive over the left field fence.

41. We saw too much when Shawon Dunston fumbled a fly ball at the right field fence, setting up the winning Braves run in the top of the eleventh.

42. This was the night when Chipper Jones sealed his rep at Shea by burying the Mets to the press after the game, suggesting we could all go home and "put on our Yankee stuff".

43. As Laurie and I moped on the 7 platform about how we were now two behind both Houston and Cincinnati with only

three to play, we ran into Jason and Emily, which seemed really bizarre considering more than 48,000 had been at Shea and here were two people we knew. . . . I thought that sort of thing happened only on *Seinfeld.*

44. With our playoff chances down to about nothing, I couldn't bear to leave my office Friday night, October 1, as the Mets battled the Pirates into extra innings, for if I left, something definitively disastrous might occur to the Mets.

45. Pretty decent things were going on while I listened, including dependable Kenny Rogers pitching into the eighth— he was pretty much lights out for the Mets during the 1999 season—and John Franco getting a generous call to strike out Adrian Brown, looking to end a Pirate threat (making me wonder whether anyone held up a sign that said THANK YOU MR. BROWN).

46. I kept putting off my departure until I could wait no longer, new headphones bolted to my ears as I rushed up Seventh Avenue to Penn Station, hewing to a path inside Penn that I knew would give me some semblance of AM radio reception and claiming a window seat so I could hear the game clearly as we pulled out of the depot and through the tunnel; this was what I'd been doing during baseball season ever since my magazine moved into Manhattan in 1996.

47. Seeing the headphones, somebody in a seat facing mine asked, "Is that the Mets game you have on? What's the score?" which was the very first time anybody had ever asked me that on the LIRR in four seasons of commuting.

48. When Robin Ventura broke out of a massive slump to single home Shawon Dunston with the bases loaded and two out

in the eleventh, giving the Mets a 3–2 win, I made eye contact with my fellow traveler and gave him a great big thumbs up.

49. I didn't say anything to anybody but smiled very broadly when it was reported after the game that in Milwaukee in the top of the tenth, Marquis Grissom pulled a David Doster on the Reds, robbing them of a go-ahead run with a diving catch in center, prefacing the Brewers scoring in the bottom of the inning and putting us only a game behind with two to play.

50. Saturday afternoon, I did two things to help the cause: a) I slipped on a GOODBYE COUNTY STADIUM T-shirt a friend sent me from a trip to Milwaukee; and b) went out looking for a bottle of Rheingold to have on hand for a potential Wild Card-clinching toast, which was the most confidence I had allowed myself to express since the Mets left the Vet six days earlier.

51. On line at Waldbaum's to pay for my Rheingold, some Yankees fan expressed surprise at finding a real live Brewers fan here on Long Island—I assured him it was a temporary condition.

52. The Brewers beat the Reds 10–6 when I got home, positioning the Mets to have control of their own destiny if they just kept winning, which only made me more nervous; the last thing you want to trust the Mets with is their (or your) own destiny.

53. In one of the most spectacular latter-day pitching performances the Mets have ever had, Rick Reed struck out a dozen Pirates—nine through the first six innings when the game was scoreless—and the Mets beat Pittsburgh 7–0 to pull into a tie for the Wild Card lead with the Reds.

54. I woke up Sunday, October 3, overwhelmed by the enormity and the reality of the situation.

55. This was gonna be it.

56. A year earlier, on the last day in Atlanta with the Mets locked in a three-way battle with the Cubs and Giants for the Wild Card, Bob Murphy opened his broadcast by noting, "There are some days in your life, and this is one of them."

57. So was this one, even more so.

58. 1999 had been the most intense season I had ever experienced, both in quality and quantity.

59. When Stephanie and I would arrive at Shea that afternoon to meet Richie and his son Richie, Jr., it would mark my twenty-ninth game of the year, five more than 1998, more to that point than in any single year—truly an embarrassment of riches.

60. I had seen, among other things, Bobby Jones (the starting pitcher) homer in the Home Opener; Tug McGraw present a motorcycle to John Franco; the '69 Mets gather for a thirtieth-anniversary reunion; Matt Franco score from first on a windblown pop fly to short; Robin Ventura hit a grand slam in the second game of a doubleheader after he had done the same in the first game; David Wells chased from the mound while protecting a three-run lead in the ninth; a bunch of broads who looked like David Wells leave the game when he did; the Mets complete their comeback on Wells's Blue Jay teammates after we stood for a fourteenth-inning stretch; Mike Piazza tear Roger Clemens a new one about 450 feet long on a Friday night; Mike tear the less offensive but no less culpable Ramiro Mendoza one that was even newer and longer the next afternoon; M. Franco beat

M. Rivera in the backest-and-forthest Subway Series game ever; the Mets retake Merengue Night from the Sammy Sosa acolytes in the crowd; Octavio Dotel outduel Chan Ho Park from seats directly behind home plate, seats where I could make out how curve balls actually curved; and that death-and-life-and-death series against the Braves.

61. Through the course of the riveting 1999 season, I had grown closer to Shea than ever before, closer to friends whose main connection to me was the Mets than ever before, closer to the Mets than ever before.

62. The '99 Mets had the tightest defensive infield in baseball history, the most imposing catcher in the game, a splendid, leakproof bullpen, and comebacks out the yin-yang.

63. The '99 Mets also had adequate starting pitching, a series of revolving outfielders, and they were tightrope walkers where the standings were concerned.

64. The '99 Mets were another Bobby Valentine production, from his brush with firing to the three coaches GM Steve Phillips took away from him to the moustache and glasses he slapped on in the dugout after he'd been ejected against Toronto to an article that showed up in the *Sporting News* right there around the end of the season asking "Why does everyone hate Bobby V?"

65. The '99 Mets were a circus, in the best sense of the word— I'd seen that over 161 games.

66. On October 3, 1999, I had the sense the most memorable was yet to come.

67. Despite having developed a phobia about highway driving some years earlier, I insisted we take the car, which wasn't the best choice since the only parking we could find was on the far side of the World's Fair Marina, keeping us from witnessing the first inning.

68. We stepped briskly to meet the Richies outside Gate D, us with a radio but no cell phone, Richie with a cell phone but no radio, thus leaving all of at least a little bit shy of optimal communications.

69. I picked up the tickets at Will Call—left for us by Dee Reed, wife of the previous night's winning pitcher and an acquaintance via Laurie who met them both over AOL back when the Internet was a much smaller place—and the four of us proceeded to the last row of Loge.

70. Richie spent much of the afternoon enjoying the back of the head of a man who liked to stand up a lot, but it was better than not being at Shea, he was quick to point out.

71. While we were marching from the Marina, the Pirates had scratched out a run off Orel Hershiser, a Met for this one season eleven years after he doomed us as a Dodger, but he settled down and started posting zeroes.

72. The Mets were getting nothing off Pittsburgh starter Kris Benson in what was fast materializing into a classic matchup of flame-throwing rookie versus grizzled veteran.

73. These two had hooked up, Benson winning, when the Mets dressed up as the Mercury Mets in July and Orel—moral as

he was in his halcyon L.A. days—found the allegedly futuristic logo vaguely demonic, fearing it wouldn't sit right "with The Man Upstairs."

74. The Mercury Mets . . . toldja the '99 club was a circus.

75. If you ever wondered what 50,111 people holding their breath sounded like, you could listen closely to all of us barely exhaling until the fourth when a little subpar Buc fielding set up our first run.

76. Then we went back to sucking it in, as inning after inning passed and the Mets didn't score and the Pirates didn't score.

77. Hershiser left with one out and a man on second in the sixth, giving way to Dennis Cook and Pat Mahomes, each of whom registered a crucial out.

78. The Mets loaded the bases in their half of the sixth, but Matt Franco, pinch-hitting for Mahomes, stranded the runners.

79. When Turk Wendell came on in the seventh, Stephanie suddenly decided she wanted ice cream, which was my beyond my comprehension, but for putting up with me for 161 games and six innings, she deserved ice cream, so we got up to get it.

80. In an absolutely empty Loge concourse—because who in their right mind wants to leave his or her seat *now*?—the Walkman told me Turk retired the Pirates in order; we were back in front of our seats in time to stretch.

81. Rickey Henderson, the all-time stolen base leader, singled to lead off the Mets' seventh and was replaced by Melvin Mora on first and in left.

82. Henderson jogged to first one week earlier in Philadelphia, and Mora was a better bet to have in now . . . but he was left on first as Benson mowed down Fonzie, Oly, and Mike in order.

83. Turk got the Pirates in order again in the eighth, one of his victims, Dale Sveum, pinch-hitting for Kris Benson, who, glory be, was out of the game.

84. The Mets did nothing to speak of against Pittsburgh reliever Jason Christiansen in the eighth except leave Agbayani on first—ten LOB in eight innings, for crissake.

85. As Melvin Mora moves from left to right, but stays in the game, Turk gets the first two Buccos before allowing Kevin Young to single.

86. Out goes Turk, in comes Armando Benitez, the ferocious eighth-inning setup guy who took over as closer after John Franco was injured—the mere sight of hulking, hard-throwing Armando filled you with confidence if you were a Mets fan.

87. After Young stole second, Armando issued an intentional walk to Warren Morris and struck out Aramis Ramirez, leaving this all, nothing, or maybe game tied at one going to the bottom of the ninth.

88. In Houston, the Astros were clinching the N.L. Central, thus removing themselves from our concerns.

89. In Milwaukee, the Reds and Brewers were waiting out a rain delay.

90. In the bottom of the ninth of what was either an excruciating pitchers' duel or a popgun target practice—the Pirates

were pathetic and the Mets were hitting down to their level—
Bobby Valentine inserted Bobby Bonilla to pinch-hit for Shane
Halter leading off.

91. Bonilla couldn't have been less popular at Shea Stadium
in 1999 had he still been a Pirate.

92. Bonilla had more downs than ups during his first term
in Flushing from '92 to '95, but he'd actually been intermittently
productive; in '99 he was an oaf all the way.

93. But when he was announced into the game, just about
every Mets fan in that ballpark stood and applauded for Bobby
Bonilla . . . this was just too big a moment to let personalities
intrude on what was a teamwide matter for all of us.

94. You could just feel Bonilla trying to make good on this
newfound faith we had invested in him: he took a serious cut on
the first pitch he saw.

95. Alas, Bobby Bo would ground out to first.

96. As he returned to the dugout, most of us stood and
applauded one more time for the guy most of us couldn't stand—
if nothing else happened on October 3, 1999, that confirmed that
this would be the most incredible game I'd ever attend at Shea
Stadium.

97. Of course more would happen . . . Mora would happen.

98. Melvin Mora, still in the game from when Bobby V pinch-
ran with him, was up next.

99. Melvin Mora was utterly unknown to us prior to 1999, befitting his true journeyman status.

100. His sojourns had taken him to Taiwan where, in 1998, he did a hitch as a Mercuries Tiger.

101. From Mercuries to the Mercury Mets in a year's time, Mora had been as fringe a 1999 Met to date as Shane Halter (who was immortalized in my "They Choked" poem with the line, *It's a shame Shane Halter can't halt this dreck*).

102. Melvin was mostly a defensive replacement and pinch-runner during the course of the season.

103. His role in this nominally ultimate game was underscored by his designation in the boxscore: PR-LF-RF-LF.

104. He stepped to the plate against Greg Hansell with exactly four hits on his major league ledger.

105. Melvin Mora collected the fifth hit of his life off Hansell, a liner to right, transforming him from obscure reserve to potential winning run.

106. The clutchest Met there was in 1999 was Edgardo Alfonzo, and Fonzie confirmed it with another single to right, which drove Mora from first to third.

107. Shea grew very loud as John Olerud, just about as clutch a performer as Fonzie, came up, but he would be intentionally walked to load the bases, a perfectly sensible maneuver by Pirate manager Gene Lamont except for one little detail.

108. The next batter would be Mike Piazza.

109. Mike Piazza had knocked in 124 RBI in 1999, the most runs ever batted in by a Met.

110. Mike had been slumping like every other Met the last couple of weeks, but he blasted a two-run homer the night before.

111. Now Lamont was gambling Piazza would hit into a double play and take his new pitcher, ex-Met Brad Clontz, off the hook and send this to the tenth.

112. Let's not oversell the ex-Met angle: Clontz pitched in exactly two games as a Met in 1998.

113. But Clontz pitched for the Dodgers in '98 before becoming a Met—and his catcher there was Mike Piazza.

114. Who would have the advantage between a catcher and a pitcher who were more than a little familiar with each other?

115. We shall never know, for Clontz threw exactly one pitch, and it was nowhere near the strike zone.

116. Gary Cohen described it my ears:

117. *Clontz is ready to go, pitching off the stretch.*

118. *Deals to Piazza.*

119. *Low and outside . . . IT GETS AWAY!*

120. *Onto the screen!*

121. *Mora scores!*

122. *The Mets win it!*

123. *The Mets win it!*

124. *Mora is mobbed by his teammates as he crosses home plate!*

125. *Brad Clontz bounced the first pitch up on the screen!*

126. *Melvin Mora scores the winning run!*

127. *The Mets win in game number one-hundred and sixty-two!*

128. *And the Mets will play again in Nineteen Ninety-Nine!*

129. What I saw and screamed was "WILD PITCH!" as if everybody couldn't see it for themselves.

130. "WILD PITCH!" I told Richie, who could make it out just fine from behind that guy's head.

131. Richie, a Little League coach, four years my elder, and something of a big brother figure to me throughout the season, grabbed me, hugged me and said in a low, serious voice, "They didn't choke."

132. No, they didn't choke.

133. Mike Piazza was a 124-RBI bystander as Mora roared down the line—the Mets were going to win the game that would win them the right to play one more, at least.

134. We got Piazza the year before and dreamed of him coming to bat with the season on the line—Mike at the plate and us winning, if not precisely as had just happened.

135. Nobody was questioning how we got here.

136. Nobody was leaving either.

137. The Mets had only clinched a Wild Card tie if that was, in fact, something you could clinch, but it was the first in-Shea celebration I was ever a part of.

138. First, as Mora was mobbed, and we mobbed each other, we heard our fight song, "L.A. Woman" by the Doors.

139. The fight part was the refrain: *"Mis-ter MO-JO RISIN'!"*

140. Instituted by Ventura in the clubhouse and seeping out to the fans, it was one of those pennant race totems that took on a life of its own, no matter how little sense it made.

141. We were all Doors fans for the duration.

142. Then it was *"Wild boys! Wild boys!"* because we were now a half-game up on the idling Reds for the Wild Card.

143. When this series started, it was pounded into our heads that only one team down two games with three to go (the 1962 Giants) had made it to the postseason.

144. Less than 48 hours later, Duran Duran was being pounded into our heads.

145. Duran Duran sounded a lot better.

146. Before leaving the house that morning, I had inscribed two initials onto the side of my cap with soap the way players did to salute their injured comrades (before the commissioner made them cut it out): LR.

147. LR was for Laurie who arranged with Dee to leave the tickets . . . and for Laurie who couldn't be there herself because she was sent to Chicago on business.

148. In the first wave of pandemonium, I borrowed Richie's phone and called her in the Midwest; on her voice mail I left a booming message (because I didn't know that you didn't need to yell into a cell) to let her know what happened and that we were thinking of her and that she was here in spirit via soaped initials.

149. On the field in real life, once the players were done embracing, they shared their joy with their soulmates: us.

150. Our nation turned its giddy eyes to one John Franco, the active major leaguer who, to that point, had participated in the most games without any of them being of the postseason variety.

151. For maybe a half-minute, the collective consciousness of Shea Stadium seemed to think, "John Franco is finally going to get his chance."

152. Diamond Vision found him and the crowd erupted for someone who had been, at best, a Rorschach test for most Mets fans.

153. *I see a reliever who saves loads of games . . . no, wait—I see a choke artist.*

154. That Cincinnati, Franco's first team, would still have to be vanquished for the diminutive homeboy lefty to finally break into postseason play wasn't immediately grasped.

155. But in the sudden team-of-destiny blitz of emotions, the Reds and their never-ending rain delay were relegated to an afterthought.

156. Instead, we stood and we clapped as the music kept thumping: Gary Glitter, Tina Turner, some schlocky Rod Stewart song that was apropos because it preached faith of the heart.

157. No matter how many times I had given up on these 1999 Mets, I kept the faith.

158. I was there, wasn't I?

159. I was there and making no move to the exits, as was nobody else.

160. Stephanie did not usually evince that kind of staying power, but she knew, she told me, "We were in it for the long haul" that Sunday, however many innings and hours that entailed.

161. "My mother would have enjoyed this," she said in the middle of all the exulting, which I found strange since my mother-in-law, who had passed away five years earlier, had never expressed the slightest interest in baseball.

162. "She liked to watch people."

163. I took that to mean somebody was getting a wee bit antsy to hit the road now that the game was over and Mojo had risen and John Franco had been properly saluted—hint taken.

164. What a wonderful, joyous affair, the Mets doing exactly what we needed them to do, putting the bad taste of 1998 forever out of our mouths, catapulting us into at least one more day, assuring we would remain Milwaukee Brewers fans well into the evening, whenever it stopped raining at County Stadium—and as we said our goodbyes to the Richies, we knew nothing could detract from the delight of this greatest day ever at Shea Stadium.

165. Except, of course, for the way things worked at Shea Stadium.

166. See, it was Fan Appreciation Day, not only in the sense of Mets 2, Pirates 1, in that it was the last scheduled home game of the season, and we were supposed to get a little prize to go with our Wild Card tie.

167. We were supposed to receive a miniature bat, each and every one of us, in appreciation for our patronage across 1999.

168. Usually, you get the token of Met appreciation when you walk in, but the Mets, being the Mets (who theoretically might blow their playoff chances on the final day; imagine that), didn't want to hand out projectiles to the same people who had demonstrated bouts of impatience across the long season, so it was announced beforehand that fans would see their bats after the game.

169. Hopped up on good feelings, we went to look for our bats before leaving Shea, only to discover a mob scene at every gate, fans putting aside their own appreciation and fighting for what amounted to $6 souvenirs.

170. We couldn't get anywhere near whoever was handing out the bats, so I scrounged up a couple of rainchecks from the ground (couldn't get near whoever was distributing those either) and figured I'd take my chances mailing them in.

171. Ah, what's a bat when the Mets will play again in Nineteen Ninety-Nine?

172. Though I have to confess I was a little discouraged that as we drove away from the Marina empty-handed, we saw some guy whooping it up with approximately *nine* bats in his arms.

173. The Reds and Brewers waited an eternity to get their game in, with almost nobody in the Milwaukee stands to watch.

174. Cincinnati won handily, setting up the one-game playoff to determine who would win the Wild Card, us or them.

175. During the Reds game, I spoke to Laurie, who told me excitedly, "Rick called during the celebration and said he wrote my intials on his cap!"

176. I probably shouldn't have revealed who that really was on the phone.

177. Hard to say that the all-the-marbles affair Monday night at Riverfront Stadium/Cinergy Field was an anticlimax, but after Sunday afternoon at Shea, anything would have been.

178. But it was the best kind of anticlimax, the kind that didn't put you on edge for very long.

179. Walking out of my office en route to the train a little after 7:00 P.M., I heard Rickey single and Fonzie homer and let out the biggest "YEAH!" Seventh Avenue had experienced that day.

180. It was Al Leiter versus Steve Parris . . . forget Parris.

181. It was all Al, all the time that night, carrying a commanding one-hitter through the balance of the evening while Jack McKeon was forced to dip into his bullpen early and often.

182. Denny Neagle walked home a run, Rickey homered to lead off an inning, and Fonzie drove in Rey-Rey, all adding up to a 5–0 Mets lead in the sixth.

183. After two oxygen-deprived weeks and six anxiety-riddled months, the Mets were finally, finally, *finally* going to do what they didn't do the year before, what they didn't do for a decade before that.

184. They were going to make the playoffs.

185. I actually had a few innings to consider how I was going to react.

186. But I forgot about whatever plans I had, whether to shout or sob, because the ninth felt just the slightest bit dicey.

187. Pokey Reese doubled to lead off the bottom of the ninth and moved to third on a grounder.

188. After the second out, Greg Vaughn walked, bringing up the dangerous Dmitri Young—Bob Murphy reported Benitez was warming up in the pen.

189. I saw a line drive, pictured two runs scoring, braced for Al leaving, Armando entering, the Mets' lead reduced to three, Hammonds up, the tying run on deck . . . and began to rekindle that familiar sense of dread.

190. Except Young's line drive was caught by Alfonzo and that was it: the Mets were in the playoffs.

191. I was levitated off the couch by forces unknown to me and performed what could best be described as a scissor kick.

192. I probably yelled something triumphal as well.

193. After a fashion, I cued up a CD with CeCe Peniston's "Finally" on it because, finally, in the 163rd game of the season, my team winning its way into the playoffs happened to me.

194. And I brought out that chilled Rheingold purchased Saturday.

195. Before Opening Day 1998, I attended a press luncheon at which Rheingold, the original beer sponsor of the Mets from back in 1962, was reintroduced to the marketplace.

196. We were each given a can to take with us and I decided I would save mine for the end of the '98 season to celebrate our eventual playoff berth.

197. After we choked that away, I opened the can, took one sip, and poured the rest down the drain.

198. The 1999 vintage Rheingold I savored for quite a few minutes.

199. About a month later, our Fan Appreciation giveaways arrived in the mail with a letter from the Mets explaining that it was the NYPD's idea not to give out the bats in advance ("citing concerns over fan safety if our game went poorly") and that, "When the crowds began pushing, grabbing hands full of bats, and shoving the promotional staff out of the way, the police insisted that we halt all distribution of mini-bats and that the remaining mini-bats be locked away."

199.9. As for the playoffs that took place during that intervening month . . .

TWENTY-FIVE

MOJO RISES, MOJO FALLS

The first transcendent, surpassing moment of the Mets' 1999 postseason is easy. Easy to identify, anyway.

First there's Pratt. No need to identify it further, except to say that when he hit it, all of Shea Stadium froze save for the ball and Steve Finley. Todd Pratt himself froze. I watched from the Mezzanine as he pulled up around first, in suspended animation, waiting to see whether the great Diamondback centerfielder was going to leap and ruin a perfectly good fly ball the way Steve Finley had been ruining perfectly good long fly balls at least once per West Coast road trip for years. I froze, but did manage to think, "You know, Tank, there is some middle ground here. It might be that it doesn't go out but that Finley doesn't catch it, and do you really want to be thrown out at second because you're standing there like a schmuck?"

Good ol' Tank, however, knew enough to hit his ball 411 feet, a full dozen inches beyond the grasp of Arizona's leapingest lizard. And then everything unfroze: first base ump Bruce Froemming twirled his right index finger; Pratt broke into a sprint; the "Mojo Risin'" refrain vibrated up and down the ballpark; confetti fell from somewhere; I grabbed Stephanie and hoisted her in the air by at least as many inches as the ball missed becoming Finley-veiled; I turned to my left and did the same with Jason, leaving him forever with the impression that I possess upper-body strength (when, in fact, it was one of those adrenaline rush, lift-the-car-off-your-baby episodes you read about on diner placemats). The Diamondbacks slithered away in dismay. The Mets piled on their catcher who, twenty-four hours earlier, was a leading indicator that things might not work out, what with Piazza and his forty home runs and his elbow all out of commission for the remainder of the National League Division Series.

Since he slugged it, Todd Pratt is synonymous with the walkoff homer of walkoff homers in Mets history, though I'll never quite get over the way someone with only three long balls on his CV in 1999 stood and watched Steve Finley try to take away his fourth. I suppose you don't get to be called Tank without rolling through life oblivious to the consequences of your actions.

* * *

Second, there's the Grand Slam Single. No need to identify it further either, but it's probably worth backing up a tad ahead of its immaculate connection to consider how it came to be on a rainy Sunday at Shea.

I wasn't there. I was there Friday night when we fell down 3–0 to the Braves in the NLCS. It was a one-nothing loss . . . a one-nothing blowout, if such a creature exists. We went down a run in the first and that was that. The only real highlight was when John Rocker, warming to the role of professional wrestling villain by now, entered and the guys in front of me augmented the standard "ROCK-ER SUCKS!" chant with "FUCK YOU ROCK-ER!" We had a good thing going:

"ROCK-ER SUCKS!"

"FUCK YOU ROCK-ER!"

In a one-nothing blowout, you'll take what you can get.

Just don't get swept, I whispered from home Saturday night, without much conviction, because maybe it would have been best to get this over with. But John Olerud had other ideas. He broke a tie in the eighth and the Mets won 3–2. They were still alive. Nobody had come back from down three games to none in baseball history, but a few had come back from three games to one—and now, I told myself, we're down three games to one.

Then Sunday, the endless afternoon turned into evening turned into night that the Mets and Braves played in the chilly rain of Queens. The first fourteen innings were foreplay: necessary, stimulating, and excruciatingly pleasant (or pleasantly excruciating, depending how you take it), but five hours of prelude. Olerud homered off Maddux for two in the first, but their guy settled down. Masato Yoshii, a figure of much stress for two years and some redemption in the last two months (before being traded for an extra, unnecessary Bobby Jones), allowed the Braves to tie it and didn't make it out of the fourth.

And that's where it stood forever. Every pitcher the Mets had or had ever had trotted in from the bullpen between the fourth and the thirteenth. First Orel Hershiser, who cleaned up Yoshii's mess. Then Turk for one batter in the seventh, a strikeout of Chipper/Larry. Then, in some Bobby V gamesmanship that worked to a tee, a Dennis Cook lefty-lefty cameo forced Ryan Klesko out of the game. Then Pat Mahomes took to the mound. Remember Pat Mahomes? Pat Mahomes was an unsung hero all through 1999, back when we could use words like "hero" to describe ballplayers playing ball and not feel shallow about it. It took four pitchers—Hershiser, Wendell, Cook, Mahomes—but the Braves didn't score in the seventh.

We didn't score either, by the way. There was lots of not scoring. As the middle relievers gave way to the closers, nobody scored. Franco gave an inning-and-a-third. Benitez a shutout inning. On the other side, Rocker shut his door. In the eleventh, we had Kenny Rogers out there. Kenny Rogers was undefeated (2–0) in seven outings at Shea since coming over from Oakland in July. And Kenny Rogers was as perfect as he had to be that night, pitching two scoreless innings.

Octavio Dotel, rookie righty, alternately glorious and atrocious since his callup, toed the rubber in the thirteenth inning. Octavio Dotel, a child, a starter, was being asked to hold the fort in what was making a bid for greatest game in Mets history, Son of Astrodome at the very least. Bobby V had used everybody else within reason. The only pitchers left were last night's starter, Reed (seven very sharp, very economical innings) and Leiter from Friday night and, with Divine Providence, the upcoming Tuesday night. So it was all on Dotel.

Keith Lockhart, one of an assembly line of Braves gnats, singled with two outs. Chipper/Larry, bane of our collective existence that fall, doubled to right. Lockhart was about to score the go-ahead run and bury, once for all, our dream of National League preeminence.

Except Melvin Mora, the guy from nowhere, is in right and throws Lockhart out by ten feet. Across this postseason, Mora had already thrown out runners from left and center. In Game Four he instigated a double steal that set up the tying and winning runs. Though we lost Game Two, he snuck in his first big league homer . . . in the playoffs. And now he's saved the season again. You could predict good things for this fella.

Dotel got through the fourteenth, too. But Mets didn't score either. In the fifteenth, you learned you could ask only so much out of one rookie, no matter how talented, only so much out of one ballclub, no matter how big its heart. We've got heart, but they've got Lockhart and he triples home Walt Weiss. Braves lead 3–2 going to the bottom of the fifteenth. It's raining and it may as well be snowing. Though to this point I've been worrying about one game—this game—the score reminds me that if we don't tie, the series and the season are over.

But a game like this isn't over until the visitors collect forty-five outs.

Shawon Dunston wasn't going to help that countdown. Shawon Dunston didn't want to be here. Shawon Dunston, the dictionary picture of a journeyman, was comfortable at last in St. Louis. They all love being in St. Louis, these ballplayers, and Dunston was no exception. He had just bought a house there. As seems to happen to every baseball player who dabbles in real estate, he got traded. To us. He was supposed to be happy. He was from Brooklyn, grew up a Mets fan. They assigned him No. 12 and he immediately recognized it as Ken Boswell's digits. Yet he never copped to being thrilled to be here.

But now it was all on Shawon Dunston's head. He led off the fifteenth. And he, like this game, wouldn't stop. He just kept leading it off. He worked the count. He got to three balls and two strikes and decided walking was not the better part of valor. So he kept swinging and kept fouling them off. He did everything but jump out of the way of a pitch at his legs that would allow Kevin Mitchell to score from third. Except for that, it was the greatest at-bat in Mets history. Mookie forgive me, it probably *was* the greatest at-bat in Mets history.

On the twelfth pitch of the greatest at-bat in Mets history, Shawon Dunston singled off Kevin McGlinchy. The tying run was on first, with nobody out. The rain continued to fall. The snow disappeared. Winter would have to wait.

With *Moneyball* more than three years from publication, Shawon Dunston immediately stole second. In the time it might have taken to point out what a dangerous play this was, he accomplished it. The rest was textbook execution. Matt Franco, who set as obscure a record as one could that season, for most pinch-hit walks, walked as a pinch-hitter for Dotel. How has Bobby V gone through every pitcher yet still have his ace pinch-hitter available? And while you're wondering that, will you look in the Mets' bullpen? The righty warming up is Rick Reed, the lefty is Al Leiter, the two starters from the last two nights and maybe the next two nights. There is no tomorrow if there's going to be a tomorrow, as the Ol' Perfesser might have said from his perch that night.

Fonzie, the best all-around, everyday player the franchise ever produced to date; Fonzie, who posted 27 homers and 108 RBI in 1999 including one and three of each, respectively, in the one-game playoff against the Reds; Fonzie who turned in a 6-for-6, 3 HR game in Houston at the end of August; Fonzie who stuck it but good to the Diamondbacks in the prior round (three dingers; one a slam; another off Randy Johnson) laid down a bunt. He moved the runners over, Dunston to third, Franco to second. That's how you get to be the best all-around, everyday player the franchise ever produced to date.

Second and third, one out. The Braves—it's still McGlinchy even though Millwood, Glavine, and Smoltz are theoretically available to Bobby Cox—intentionally walk John Olerud. The bases are loaded, there's one out, the Braves are still winning, the rain is still pouring, and summer's coming back to life.

Todd Pratt is up. Pratt's been doing some serious caddying this month. Mike's aching elbow has limited his effectiveness, his mere utility. In the game that will now define the fortunes of the New York Mets, what 1999 was, what the future will be, Bobby V took Mike out to start the fourteenth and inserted Todd Pratt, the only other actual catcher on the team. Matt Franco is considered the emergency catcher, but he is now pinch-run for at second by Roger Cedeño, the last bench player, otherwise out with a bad back. The Mets are physically and numerically disappearing. They have gone through everybody. Of a twenty-five-man roster, twenty-three have now played. The other two are warming up. This isn't an All-Star Game, it's as close to life or death as a baseball contest will allow us to get. And at this very moment, though death is ahead on the scoreboard, I wouldn't bet against life.

Todd Pratt was a backup catcher until last Saturday. Now he's Tank, the guy who went all Mazeroski on Matt Mantei, ending the Division Series with one swing. Todd Pratt, it is now official, can do anything he wants.

Todd Pratt walks. Shawon Dunston trots home, Cedeño to third, Olerud to second, Pratt to first. It's Braves 3, Mets 3.

Up steps Robin Ventura. And he needs a sac fly. That's all. A sac fly will do very nicely. A base hit or a walk or an error or a wild pitch or a passed ball that bounces far enough away will all do the trick, but all we really need is a fly ball hit long enough to allow speedy Cedeño to tag up and run ninety feet. If Robin Ventura, who's had an MVP-worthy season (32-120-.301, Best Infield Ever anchor, the dude who came up with "Mojo Risin'") but a bone-chipped month of misery, can do that, he will be Tank times ten.

He will be Tanks a lot.

I didn't think anything could rate with Melvin Mora scoring on that wild pitch on October 3. Six days later, there was Pratt. And when you think it can't possibly get any better than Pratt winning the final game of a postseason series, here, eight days after that, comes Robin Ventura, unloading on Kevin McGlinchy not just a fly ball . . . not just a fly ball that clears the right-center field fence . . . not just a fly ball that clears the right-center field fence with the bases loaded . . .

. . . but a single!

While I was processing what seemed to have just happened— *That's more than a sac fly! That's a grand slam!*—Robin Ventura's teammates, led by Todd Pratt, decided en masse that the rules didn't apply to them. Lawful Robin wanted to circle the bases. Territorial Tank said, sorry you, game-ending homers are my department. You take a single and we'll take the win.

Todd Pratt, it is now *truly* official, can do anything he wants.

In retrospect, I'm surprised Cedeño remembered to run home.

That, as we all know, was the Grand Slam Single. Robin Ventura hit a home run that didn't count because his jubilant teammates wouldn't let him round the bases, a feat destined to be discussed in the same vein as mythical feats from another even more distant age. The Called Shot. The Homer in the Gloamin'. The Grand Slam Single. Robin Ventura's face should be on a stamp, even if he's only retired and not dead.

Those five hours and forty-six minutes of baseball left me literally speechless. For the only time in my life, I think, I didn't know what to say about the Mets. I could only react viscerally. My wife and I were sitting on the carpet in front of our TV when Ventura swung. I rose as his ball did, and when it drove in one if not four runs, I could say absolutely nothing.

So I jumped her. I leapt atop Stephanie as if we were on our own pitcher's mound—Grote to her Koosman, Gary to her Jesse, Tank, come to think of it, to her Robin. It was the only reaction I could express with any clarity. Our phone rang and it was my friend Chuck. "I'll call ya back, I can't talk," I said. I wasn't kidding. There were no words. Except, perhaps, that the Mets had come through for me once more.

When my head cleared, I looked less at what had just occurred and more at what might happen next. Nobody had come back from down three games to none in baseball history, and a few had come back from three games to one. But a whole bunch of teams had come back from three games to two, and that's who we were now. We weren't making history. We were playing a sixth game, Tuesday night, in Atlanta. If we won that, we'd just be another team tied at three, playing a seventh game. And if we won that, we'd be playing the Yankees in the World Series.

* * *

This is where it gets difficult to discern. There is a third transcendent, surpassing moment to the Mets' 1999 postseason. It's in there somewhere, specifically inside the sixth game of that very same National League Championship Series that Pratt made possible, that Ventura left indelible.

No, it's not Kenny Rogers walking in the winning run. That's not fair. Well, it's not fair that he walked in the winning run, but that's not what I mean. Game Six against Atlanta shouldn't be remembered for how it ended; how it wound up in the bottom of the eleventh tied at nine and then suddenly untied in the wrong direction; how ball four wrecked the dream of coming back from down three games to none.

What should be remembered is that the Mets got to the eleventh inning. After Senator Al's perfectly Turner Field first inning—no outs, five runs—the Mets fought back.

They fought back to 5–3, only to have it slide away again to 7–3.

Then they fought back to make it 7–7. And take the lead 8–7.

They let it slip and allowed the Braves to make it 8–8. But *then* we went ahead 9–8!

How the fudge did we lose that game?

I blame Al Leiter's inability to retire a single batter in the first inning (I move the Senator yield the floor).

I blame Turk Wendell for hitting Jordan to lead off the sixth just after the Mets had closed from 5–0 to 5–3.

I blame Dennis Cook for surrendering two runs with two outs via that human canker sore Jose Hernandez a few batters later.

I blame John Franco for giving back an 8–7 lead—we were ahead, honest-to-goodness ahead—with the same kind of stuff on which he gave back too many leads for the entire decade that preceded that particular giveback.

I blame Armando Benitez for giving back a 9–8 lead—we were actually ahead after spotting the Braves five runs in the first *and* after letting them tie us in Franco's eighth—and revealing in the harsh light of do-or-die that we could never live peacefully with him as our closer.

I blame John Olerud, Shawon Dunston, and Robin Ventura, three genuine giants of October 1999, for letting an unremarkable righthander named Russ Springer off the hook in the top of the eleventh. Once those guys couldn't or wouldn't or didn't touch Springer, I sensed it was only a matter of time.

I blame everybody all at once and, honestly, I blame nobody. How could you get down on the 1999 Mets? All right, maybe Bobby Bo (though he pinch-singled in the fifth of Game Six), but that's it. I don't blame Piazza for being too sore to make it to the bottom of the ninth, a half-inning he helped ensure with his laser in the seventh (it was his *Cobra* shot: Smoltz was the disease, he was the cure). I don't blame Rickey, who drove in a run in that same seventh, for his legendary card-playing once he was taken out of the game; he was ineligible to come back in, no matter where he decided to sit. I don't blame Ordoñez for his general offensive ineptitude because he sacrificed successfully in the eighth and threw out more guys in the course of the evening than anybody else.

I can't stay mad at anybody on that team. That is my favorite Mets season of them all and Game Six was the greatest baseball game I ever saw.

Greatest baseball game I ever saw. *And we lost.* That's how good a game it was.

So where's the transcendent, surpassing moment that allows it to reside in the pantheon with Pratt and the Grand Slam Single and, for that matter, Mora?

It might have been when I abandoned all precedent and protocol and *voluntarily* turned off the television and left the house in a state of radio silence for ten purposeful minutes while I picked up some Chinese food I was too nervous to eat.

It might have been when I shoved my thirty-six-year-old body into a Mets jacket designed, literally, for the eighteen-year-old me and took what I hoped would be a shutout-shattering walk to Fu Yu kitchen, bursting from my satin but maybe picking up some good vibes in addition to the chicken and broccoli.

It might have been when I returned home with the Chinese and discovered we were scoring our first three runs.

It might have been when Turk hit Jordan and Jordan glared at him and I screamed, "GOOD! GOOD! I HOPE HE BROKE HIS WRIST!" which is a nice way to kill your karma.

It might have been when I realized I had to repent and say to Stephanie, the cats, and the television that the Braves were the finest team in the land: *People don't realize how great a player Chipper Jones really is; John Rocker may talk a lot, but he backs it up; Bobby Cox is an awesome manager.*

It might have been when I blew my karmic cover after Benny scored the last Met run of the century ahead of a throw from Andruw Jones in the tenth and I exclaimed to the heavens, "ANDRUW JONES HAS THE BEST ARM IN BASEBALL AND I'M NOT BLOWING SMOKE!" Once I gave the gods a chance to question my motives, we were dead.

Kenny Rogers's final pitch shouldn't be the button we sew atop Game Six's legacy. Nor should the last image be that of the three logos NBC plastered on the screen after Gerald Williams scored: the Braves', the Yankees', and the 1999 World Series'.

Is "UCCHH!" a word? It's the one I used at that moment.

But forget those logos. Forget Andruw and Chipper and however many other Joneses we never managed to keep up with at Turner Field. Forget how crushed the great Bob Murphy, the most optimistic man in America—with Murph at the mic, we were never down five runs; we were simply a few baserunners from getting the potential tying run to the on-deck circle—was by how it ended:

The count is three and two. Now the pitch . . . he walked him! The season is over for the New York Mets. Kenny Rogers walked Andruw Jones forcing in the winning run from third base, Gerald Williams heads into score, and it's celebration time for the Atlanta Braves. What a horrible loss for the New York Mets.

Forget Kenny Rogers, even.

Remember what it was like to watch those 1999 Mets scratch and scramble and survive.

Remember how losing those three games in Atlanta in September never made you believe they wouldn't win two there when they really needed to in October.

Remember how Amazin' 10–9 was when it followed hot on the heels of a series that was, for five games, 4–2, 4–3, 1–0, 3–2 and 4–3.

Remember how exhausting the Mets could be and that nothing else mattered if it didn't have to.

Remember how we were gonna win Game Seven, how Reed was gonna beat Glavine, how we were gonna ride that wave straight to victory in the Subway Series (hey, prove me wrong).

* * *

I called in sick for the next day as soon as I could find the strength to push the buttons on the phone for my magazine's voice mail. It wasn't that I was afraid to show my face. It's that I could barely move my face or my head or any of the brains inside it off anything but the Mets. A friend told me word at the office was I needn't have bothered calling in. "Nobody expected you to come in after that," she said.

I don't know that I expected the Mets to come back from three games to none. I was willing to expect it, but I don't know. Still, they got us there. They raised my hopes. They didn't let me down. They just kept me hanging on. In a way, because of what they did in September and October 1999, I am still hanging on.

Maybe that's the transcendent, surpassing moment I've been looking for.

TWENTY-SIX

THE NINE-TEN YEARS

Stephanie and I were taking a walk through East Rockaway one Sunday afternoon in the summer of 2000, long after the postgame edition of *Mets Extra* had wrapped, when I noticed, lying on the ground, a used Shea Stadium parking stub.

"Wow," I said, "that's weird. I was just thinking about the Mets and there's a thing from Shea."

"What's so weird about it?" she asked. "You're always thinking about the Mets."

Yes. Yes, I was. I still am, I suppose, but those years, those years encompassing the Mets' rise to viability in 1997 through the clinching of an overdue pennant in 2000 . . . I think those are my years more than any others.

Those were the Nine-Ten Years, years that called for passion from us, the fans, because it was generated—and returned in spades—by our players. On a scale of five to ten (because, let's face it, it was never going to dip into low single digits), how much did the Mets matter to me then? Somewhere between nine and ten.

The needle never saw eight.

How did that happen? Was it just a matter of being starved of contention for so long that once I got it I had to gorge on it? Was it the new fount of Mets fans to which I had access through the Internet after so many years of feeling like the Bee Girl in the Blind Melon "No Rain" video—wearing my Mets stuff in front of others and being chronically mocked for my essential nature until I found a hive of people like me? Was it the team itself, an imperfect vessel for our hopes and dreams but, boy, didn't you get the feeling they were always trying?

All of it, I guess. I say "I guess" a lot because as Met nemesis Joaquin Andujar once said, you can sum up baseball in one word: you never know. I don't know exactly why in my mid-thirties the Mets became, somehow, more woven around my being than at any time before, even if baseball is supposed to be a kid's game.

It is? I would guess not. As much as I loved baseball as a kid and as much as I tried my unskilled hand at it, the Mets were a fairly lonely proposition to me in childhood. It was me and Channel 9, me and Topps, me and *Baseball Digest*. It wasn't me and Jason or me and Laurie or me and the passel (to use a Gary Cohen word) of folks I would get to know pretty-to-very well during these Nine-Ten Years. My family was benignly supportive of my mania, supportive as they could be considering they never really got it. But the friends I depended on to hear me out on why Steve Phillips was killing us or why Todd Zeile replacing John Olerud was a misguided notion or why Fonzie was the coolest, were, in the realm of the Mets, more like a family than my own family was during the baseball-intensive period that climaxed in 2000.

My Mets-above-all Zeitgeist had been in effect since 1997, when Bobby Valentine first truly insinuated himself into my well-being. He and his charges gave me reason after reason to worry about them. My angst on their behalf was well-honed by October 2000 but it was also extremely genuine. I cared because I couldn't not care.

With me every step of the way, even more than Mike and Robin and Al and Rick, were the Mets fan friends I had made and kept. With baseball serving as our common denominator I realized I knew little else about these people—their politics, their musical tastes, their favorite TV shows, all of which are subjects I carry strong opinions about. I didn't know much if anything about their jobs, their parents, their children, their backgrounds, their hopes, their dreams, their aspirations.

All I knew is they, like me, wanted the Mets to win. I didn't need to know a whole lot more. As the years went forward, I did get better acquainted with most of them and I was never sorry I did.

* * *

When I was in college, I tried intramural softball once and when a ball flew over my head in left field as I broke in to catch it, I called it a career. What I did do in college when none of my various roommates were around was stand in front of the mirror and—good lord, I'm glad nobody ever walked in on me in the middle of this—practice cheering the last out of the next World Series the Mets won.

All I ever really wanted to do was be a Mets fan. And *that* I got good at. I was never better than during the wistful winters, the restless springs, the high Bobby V summers and the crisp autumn nights of 1999 and 2000. That was when I could be who I was meant to be and be with whom I was meant to be—my wife, my cats, and my fellow Mets fans. My friends. In my tribe. Maybe it helped to be not so young anymore. I was old enough to enjoy it, understand it, and savor it without self-consciousness in all its unlikelihood.

* * *

As has been the bad habit formed by luck, cynicism, and the universal cry for gratification, seasons that don't wind up wrapped in ultimate triumph are usually written off as the stuff of losers if they're written at all. The Mets of the Nine-Ten Years fit quite comfortably into this narrative as they found a way to lose almost everything a team could lose while still being good. They lost the Wild Card on the last day of the season in '98, the pennant in excruciating fashion to their archnemeses in '99, the World Series to their most bitter psychic rivals in 2000, and, as a coda to the era, came up short of a division title after rushing furiously toward one late in the 2001 season.

They lost a lot when there was a lot on the line, but to me they never felt like losers. Rooting on their behalf was too compelling. I gained something back then. I gained a sense of purpose. I hated not winning World Series Games One, Two, Four, and Five to the Yankees, but I never felt more an essential part of something than when I'd sit myself down at the computer and send out "buck up, it's gonna be OK" messages to the ad hoc e-mail group I crafted from various elements of my Met life. The AOL people, the people from high school, the people from college, the people who used to work with me, the people who worked with people I knew . . . even a few sympathetic non-Mets fans. It was the only community of which I ever felt a part. Being in the World Series with those people, even if I never scored a ticket to any of the World Series games, made that the most interactive World Series I ever experienced.

That whole 2000 postseason was laced with High Holy Nights, so having a Mets World Series in our home felt like both a blessing and a tremendous responsibility. I placed a WFAN LET'S GO METS! sign in the living room window to let our neighbors know exactly where we stood, and we planted ourselves on the couch for this once-every-fourteen years epiphany. Bernie and Casey, our steadfast cats, took turns wearing a new orange Mets cap I bought in one of my many Officially Licensed Merchandise frenzies; they took turns squirming out from under it as well. Stephanie, who had jabbed her right index finger silly trying to get through to Ticketmaster, admitted she was perversely kind of glad I hadn't gained World Series admission. She wasn't going to join me at any stadium for games that were late and cold but she was happy we could watch them on TV together. Hell, she even picked up my superstitious vibe.

"Why won't you reassure me that everything's going to be all right?" I asked after fretting—thanks to Timo Perez trotting around the bases on a non–home run—about winding up on the wrong side of the Subway Series tracks.

"Because I'm afraid if I say they'll win, they won't."

As helpful as it would have been to have had one of us remain sane, Stephanie's once-and-for-all absorption into the Metsopotamian culture was even better than finding out she knew who Tom Seaver was back in 1987.

* * *

I perfected my clean-and-jerk routine that October. When Benny Agbayani sent an Aaron Fultz pitch soaring almost before our eyes in the left field Upper Deck in the third game of the 2000 NLDS . . . up, up and AWAY! until it cleared the fence for a thirteenth-inning win, I was transported back to Pratt. Laurie, lighter than air, was an easy lift. Jason, just a little less so, but Benny let out the dogs, so the animal came out in me.

Every time I hear "Who Let the Dogs Out?" for the rest of my days, no matter how derisive the context (it's usually played as part of some sort of Worst Sports Song ever countdown), I get goosebumps. Or dogbumps.

The Mets' incongruous good luck song played again the next night when the normally hapless Bobby Jones finished off the San Francisco Giants. A one-hitter that, technicality of a Jeff Kent double aside, stands as a perfect game. When Jay Payton caught its last out, I did more hugging, if not as much hoisting. My friend Joe was to my left. I'd met Joe in the waning days of the Johnson administration (Davey Johnson, that is) and our friendship was forged at the Shea of Anthony Young. Now we had our reward and our embrace. I turned to my right and there was Richie, not as constant a companion as he was in 1999 for Matt Franco and Melvin Mora, but still my brother in Mets. Another hug for another incredible October win.

* * *

The NLCS this time was as stress-free as something like that could be at Shea Stadium. The Mets came home from St. Louis up two games to none, lost an "oh well" Game Three, rocked the Cardinals with five doubles in the first inning of Game Four, and brought us to a potential clinching in a state free and clear of cold sweats. Game Five felt almost like a formality.

Me and my friends sat in the Mezzanine level for Game Five. I'd arranged to meet Rob, an old coworker, outside Gate E an hour ahead of the first pitch, but we missed each other from a range of twenty feet and barely made it in for the start. That was the only gaffe of what became the single most magical night I've ever experienced at Shea Stadium.

Mike Hampton pitched flawlessly.

Timo and Fonzie fueled a three-run first.

Todd Zeile drove in three more himself.

And the National League pennant was counted down to, out after out after out.

Matters seemed so settled that I could really notice where I was. To my left was Jason, the Mets fan I met online as if through some jock-obsessed dating service. To my right, Rob. I met them both when New York's bout of Mets fever was in remission. That means that no matter how I found them, they were pure of heart. Like me, they never stopped rooting for the Mets.

Rob, my friend since 1992, and Jason, my friend since 1994, were the two people with whom I hunkered down most intently during the victory drought of the early and mid-'90s. Maybe I would've been pals with each of them if we had met when the Mets were on the upswing, but meeting them when they weren't made my friendship with each, on this pinnacle night, that much more meaningful.

I can't swear to it, but I doubt I would have gotten to have known either of them without the Mets. I hate to think of how many people I wouldn't have gotten to have known if not for the Mets.

When Rick Wilkins lofted a fly ball to Timo Perez in center to crown the New York Mets champions of the oldest established league of professional baseball clubs, there was no heavy lifting. I turned left and hugged Jason. Then I turned right and hugged Rob. (Rob never struck me as much of a hugger.) It was the moment I had waited fourteen years for and I was between exactly the two people I would've wanted had I ever practiced it in front of a mirror.

* * *

Normally I would take the subway to Woodside or, depending on the vagaries of the LIRR, Penn Station. But Rob, who also lived on Long Island, had his car, so I parted ways with Jason and Emily and went for the ride home. Rob had parked in the lot across Roosevelt Avenue and given the milling of the sellout crowd, we had to take a long walk to get there. We said almost nothing to each other. Rob was always quiet. I was just mesmerized by what I was watching.

Did you see ever the film *Avalon*? It's mostly manipulative pap (if you're not watching it in 1990 five months after your mother has died), but the opening scene holds up. An old man flashes back on arriving in America on the Fourth of July in 1914. In his mind, children are running through the streets of Baltimore waving sparklers. There's no sound in particular. That's what the outside of Shea Stadium and Roosevelt Avenue reminded me of on Monday night, October 16, 2000. There was noise to be sure. There was honking and yelling, but it all felt like it was taking place in dreamy, occasionally stuttery slow motion. People waved instantly bought T-shirts and climbed up on light poles and were just happy. Neither Rob nor I had to say a word. The night said it all to us.

The Mets had won the pennant. On a scale of five to ten, it was off the charts.

Twenty-Seven

BEAUTY, PAIN, JOY

After being introduced to baseball by the 1969 Mets; after learning the tenets of faith from the 1973 Mets; after ascending to unprecedented heights on the shoulders of the 1986 Mets; after taking the ride of my life with the 1999 and 2000 Mets . . . what more could I want from this team?

More. Always more. That's the beauty, the pain, and the joy of baseball. It has one season after another, so you never really get off the ride. There is no definitive conclusion to what you're trying to attain or accomplish. You don't get even with the team that beat you the year before (say, the '85 Cardinals) because that team can come back and beat you the year after (like the Cardinals in 1987). Every year is its own narrative device and every year is no more than a component to the greater story arc. As long as you're alive and rooting, there is no obvious conclusion.

So we keep rooting, even when the arc takes a dive. The years after the Nine-Ten apogees were bound to level off. And they did, starting, I suppose, with the moment Bernie Williams wrapped his glove around Mike Piazza's fly to deep center in the fifth game of the ill-fated Subway Series. But it was still the Mets and it was still baseball, even if it was, for a while there, only a fraction of its more satisfying incarnation.

The Mets would stop contending after coming up shy in a late, well-intentioned rush to redeem 2001 at the very moment the people around them were seeking beauty and joy . . . and a refuge from pain. Some people said it was Mike Piazza's home run in that first game at Shea after 9/11 that showed them things might be all right. For me, it was Brian Jordan and the Braves doing in our unlikely divisional hopes two days later in an extra-inning heartbreaker. I was wildly pissed about a baseball game on September 23, 2001. If I could feel that, then maybe everything about the world hadn't changed.

After some 2002 roster renovations went awry, it was time to hastily deconstruct, if not wisely rebuild. Bobby Valentine would be fired; Edgardo Alfonzo, his productivity declining due to a chronically bad back, wouldn't get a new contract; Bob Murphy would retire; a Mike Piazza statue would be erected at first base—whoops, sorry, that was actually Mike attempting to play first. Three years of bad ideas would come and go. I'd leave one beverage magazine to start another. That lasted not quite as long as Art Howe. I returned to my freelance roots in the summer of '04. Howe would be sent packing with his guaranteed contract in October. The Mets lose in copious amounts, chaos ensues; the drill was familiar.

When your team is bad, life is about getting better. That's all you can think about. That's all you can focus on. Stop being bad; start being good. Any sign is a welcome one.

Enter Omar Minaya. Enter Willie Randolph. Enter Pedro Martinez. Enter Carlos Beltran. New era. New Mets. Only a few holdovers. That kid Reyes, brought up in 2003, who ran wildly, fielded beautifully and hit occasionally. He was hurt a lot, but he was bound to get better. That kid Wright, promoted in 2004 and living up to the hype instantly. After one of the *Not Again* era's oases of awesomeness, an 11–9, twelve-inning win over the Giants at Phone Company Park (decided on a fly ball lost in the sun), it was reported that the great Barry Bonds acknowledged our Diamond Dave. He landed on third after a triple, and young

Wright reportedly told him, "You're as good as advertised." Bonds, who was watching David go 4-for-6 himself, told the rookie, "Keep swinging it."

If David Wright could make the Bonds monster seem human, then gosh, maybe he could help us win.

Those kids and those free agents—this was a franchise, mind you, that sated us in years past with *Rigo* Beltran and the *other* Pedro Martinez (and, for that matter, *Mike* Maddux)— and new management that couldn't have been any worse than old management . . . you know, 2005 might be better than its preceding seasons.

And it was. Not knock-my-socks off 1980 thrilling or no-doubt 1984 contending or mindblowing 1997 arriving, but good. Good, solid, winning baseball. A flirtation with the Wild Card. A months-long tango with .500. A finish above it. A living as a consultant that helped to pay for the co-op apartment my wife and I bought about ten minutes before I lost my last magazine job. And a blog written by Jason and me, read by other Mets fans and occasionally commented upon by them.

Blogging revealed itself to me as Banner Day's logical and technological successor. Mets fans are always dying to tell you about being Mets fans. We each fancy ourselves Mr. Met, except Mr. Met is mute and never stops smiling, whereas we never shut up and expend loads of bandwidth contemplating, complaining, and, only on infrequent occasion, complimenting.

I took to blogging the Mets in 2005 like I took to rooting for the Mets in 1969.

* * *

I'm glad Shea got 2006 and one more first-place season. The unmourned announcer Fran Healy—how *did* he keep his gig for twenty-two years?—loved to hype the Mets with his estimation that "Shea Stadium will be *rocking*" on Paper Towel Night or whatever, but in '06 (the year Healy was excused from any longer delivering his fevered pitch), Shea Stadium really did rock.

It rocked first and foremost for the coming of age of young David and Jose, princes of our part of the city. WRIGHT 5 jerseys seemed to have been issued as if by government fiat. Jose, healthy and hitting, did a little of everything: a cycle in one game; three homers in another; an inside-the-park job, too. I think he could have gone for five bases on that deep drive to center. Beltran lived up to his contract, illustrating what it meant to have a "five-tool player" only a decade after we were fraudulently introduced to the term by appraisers of Alex Ochoa's talent. Carlos B. was joined by Carlos D.—Delgado—that rare species of established power hitter who came to Shea and hit with power. Billy Wagner and Paul Lo Duca more or less exceeded the expectations attached to their billing. Pedro, One of Us from the second he arrived, pitched brilliantly until he couldn't pitch anymore. Everybody Willie Randolph deployed clicked; even unwelcome Tom Glavine, a Met more in name than emotion since taking our money in 2003, finally looked to be at home.

* * *

The beauty of 2006 was in beating the hell out of everybody 1986-style. The beauty of 2006 was in having a magic number countdown commence in earnest in August. The beauty of 2006 was in falling in love with the Mets all over again as part of a mass movement. Shea, Healy might have noted as he watched from home, really did rock that year. It rocked for David, for the Carloses, for Billy the Sandman, for Lo Duca and his easily blown top, for Orlando "El Duque" Hernandez and Endy Chavez and Chris Woodward and Julio Franco and Lastings Milledge and, with a flair that would have fit snugly amidst a high-five between Ray Knight and Wally Backman, Jose Reyes. *HO-zay! Ho-zay-ho-zay-ho-zay . . . HO-ZAY!* His chant was the best thing since Let's Go Mets.

It was kind of a technicality that the Mets hadn't won a division title since 1988. The Wild Card seasons of 1999 and 2000, with all the October drama they wrought, were definitively not chopped liver. But for a team that, to my mind, invented the National League East in 1969—for whom it was urged LOOK WHO'S NO. 1 when they took first place—there was a bit of a hole on the wall of postseason markers in right. After eighteen years, it would sure be nice to practice some long division.

In 1986, the Mets (probably unintentionally) failed to clinch the N.L. East on the road when given every opportunity. It made for a better story, if a more pockmarked field, when they returned to Shea and made it official. Same thing in 2006, save for the pockmarked field, 'cause they've had horses to keep you off since then. The Mets could have won the East in Pittsburgh, but theatrically got themselves swept. The second-place Phillies made a last stand, sweeping in Houston, so the magic number remained an uncomfortable 1 on Monday night, September 18.

It wasn't uncomfortable for long. Steve Trachsel, probably the most unembraceable starter of tenure in any Met rotation, pitched to the high end of his capabilities. Jose Valentin, the second baseman of last resort who worked out beyond anybody's dreams (the way those things happen when you're en route to a championship), poked two homers. And Cliff Floyd, lacking only the health that made him such a threat in '05, snapped his glove shut on a Florida Marlin fly ball with two out in the ninth.

The Mets were champions of something again.

There was no real suspense, but we could play-act as if there was. Jason and I embraced like it was 1999. Laurie, too. She was sitting somewhere in the Upper Deck but joined us in Mezz for the final three outs, sneaking three tiny bottles of champagne into her purse so we could toast and guzzle and do everything but storm the field. Those horses guarding the foul lines looked pretty formidable. That champagne tasted pretty wonderful.

* * *

The joy kept flowing as the postseason got underway. The Mets were short of pitching—Pedro was done and El Duque, a midseason addition to the party, was sidelined as you kind of knew he would be sooner or later—but they were rolling in heart. The Dodger series started on a Thursday afternoon at five after four. It was more or less over before five o'clock. I didn't check my watch, but I'd mark L.A. DOA in the top of the second when Lo Duca tagged out Jeff Kent and J.D. Drew at home on the very same play. From way the hell up in the Upper Deck, I saw Kent thrown out and, while I was still exulting, heard Drew get it. *Why did everybody cheer again?* I wondered. The scoreboard said there were two outs . . . Drew kept running even after Paulie tagged out Kent? Yes, he did.

The Mets were a little shaky through the Division Series, but Shea was even shakier. It rocked in ways Fran Healy could only imagine. It rocked in the middle of the Cardinal series in 2000, during all those doubles in Game Four, but everybody had grown louder and jumpier in the ensuing six years. I never heard or felt Shea thunder the way it did it in October 2006.

Ultimate NLDS achievement was secured at Dodger Stadium hours after the Yankees were eliminated from the American League playoffs in Detroit, ensuring October 7, 2006, would be known forever more on our blog as Holy Saturday. It hit me as Wagner nailed down the final outs of the third and final game that this was the first time I was watching the Mets win a postseason series via television since Jesse Orosco threw the last pitch to Marty Barrett in 1986. The players had changed in twenty years, not just on the screen. My mother was gone. My father was doing whatever he was doing, almost certainly not watching a silly baseball game. Now it was me and Stephanie and a new in-residence pair of cats, Hozzie the recluse and Avery the aggressor, worthy successors to our beloved Bernie (1992–2005) and Casey (1990–2002). When I turned the TV sound down and the radio up, it was Howie Rose instead of Bob Murphy (1924–2004) painting the word picture. I was forty-three, not twenty-three.

Some things hadn't changed, though. I still hugged a Mrs. Prince when the last out was made. And I still threw my cap—the very same cap I wore October 27, 1986, one I received for attending the first game after the strike of 1981—toward the ceiling.

* * *

Into this dreamiest of beauteous Metscapes, I couldn't foresee pain. Not for our 2006 Mets, not when Glavine and Beltran staked us to a 1–0 lead in Game One, when my only problem was being pelted in the mouth by a stray sack of peanuts intended for the guy sitting behind me. When I got off the LIRR at Shea before Game Two, I had to fight off notions that this would be the first 11–0 postseason in major league history, that we'd plow through the Cardinals with ease and that whoever the American League threw at us would be mere championship fodder. It wasn't just that we'd won our first four postseason games with élan. I was just so caught up in the momentum of being a Mets fan. More than thirty years of getting off LIRR trains at Shea and only now, in the fall of 2006, was everybody dressed for the occasion—teenagers were wearing their fathers' '86-era Starter jackets—and only now was everybody chanting for it and singing for it. It was a loop: *Ho-zay! Let's Go Mets! Meet the Mets . . .*

Yes, we were actually singing "Meet the Mets" as we crowded along the platform. Even the underknown second verse celebrating butchers and bakers and people down the street.

The pain was in the reality that the Mets, without Pedro, without El Duque, with Steve Trachsel teetering back to his usual Trachsicality, didn't have enough pitching to quell the Cards.

The pain was that Wagner wasn't infallible; that August pickup Guillermo Mota—whom most of us conveniently stopped holding a grudge against from his throwing at Mike Piazza—was available late in summer for a reason; that Willie calling on the bullpen was riskier business since Duaner Sanchez became a victim of a cab accident in Miami; and that clutch hitting had become a perishable commodity. The Cardinals unleashed all manner of pest on the Mets: So Taguchi, Scott Spiezio, Ronnie Belliard. We lost Game Two, then two of three in St. Louis.

The Mets were on the verge of elimination when the series returned to Shea. This was highly unscripted. Even more unexpected was an e-mail from Jason the morning of Game Six. Somebody was offering him two Upper Deck tickets for that night. It would be $150 apiece, the most I'd ever been asked with a straight face to pay to see a baseball game. I don't know if it was the price, but I had to stop and think about it.

If there was ever a sign that something was off about the 2006 postseason, that was it. I was like "I dunno." Jason was like "me too" (we weren't feeling terribly articulate either). Who wanted to pay through the nosebleeds to watch the Mets get eliminated? Then we remembered that Mets playoff games don't come along very often and that if you're going to blow $150 on anything, it should be on that.

And that, of course, you gotta believe.

For eight innings, it was every bit the autumnal festival that Game One against the Dodgers had been, that 2000 and 1999 were when I was in attendance. In the ninth, it became a breath-holding contest. Billy Wagner was getting nicked and cut and jabbed and *oh no, he's gonna blow it, we're gonna blow it, we're gonna lose, we're gonna be eliminated, everything is ruined, this isn't 1986 at all.*

Then he got a third out and we won. "Takin' Care of Business," that season's unimaginative update to "Mojo Risin'" and "Who

Let the Dogs Out?" blasted and I should've been happier. I was only relieved—barely. I never crumpled into my seat after a win the way I did when Wagner *finally* got David Eckstein to end it. Then again, for $150, I should have gotten as much use out of that seat as possible.

* * *

Pain had the last word in 2006. I didn't have a ticket, not even a $150 ticket, for Game Seven. I had been to every NLDS and NLCS game this year and in 2000 but I wasn't going to the last one Shea would ever host. Deprived of access to my natural October habitat, it was dangerous letting me stalk the living room for an all-or-nothing night. I didn't know what to do with myself. I was used to taking my cues from Diamond Vision. I was used to cramming myself in among 56,000 soulmates. I was used to yelling horrible things at Albert Pujols. I'd had chants and songs in my head all month. It was normal to express them in a crowd. It was weird doing it in front of Avery the Cat.

These were no longer the mighty Mets of April to September. We were reduced to using Oliver Perez, a trade deadline afterthought, no better than sixth on the rotation depth chart. But desperate times were calling and desperate measures were answering. Perez, like the barely tested John Maine the night before, overcame our perceptions and kept the Cardinals at bay. Jeff Suppan from St. Louis was better. The score was tied into the sixth. Ollie (if he was our last, best hope, we might as well get familiar) allowed the enduringly cretinous Jim Edmonds a one-out walk. Scott Rolen came up and all but homered.

That is to say, like Robin Ventura seven years earlier, he hit a ball out of Shea Stadium but wasn't credited for a home run. He didn't even get a single out of it.

With Cliff Floyd hobbled, Endy Chavez, a do-no-wrong fourth outfielder through the course of the year, played left. He wasn't necessarily playing anywhere near where Rolen hit his ball, but Endy had a way of getting where the action was. He ran, he leaped, he nabbed, he threw. Rolen was out. Edmonds, who couldn't have been blamed for thinking he was homeward bound, found himself doubled off first.

Stephanie said she thought she heard a Warner Bros. cartoon on in the living room. My noise amounted to something to the effect of *"SQUOH! SQUOH! SQUOH! SQUOH!"* If it's not a word, it should be.

Many Mets fans will tell you that when Endy preserved Ollie's effort with a catch that immediately lined up alongside Mays's and Agee's and Swoboda's, they knew there was no way the Mets could lose. I suspected different. I assumed this was a set-up. It would be the mythic Mets thing to ride a once-in-a-generation catch to a rally, but it would be the more likely post-1986 thing to make you wonder how they couldn't go ahead ASAP after receiving from the heavens a gift like that.

During the commercial break between the top and the bottom of the sixth, I tried to believe, but I realized 2006 wasn't 1986.

No, the Mets didn't score. And yes, Yadier Molina inscribed his name as the Cardinal pest of pests when he stuck Aaron Heilman with the goat horns in the ninth. And no, Carlos Beltran did not swing successfully at any of the three pitches thrown by Adam Wainwright. The Cardinals, not the Mets, became 2006 National League champions. The Cardinals, not the Mets, defeated the Tigers in the 2006 World Series. The Mets, not the Cardinals, were left waiting for their first world championship in two-plus decades.

Oh, the pain. But not a little beauty and joy en route.

TWENTY-EIGHT

TO THE TRACK, AT
THE WALL . . .

On September 30, 2007, I would eventually turn my back on the field that I watched so intently from plastic seats thirty-five separate times during the star-crossed year that had just finished, including its final five dates. It was Sunday; I'd been at Shea since Wednesday night, essentially leaving just long enough to nap, shower, change, and commute back. I had earlier in the season become surprisingly used to coming to the ballpark as a matter of course, as if watching home games from my couch was the anomaly. Now I was so used to being at Shea that it was strange to realize I was leaving it for six months, that I was going to nap, shower, change, and then do something else altogether until April.

My back was soon turned on the Upper Deck, then Mezzanine, then Loge and the rest. I had grown used to living inside a baseball season. As badly as this baseball season had ended, I'll always regret walking down its last ramp.

It was the penultimate ending for Shea Stadium, the beginning of putting it all behind us.

* * *

When Luis Castillo struck out with two down in the ninth that Sunday, September 30, a baseball season was completed. Like the

Mets themselves, 2007 at Shea Stadium vanished in a blink. We 54,453 who witnessed it would never forget it, albeit for all the wrong reasons (primarily Marlins 8, Mets 1, knocking the Mets out of the playoff picture but good), yet institutional amnesia set in immediately. I'd been to fourteen previous Closing Days at Shea. I thought I knew all the team-driven postscripts: warm; celebratory; indifferent; anticipant; relieved; sad. But what was the actual moment of official appraisal for these Mets in terms of Diamond Vision or any kind of reaction? *Nada.* The Mets turned off the figurative lights as soon as they could. If you didn't know it was the end of September, the end of the season, you wouldn't have thought a year had just been put eternally in the books.

This wasn't just a Closing Day. This was a day that would live in infamy.

In past years, the better ones, the players would assemble on the field, particularly if there were no road games remaining. They would wave. They would autograph. They would toss a cap or two. Go try and find a Met that final Sunday in September '07 who wasn't hustling into the clubhouse at the end of this trying day at the end of this trying month (when the whole concept of "trying" seemed alien to certain Mets).

Once the score went final, the Marlins rushed each other as if they had won something more than their 71st game; their relievers raced in from the bullpen faster than they had for Saturday's brawl. Backs slapped, they filtered into their clubhouse, presumably to toast their rousing last-place finish. Without Marlins and without Mets, the field belonged to the grounds crew. A few workers took to the plate and the mound for a little manicuring. Maybe they were ordered to keep up appearances in case the Nats scored six quick runs in Philadelphia. More likely, they were just securing the summer house before the last ferry out. I wondered how soon they'd disassemble the special VIP boxes by the dugouts, the ones set up for the playoffs that weren't to be.

The Mets dugout was now conspicuously devoid of Mets. The only uniformed personnel apparent were a couple of batboys rounding up equipment and whisking away the remains of eighty-one days. These kids' uniforms said "Mets 07" on the front. Even from the Upper Deck, they didn't look like big leaguers.

Then again, neither did the Mets.

On the scoreboard—to the left and right of the brand new Budweiser ad that heralded The Great American Lager and was no doubt supposed to show up behind every fly ball to center on TV in the coming weeks—the Marlin and Met lineups disappeared instantly. The out-of-town scores stayed lit just long enough to confirm what everybody assumed: F WAS 1 PHI 6. Then those, too, vanished. History was erased as fast as it could be. The end of summer is truly a blank scoreboard.

The colorful message displays generated only a generic THANKS FOR COMING. "Thanks for coming"? It could have been April. It could have been June. No acknowledgement that it was the last day of September. Not even a nod to the record-breaking attendance of 3,853,955. Certainly no video presentation of 2007 highlights, no chance to relive the 134 consecutive golden days between mid May and late September when the Mets held first place by themselves. If there was such a film in the can, it wasn't about to be fired up. Probably good thinking given that nobody cared any longer about the story arc that got us to this final scene.

I looked around some more. Blue sky, punctuated by a few of Bob Murphy's clouds. Perfect day if you didn't know any better. I was sitting in shirtsleeves outdoors as if I were always going to be doing that, as if that's what people do every day, as if that's what I would be doing for the next six months because that's what I'd been doing so often for the last six months. It was occurring to me that I would not be doing this anymore for quite a while.

Turning my view left, I observed the left field cutoff. It was where Section 48 ended, as if they ran through their construction budget before they could tack on a Section 50. Of all that was familiar to me about Shea, it was that view of the way the Upper Deck cut off and became sky that struck me as most iconic. I saw it on television when I was six and it instantly said Shea to me. I knew a player traded to the Mets had truly become a Met when he had his publicity photo taken with that particular backdrop of seats and sky over his right shoulder. In 1994, they added the Tommie Agee marker up there. It served to commemorate the longest fair ball ever hit at Shea Stadium, but also as a warning track for those who would venture that high up and that far out: walk too much further, and it is you who will become puffy and cumulus if you're not careful.

That view . . . it would be gone after next season. Whatever angles the successor to Shea Stadium provided us, they would not have that feeling of infinity to them. Come to think of it, Jeff Wilpon had already gone on record, quite proudly, as describing Citi Field as "a ballpark that will envelop you." Hmm . . . I'd always liked the way the ends of Section 48 in left and Section 47 in right, cutting off and revealing heavens, achieved precisely the opposite effect. They gave you the impression that if you sat in Shea Stadium, you could see the world open up before you, offering a rare vantage point of unlimited possibility.

If 2007 taught us anything—and as Closing Day reminds us annually—baseball is more finite than that.

* * *

I would physically leave Shea in 2007, but I don't know that I left it behind so easily. As long as I stayed up there in the Upper Deck of my mind, Tom Glavine was still out there surrendering—like Cornwallis at Yorktown, like Lee at Appomattox, like Rogers at Turner Field—seven runs in one-third of an inning to the last-place Florida Marlins; Tom Glavine was still out there throwing but not pitching, presumably trying but definitely not succeeding, fooling no one and enabling what was already catching on in the baseball lexicon as The Greatest Collapse In Baseball History.

The Mets played dead for fewer than three weeks and they already had a name for it.

If you cling to your seasons until they all become one season, Glavine may have left the mound but he's still in the clubhouse, which means he's still calmly (too calmly) answering questions. He's disappointed, sure, he tells the reporters, but he's not devastated. This, too, becomes part of our common tongue. No Mets fan will ever again hear "disappointed" and not feel the need to match it with "devastated." We could go on *Password* and win valuable prizes if the password were either one of them.

* * *

Having to consider Glavine and the Manchurian Brave–style revenge he so successfully wrought on us was part of the collateral damage of dwelling on and lingering in September 30, 2007. But I dwelled there and I lingered there for months. I didn't do it for Glavine.

I did it for Shea.

Shea—unlike the bottom-of-the-first, bases-loaded, two-out blast off the bat of Ramon Castro that died at the left field track (dropped into Cody Ross's glove by wind currents forever corrupted by the intrusive shell of Citi Field)—was truly going, going . . . it would be *outta here!* by the end of September 2008, give or take a playoff bid. Next year on that occasion, I knew I'd be back, probably in this very same deck. It was my conviction, as if it were mine to have, that Shea wouldn't be shushed as easily. Even the Mets would kiss it goodbye with some pomp and some heart and maybe some guts. Even the Mets would know enough about their fans to pretend to care that much. Surely they would avoid an ignominious ending along the lines of 2007.

Wouldn't they?

TWENTY-NINE

IT'S OUTTA HERE

I don't love the Mets because of all their October participation. If that's what I came for, my love would be pretty darn intermittent. They're 7-for-40 getting there on my watch and 2-for-7 when there are playoffs to watch. Two world championships in their and my lifetime. They were awesome, but they're not why I love the Mets.

I don't love the Mets because they are such a well-run organization filled with the kind of people to whose baseball acumen you'd willingly trust your fate. There are less successful franchises all about, but I swear only the Pirates and their sixteen consecutive losing seasons sit between the Mets and rock bottom in terms of reasonable return on resources.

I don't love the Mets because they treat their customers with care and respect. My almost-mandatory attendance at every single home game in September 2008 indicated to me that it is company policy to approach us with unsurpassed indifference and hold us in utter contempt. On any given night, we were 50,000 walking cash machines or, perhaps, the reason a whole lot of people couldn't knock off early.

I don't love the Mets because of the great mass of Mets fans who surround me too often. Too many Mets fans come to Mets games for reasons that apparently have nothing to do with supporting the Mets. These are the kinds of people who stand in your way in supermarket aisles and cut you off on the Southern State Parkway and boo their cats for not being dogs.

I don't love the Mets because of the players who composed the most recent Met roster. The players on the Mets, individually and as a unit, don't automatically forge an instinctual connection with me. I had nothing against Shea's final edition, but I found myself with little in particular *for* them. Some struck me as talented, enthusiastic, and good-natured, and I appreciated their efforts on my nominal behalf. Mostly, though, I didn't feel the 2008 bunch all that much. And, though it's not a hanging offense, they just weren't very good.

I don't love the Mets because I'm rebelling against or reacting to the presence of some other team . . . *any* other team. The Mets are front and center. Everybody else in the majors is tied for second through thirtieth (OK, second through twenty-ninth; thirtieth is reserved for that bunch in the Bronx, but they're of peripheral concern most of the time).

I don't love the Mets because it gives me license to behave as a "crazy fan." I don't know whether it's crazy to give one's mental well-being over to the fickle physical fortunes of a batch of youthful millionaires. I don't know whether it's crazy to risk vast quantities of disappointment in the longshot search for a modicum of solace. I don't know whether it's crazy to think the angst I incur as a preoccupational hazard is, in fact, maybe its own reward. But I'm a big fan. I'm not a crazy fan.

I don't love the Mets for the reasons that are often cited for loving the Mets. Oh, I love the Miracle, Magic, Amazin', Believe ethos. I love the Black Cat and Bill Buckner and the Grand Slam Single. If I drank more, I'd drink only Rheingold. If my DVR would dispense them, I'd watch nothing but Met-tinged episodes of *Seinfeld* and *The Odd Couple* while eating nothing but warm Kahn's Beef Franks topped with nothing but Gulden's Brown

Mustard, the mustard Sharon Grote served to her family. I love all that stuff. But that's just part of the deal, not the deal itself.

I love the Mets because I love the Mets. Call it circular reasoning whose perimeter permits no logic to permeate. I love the Mets because I love the Mets even though there is, at certain times, almost nothing on the surface about the Mets that I can stand.

I love the Mets because I have always loved the Mets. It's no more mystical than that. I picked them up at six and stayed with them. It occurred to me at nineteen that by then the Mets had been the only non-familial constant in my life dating back to when I could account for my constants. It's only grown deeper since I was nineteen, which was 1982, which was a terrible season (65–97), but that didn't stop me. None of the terrible years has ever stopped me. It doesn't necessarily reflect on the purity of my character except maybe for its streaks of stubbornness or loyalty. It doesn't necessarily confirm that I automatically value the perennially put-upon underdog versus the well-fed overcat. It doesn't necessarily illustrate how not bad I might look in blue and orange. I've enjoyed reflecting on how these past forty seasons have transpired and what these past forty seasons have meant to me, but I could have wrapped this thing up in less time than it took Johan Santana to wrap the Fish inside his complete game three-hit short-rest shutout on the final Saturday of 2008:

I was little.

They were local.

It was 1969.

From there, it was easy. I was a Mets fan then, I'm a Mets fan now.

* * *

As a creature of habit, constancy surely plays an outsized role in my considerations of the Mets. (So would continually banging my head into a wall for four decades, I suppose, but never mind that right now.) No presence was more constant from the moment I found them than Shea Stadium. It wasn't so much my destiny as it was my destination. Dreamed of it when I was six. Broke through its doors when I was ten. Settled in there when I was thirty. You couldn't drag me away from there in 2008, the season I was forty-five.

I went to forty-four games at Shea Stadium in 2008. I went to forty-three games there the entire decade of the 1980s.

2008 was injury time, in soccer terms. It was to make up for all the games nobody took me to or I wasn't able to make. It was, more pointedly, last licks. Don't go to Shea in 2008, you're not going to get there in 2009.

So I went. I went like I never went before. I went like hell.

I went to see it again, against almost every team, from almost every angle, for almost every event. Everywhere from what they hifalutinly called Diamond View Suites to the groups-only Pepsi Picnic Area fell under my purview in 2008. Somebody repeatedly got me into the Metropolitan Club seats of the generally off-limits Field Level (for years I fought the usher law that kept me from my beloved Daruma of Great Neck sushi stand and, in 2008, the usher law didn't win). I saw Shea's last doubleheader. I saw Shea's last day-night doubleheader, both ends. Until you've shown up early, left for dinner, come back at dusk, and stayed 'til eleven for a split, you haven't lived . . . or lived at Shea.

That's what I was doing all through 2008. It was for Shea, it was for the Mets, it was for constancy's sake and a yen for completion. It was for me—the rhythms of my days, my nights and my seasons—but not me alone.

It was for me and Richie and Rob, all of us Subway Series veterans of varying degrees of gratification. (Richie and I got Matt Franco in '99; Rob and I got Mel Rojas in '98.) We got one final shot at the seriously hated Yankees and, thanks to Ollie Perez, hit the target. I kept thinking after that late June intracity triumph that it might be nice to see each of them at Shea again. Then I decided it wasn't going to get any better than beating the Yankees and let them be.

It was for me and my three best friends from high school, Joel, Larry, and Fred, who converged from across the country at Gate E to join me for a day game against the Padres in August. I'd been to Mets games at Shea with every possible combination of the three of them except as the four of us together. We saw David Wright hit the first walkoff home run of his career. I swear the kid did it for us.

It was for me and Joe, Joe and his relentless scorebook. Joe scores every game he goes to. Sometimes he scores at home. Then he adds up the totals for each player from every game he's ever scored and lets me know, for example, that Tim Bogar is batting a hundred points higher for Joe than he is for the rest of us. I'd been sitting beside Joe and his scorebook since an exhibition game in 1991. When it occurred to me, in the ninth inning of the second game of that day–night affair, that the three of us wouldn't be in this same place conferring on whether that was a wild pitch or a passed ball that just got by every catcher from Charlie O'Brien to Brian Schneider . . . I didn't say anything. I couldn't.

It was for me and Laurie, Laurie who had been, since 1996, cataloguing for me in a totally non-stalkerish way which Mets were "boyfriends," which ones were "husbands," and who was The Man. Since 2005, once Mike left, Pedro became The Man. We were together when Pedro Martinez left his final Mets game of 2008, considered likely his final Mets game ever. Pedro waved in our direction. Pedro waved in everybody's direction. Pedro had the presence of mind to know he was leaving the stage. Laurie knows from who's The Man. Laurie knows a lot.

It was for me and Jim. Jim's my art director and I'm Jim's editor, even though our professional collaborations have dwindled from daily to once in a very great while. Jim and I share a certain fatalism about life even as we try to subscribe to that essential Gotta Belief in the Mets. It's often more fun to talk through our baseball spirituality than it is to see it play out. Jim and I went to four games together at Shea in 2008, all of them played on Friday nights, including the last Friday night. The Mets went 0–4 with Jim and me on hand, 0–10 in our last ten night games since '05. It was fate. But you gotta believe it was fun.

It was for me and Jason, my blog partner since 2005, my Tuesday/Friday partner in 2001 and '02, my playoff partner almost every time we got lucky since 1999. Jason and I alit at Gate D on a blind fan date on a scalding Saturday afternoon in June 1995 for the coming out of Bill Pulsipher. We met at our soggy seats on the final damp Saturday afternoon in September 2008, practically an old married couple in fan terms.

This place is falling apart. I want a new ballpark.

It's fine. Besides, a new ballpark will be too expensive.

Why can't we ever have nice things?

Do you mind? I'm trying to watch a game here.

Then we both revved up our man crushes on Johan Santana before returning home to our wives.

It was for me and those I'd known for twenty years, and for me and those I'd known for twenty weeks. It was for those I grew up with, got schooled with, went to work with, exchanged e-mails with, blogged with, to, and among. The Mets couldn't produce nearly enough runs when it mattered, but by saving me a couple of seats at vast Shea Stadium, they represented a veritable friend factory for me. I always had something to talk about with someone. We always had the Mets. We were in this together.

I went to Shea for that as much as I possibly could.

* * *

Little of our history is grainy black-and-white footage. Shea was too infused with life from the start to deprive us of

Technicolor. "You've gotta see this stadium," Bob Murphy urged in the opening to the very first radio broadcast from Shea, April 17, 1964. "Every seat is an individually painted beautiful seat." Colorful seats for the color television age into which I was born. This was meant to be my stadium.

Soon enough, a new generation of Mets fans will come of age at Citi Field. They will see pictures of that funny blue thing with its almost kaleidoscopic arrangement of seats—orange to blue to green to red—and they will be too young to possibly remember it. Shea will be their Polo Grounds. Yet I don't get the sense Citi Field's been built, regardless of the distracting doodads installed around its edges, for anybody's kids.

My place, my field of dreams and drains, that was Shea. It may have taken me until I was ten years old to set foot inside, but it was always mine, always ours. The superb. The supernatural. The subpar. It was mine. It was ours. Casey to Mookie. Rocky Swoboda to Robin Ventura. Agee to Endy. Del Unser to Delgado. John Lennon and Paul McCartney to John Maine and Paul Lo Duca. Billy Wagner to Billy Joel. Broadway Joe to Broad-Shouldered Johan. They were there for all of us. We were there for all of them.

Shea barely functioned sometimes, but it worked for me . . . on every level.

Into each life a little rain must fall. Rain poured on Shea. Wind howled into it. It was allegedly supposed to be covered by a dome or at least be closed off. It didn't and it wasn't. If you believe Robert Caro's assertion that Shea was Robert Moses's "answer to the Colosseum of the Caesars," it was never going to be.

Hence, Shea was immune to nothing. Nor are we. We sit outside too long. We sniffle. We hurt. We don't hold up perfectly in the course of a long year. Our calves are perfectly capable of making like El Duque's in October 2006 and going south at the worst possible juncture. Whether we throw or we house or we cheer, we're all bound to be a little rickety in our forties.

But we are who we are. We don't march in lockstep. We are not of one mind. We don't all don navy windbreakers or red caps. We're a little raggedy in spots. We are individuals with our own quirks. Half a row loves the Met who's at bat, the other half is actively demanding he be packed off to Seattle ASAP. The bon mots share vocal space with the "You Sucks." We are individuals woven together for a common cause. Shea, in that sense, was one of us.

I never saw it as a cookie cutter—unless a chunk of cookie got stuck in the pan. Quick, how many other stadia have looked like Shea? Even in the multipurpose '60s, nobody else mimicked the Colosseum. Shea may never measure up in historical appraisals to the antiquities its generation replaced, but it was also never the Vet or Three Rivers. It was open. It was inviting. It was distinctive, even.

To really get Shea, you would have to sit in its Upper Deck, in left field. From high on in Section 36, say, as I did for the balance of Shea's last twinbill, against the Braves in mid-September 2008. From there, you see it all. You see why we're where we've been since 1964. You see the lush meadows Moses yearned to develop into New York City's premier park . . . the highways that link to create the heart of the Metropolitan area . . . the Long Island Rail Road station—"your steel thruway to the Fair gateway," as it was advertised in the 1964 yearbook—originally opened to usher visitors to baseball over here and Peace Through Understanding over there . . . the IRT, also known as the 7 train, because, well, this was a City field.

That day I understood anew the great truth of Shea Stadium. It was built for us. It was built for us kids, many of whom had parents who moved east, from Brooklyn, from Queens. It was meant to be our playground, our day care center. "I used to say," Ron Swoboda once recalled, "that the Mets were the biggest babysitting service in the city."

"Everybody gets buck wild over here when they watch a ballgame," Benny Agbayani said during the 2000 postseason. "This is the most exciting place that I've been to, where the fans are into the game from the first inning to the ninth. I can just imagine the people who don't have tickets, at home. They probably wreck their TVs."

We raised a fuss and made a racket, but that was all right because we helped drown out the planes (does anybody even still notice the planes?). There's a reason, I decided, home plate more or less faced Long Island—Great Neck, maybe—without decisive obstruction. It was gesturing toward us, the children of post-postwar suburbia, to come on over and come on in and come play. It was big but not daunting. It was bright: yellows, later, oranges. It had to be designed for or by children. "Tinker Toy architecture," somebody described it. The ballpark, like the team, was a gift to us, the kids who toddled out of the early '60s. Did it have to be left open at one end? Let's just infer that Mr. Moses and Mayor Wagner simply didn't finish wrapping it in time for Christmas morning, April 17, 1964, and we were too anxious to wait another minute.

* * *

I traded a degree of fascination for a surfeit of familiarity by going to Shea as often as I did as an adult. It was more important to me to be a regular at Shea than to be amazed by Shea. Remember, I got into baseball because I thought it was the normal thing to do. It's normal to go to baseball games by my reckoning. It wasn't normal to be a kid and be kept from the ballpark. Thus, I was a chronic goer in Shea's last years. I wouldn't have had it any other way, but it was tough to look at Shea as if for the first time after seeing it more than 400 times.

I tried at the end, though. I tried on September 28, 2008, to remember July 11, 1973, that bus trip from Camp Avnet. The weather was just as muggy and murky as it was then. Then I had Marvin the counselor and the yearbook with all the Met All-Stars on the front, including Jim Fregosi whether I wanted him or not. Now I had my wife but I forgot to buy a collector's edition program until they were all sold out. It was a rookie mistake.

If I had to strain to hear echoes of 1973, I had no problem making out the shadows of 1999 and 2007, when Closing Day held in its result immense consequences. This, too, was a Closing Day when a win was imperative—that and some help on the out-of-town scoreboard. For a while after I sat my final Shea Stadium sit (Upper Deck Section 3, Row Q, Seat 16), I was obsessed with what we were going to do win-wise and what the Brewers, our sudden enemy in our lunge at a severely discounted Wild Card, were going to do. They were playing the Cubs. The Cubs had already clinched their division. The Cubs played with indifference at Shea earlier in the week, yet we could only take two of four from them. The Brewers were pitching CC Sabathia, their version of Johan Santana. They lose and we win, there's playoffs at Shea. They lose and we lose, or we win and they win, then there's a one-gamer here Monday and maybe some playoffs to come.

We lose and they win? A despicable possibility . . . except it would solve the mystery of whether this was going to be the Last Game Ever at Shea Stadium or not. I was rooting for "not" with my head. I wasn't sure in my heart. I'd really wanted to be here on September 28 for the goodbye. Not to say "I was there," but to actually be there. For Shea. For me.

It had been nine years since Melvin Mora sprinted home giddily. It had been precisely fifty-two weeks since Tom Glavine trudged away sans devastation. Given that there was nobody left on the 2008 Mets from 1999 and plenty of 2007 Mets still around, did I really have to think whether or not this day would be the last day?

* * *

Sabathia did his Santana job in Milwaukee. Scott Schoeneweis and Luis Ayala allowed home runs to Wes Helms and Dan Uggla, respectively, to put us down by two. Ryan Church came up in the bottom of the ninth with one on and two out and, amid digital camera flashes, swung. Visions of Mike Piazza belting one deep to center in 2000, in the last World Series game played here at Shea danced in my head.

We lost that one, too.

We finished one game behind the Brewers one year after finishing one game behind the Phillies one year after finishing, in essence, one game behind the Cardinals. To paraphrase from Peter Gammons, back when he was reduced to making sense of the latest Red Sox letdown, the Mets killed our slightly younger selves and now the sons of bitches were coming for us.

We've got to stop melting like this.

So that was it, 4–2 Marlins, no more baseball at Shea. Everybody booed the Mets. Well, not everybody. I didn't. Stephanie didn't. Some were reserved. Others were dazed. Most seemed to just let loose. We had been held captive in the Upper Deck, Section 3, Row Q, Seats 15 and 16, by the piercing screams of someone whose team I was rooting against all day even though technically he was rooting for my team. "BULLPEN IS PIG PEN!" he kept yelling as he'd been doing since long before a single reliever took off a single jacket.

The best part about the Mets losing this final game wasn't that I could now confirm that I was at the final game. The best part was enough shortsighted screamers scrammed after the final out but before the closing ceremonies so Stephanie and I could move down about fifteen rows to partake of the ritual we really came for. We could still hear the "PIG PEN!" guy, but at that distance we could ignore him.

Harder to ignore was my lingering disgust with the 2008 and, by association (it could no longer be coincidence), 2007

Mets. It was difficult for this crowd, the diehards who refused to go—the way I and a few like me refused to go when there was nothing but scenery to gaze upon a year earlier—to overlook the competitive implications of this very date in Mets history, 9/28/08, the second consecutive Closing Day when the Mets closed their season ahead of expectations. But, shoot, I'd given up on expectations.

Except I did expect something after the game. I expected a proper farewell. I expected it sooner than later. Even that, it appeared, the Mets were capable of screwing up. The game ended a bit after five. Then we waited. And waited. And waited. Armies of grounds crew personnel and security personnel and event staff personnel emerged onto the field. There were lots of golf shirts and headsets. There was some very careful measuring in the outfield that had nothing to do with the good ol' 410 sign (which the ghouls charged with selling off pieces of the deceased rushed to replace before the weekend). There were these, I don't know, sandwich boards. They had pictures of Mets and great Mets moments and I assumed there would be some purpose to them. Maybe Rusty Staub would line up by his. Or pop out of a cake (or a rack of ribs) behind it.

They did nothing. Like the Mets.

The half-hour cooling-off period probably wasn't the worst thing to happen after the way this season and the one before it ended. After an afternoon of "what have I done to deserve this?" echoing through my mind in deference to the collapsing and the choking and what-not, I flipped the question. Like the Candy Man (Sammy Davis's, not John Candelaria), I found it was best to separate the sorrow and collect up all the cream.

I was with my wife, our first date having taken place in an Upper Deck Box in Section 8. I was at Shea for the 415th Mets game of my life. I, like John Lennon, saw the top of the mountain at Shea Stadium. I lived out my childhood dreams hundreds of times there. My childhood dreams all involved going to Shea

Stadium. Seriously. And I got to do it over and over and over again. *Talk about your childhood wishes.*

I overcame the losses and came right back. I saw the place I salivated over on TV in person. Nobody made me and nobody stopped me. I had practically lived here in recent years. When confronted by all manner of unpleasantness, it bounced off me. I was back the next night, the next homestand, the next season. It always made me happy.

What did I do to deserve *that*?

* * *

The Mets trotted forty-three former players out onto the field that Sunday. It wasn't nearly enough.

Where was Mike Vail and his hitting streak? Steve Henderson, permanent resident of June 14, 1980? My old ticket benefactor Rick Reed? Rey Ordoñez, one-quarter of the greatest infield ever? Why not Anthony Young, who never won but always tried? Where was Rico Brogna, the man for whom I forsook all Thanksgivings? Is it possible John Olerud, the artist who had more big hits in the late '90s than Mariah Carey, had somewhere better to be? Great names (literally) like Ray Sadecki and Joe Orsulak unspoken for? George Stone still passed over? Ron Hodges and Bruce Boisclair, lifetime Mets—not here? How is that even possible?

I don't know how the guest list was comprised and I'm not sure who wasn't invited as opposed to who didn't come (Howie Rose read off a list of absent notables, including Mookie Wilson, Nolan Ryan, and Davey Johnson), but there should have been more Mets. You can't go wrong with more Mets as long as Vince Coleman isn't one of them.

OK, got that out of my system. Enough with who wasn't there. Who was?

For starters, there were what passes for the "old guys" in Mets lore and my 1969-forged estimation. The Mets have only been around a little longer than I have. They don't have that many old guys. But for those who played before I was paying attention—Jack Fisher, Ron Hunt, Frank Thomas, Al Jackson—I made a conscious decision to go nuts. I stood, I applauded, I yelled out "YAY!"

Yes, "YAY!" It was something I wouldn't have been caught doing at my first game in '73 or any game since. But there was never going to be another chance to cheer a Met at Shea Stadium. Use it or lose it.

The first Met from my own memory was Jim McAndrew. If I was all "YAY!" for guys I never saw as Mets, you can imagine that the YAYs! only intensified for the ones I did.

Jim McAndrew pitched in relief my first game at Shea. Jerry Koosman started. Wayne Garrett was at third, Felix Millan at second, Rusty around in right, Cleon in left, Buddy at short, the great Willie Mays at first. I saw them all the first time I came to Shea. They were all introduced to the crowd again the last time I came to Shea.

Either all of us—the stadium, the players, and me—were too young to be in on this kind of memorial or we all grew thirty-five years older while I was busy quietly going YAY!

No need for quiet now. YAY!

YAY! for everybody who came out, whether from '69 but not '73 (The Glider Ed Charles; never just Ed Charles), '73 but not '69 (George The Stork Theodore; never just George Theodore), the fallow years that followed (somebody remembered to invite Doug Flynn! And Sky King!) or, in one case, every Met year that came and went in the '60s and '70s (Eddie Kranepool, of course). YAY! as well for the eventual renaissance of the '80s.

Keith and Ronnie and HoJo were around all the time these days. Darryl had been gone a bit but he was back in the fold. Gary tried to talk himself out of everybody's good graces a few months earlier when he suggested, with minimal provocation, that he'd sure be willing to take Willie Randolph's job should it be offered. It wasn't, but there's no keeping Gary Carter away. Nor should there be.

YAY! for 1986 and the 1986 Mets.

YAY! for the Bobby V Mets who trickled onto the scene, bringing with them, if not Bobby Valentine (presumably busy outsmarting some Japanese manager somewhere), then memories of the last almost indisputably great era in Shea history. We thought the one we were living in was the last indisputably great era in Mets history, but two years had passed since Endy made that catch, so maybe not. These guys—Leiter, John (though not Matt) Franco, Zeile, the Grand old man Ventura—would have to do. And they did fine. YAY!

I gave like five YAYs! to Edgardo Alfonzo. I'd been angling for his return since he was permitted to walk away in December 2002. It was when I saw him in No. 13 as he belonged that the 2008 Mets ceased to exist as a going concern. *Did we play a game today?* It would have been nice if a Wright or a Reyes or a Pedro (Pedro was never booed) had stuck his head out and represented 2006, if not the two years that followed, but they didn't.

Fonzie? YAY!

The YAY! factor rose exponentially when the missing Met of Mets walked down the third base line. It was Doc Gooden, the man who touched a hundred on the radar in Pittsburgh the day my mother died, the Duh-wight who touched everybody in '84 and '85, the soul who lost his way to drugs too many times to count, the legend who finished his career everywhere but here. And now No. 16 was where it belonged, and he who wore it was where he belonged.

I didn't have nearly enough YAYs! to go around.

After Doc came Willie Mays. Willie—the baseball giant who was larger than life when he left San Francisco and did what he could as a Met. Some people actually aren't impressed that Willie Mays played for the New York Mets. Those people are people I don't have much to say to.

But I say multiple YAYs! to Mays.

Then Mike Piazza. In Mets colors again. Not a Padre, not an A. YAY!

Finally, Tom Seaver.

What, you were expecting maybe Tom Hausman?

YAY! for Seaver. YAY! for all of them. YAY! for all of us.

YAY! Stadium.

* * *

I half-expected THANKS FOR COMING on the scoreboard and an usher to hustle us to the exits because they needed the joint for a Sunday night Bar Mitzvah. Not quite.

Howie announced that each of the forty-three Mets, by now lined up between first and third, would touch home plate.

They're gonna what?

Half of the guys would be approaching home from the direction of first, not sending the best of messages on behalf of a team that scored only five runs the entire weekend. Each man, still a jock to his core, gave off a vibe that they found this, quite frankly, a bit fruity. But they shrugged and went along with the program.

Willie Mays went first. He needed assistance, but made a point of bending over and touching home with his fingers. Gentlemen, if Willie Howard Mays of the New York Giants and the New York Mets, the man who touched home for real 2,062 times—seventh-most in major league history—could partake in this little oddball ritual in a way that showed it meant something to him, then you can all take a turn.

Those who were not Willie Mays and would never be mistaken for Willie Mays went next. I treated each former Met as if he were, in fact, Willie Mays: with applauding, with cheering, with crying by now.

The players kept stepping on that plate. If only it were that easy for the Mets to score forty-three runs in real life.

Doug Flynn strolls across. The Stork gives it some oomph. Buddy seems to score a winning run. Fonzie points skyward the way he might have had he just blasted a big fly off the Big Unit.

The guys came and crossed. The line on each side of home grew shorter. The gloaming was overtaking the sky. And then it hit me what I was watching: My life flashing before my eyes; the single most important edifice in my life, its seconds ticking down. The players, as great as they were, as Mets as they had been, were no longer the players.

Those were the years of my life crossing home plate.

Here comes my family. Here comes elementary school and junior high and high school and college.

It was everybody and everything, the sums of all the seasons that came before the one we were in—and now this one that had just ended.

Keith touches the plate and makes with his batting stance. Jesse raises his arms in the air as if it's October 27, 1986. Cleon recreates the last out from October 16, 1969.

Here come the clueless freelancing years, my long beverage magazine hitch, my consulting gigs. Here comes the blogging era.

Jobs changed, careers changed. I never did. I never stopped coming here or wanting to come here. It's a little frightening to realize you're never really going to change, but it's also more than a little reassuring.

Yogi misses home. Darryl crosses safely. Doc blows us a kiss.

I can see Stephanie and me. I can even see Bernie and Casey; and Hozzie and Avery. You can't be at Shea Stadium and not see a few cats.

The New York Mets and Shea Stadium infiltrated all of it, all of me—every corner of my life, every facet of my being. We were a fan and a franchise, growing up in tandem. Now we'd be moving on.

Piazza touches the plate. Seaver touches the plate.

There's only one thing left to see before the hazy Shea of winter sets in and begins to obscure the thirty-six seasons I've spent watching these Mets in this stadium.

1973 takes to the mound and fires one final pitch to 2008.

It's a perfect strike.

FROM GREER TO ETERNITY
WITH GARY COHEN

During the last week of the dismal 1993 season, I sat at my desk in Great Neck working quite late. Twenty or so minutes to the west, Gary Cohen was doing the same. He and Bob Murphy kept me riveted to a Mets-Cardinals game that reached the seventeenth inning in a state of scorelessness. Kenny Greer, just acquired from the Yankees for Frank Tanana, made his major league debut and only Met appearance ever in the top of the seventeenth, setting down St. Louis in order. When Jeff Kent doubled home Eddie Murray in the bottom of the inning (and how is it possible the 1993 Mets had two Hall of Fame-caliber players?), I reveled alone in the Mets' 55th win of the year, momentarily oblivious to the fact that it came attached to 103 losses. That excitement was all the doing of Murph and Cohen keeping me entranced the way only they could at the end of one of the worst years any baseball team has ever known. Three autumns later, I attended a discussion of baseball broadcasting at the Museum of Television & Radio and stuck around afterward so I could tell Gary just how exquisite I thought he and his partner had been that night. Before I could spit out my scene-setting details—"it was late in September and it was nothing-nothing and . . ."—he casually confirmed, "You mean the Kenny Greer game?"

Exactly. And that's exactly why so many Mets fans have come to revel in the sound of Gary Cohen's voice, whether it comes through their radio, as it did almost every baseball day and night from 1989 through 2005, or emanates from their TV as it has since 2006 on SNY. Beyond what he describes and how he describes it, just about every Mets fan I know appreciates mostly that when Gary Cohen—like his WFAN counterpart Howie Rose—talks, it is with a fan's grasp of Met history, Met detail, and Met emotion. You can't teach that stuff at the Connecticut School of Broadcasting. You could only learn it as those two guys from Queens did: growing up with it, living it, never letting it go. We're fans of theirs because they're fans like us. As was the case when we had Bob Murphy, Ralph Kiner, and Lindsey Nelson looking out for our best interests, our ears are in good hands with Howie Rose and Gary Cohen.

Almost twenty years after he joined Murph in the 'FAN booth, fifteen years after the Kenny Greer game, and a dozen years after we exchanged pleasantries that night at the museum, I had a chance to spend quality time on the phone with Gary Cohen, batting around the end of days at Shea Stadium and a few related topics. After all these years of him talking to me through the speakers and me yelling in the general direction of my radio or television, it was no surprise to me that it felt like a friendly chat between two longtime Mets fans.

* * *

You showed up that Sunday knowing this may or may not be the final game ever in this ballpark you'd been coming to for more than forty years. What was that like?

"I was struck, going into Sunday, after the joyous events of Saturday, by the lack of finality, the lack of knowing, despite the ceremonies that were planned postgame, whether indeed it was going to be the last game.

I had taken stock quite a bit over the course of the year, made sure to look around and walk around—maybe walked to parts of the ballpark I hadn't seen in a number of years just knowing it wasn't going to be there much longer.

I think what made the whole process difficult as not only someone who's been broadcasting for twenty years, but someone who's been spending large chunks of time in that stadium for over forty years, isn't just that they would be moving to another ballpark, but the fact that this place we had come to know as home would cease to exist. The spot I was sitting in the television booth . . . there would be nothing there. There'd be a parking lot several stories underneath where I was sitting, but there'd be no structure, and it's almost hard to conceive of.

So walking in that day, all of that came flooding through. At the beginning of the day, the lack of knowing whether indeed we'd be there the next day or the next week or for the next month made it difficult to reconcile."

The day was already a little surreal—the rain delay, the former Mets piling in to Shea for the closing ceremonies, the overtones of the pennant race. As you start doing the game and seeing the competitive contours of it unfold, with Schoeneweis and Ayala giving up the home runs and the Brewers winning in Milwaukee, how did your feelings evolve?

"There was still hope for a long time, but unfortunately the M.O. of that team for the last two months was if it was close late, the chances weren't real good of finding a way to win. I used the expression very often during the season that the Mets had to outscore their bullpen. It was clear this wasn't one of those days when the offense was up to that task.

I think the way 2007 ended was a bit more stunning because of the size of the lead they let get away, but in so many ways, the pennant race circumstances of 2008 really mirrored what had happened the year before—especially the last two days and the fact that you got this extraordinary pitching performance the final Saturday to buoy everybody's spirits and keep hope alive and make everybody believe for one day that they weren't going to let this thing slip away.

But once the two home runs were hit, the entire ballpark sagged, almost as though it was readying itself for the coming executioner.

I don't think you ever lose hope in situations like that. As a chronicler and as a fan, you always try to look for scenarios where the team can pull it out of the fire and Ryan Church's ball leaves the ballpark and everything changes. But deep down, given everything we'd seen over the preceding two months, it didn't feel as though there was a comeback in the offing."

I went into that game and wanted the Mets to win, of course, but I just wasn't there for that that day. It almost—almost—didn't matter to me that the Mets weren't going to make the playoffs on that particular day.

"Really?"

This may be rationalization, but I really wanted to be there for Shea Stadium's final game as opposed to worrying about what else might happen.

"The strangest part of all was the possibility of having the game, the ceremony to close the ballpark, and coming back to play the next day in that ballpark that had just been closed for good. The very fact that they had lost and the fact that the ceremony did close down the stadium made the ceremony that much more poignant. If you had had the same ceremony under the circumstance of them coming back to play the Brewers the next day, what would have that really meant? What would have we really seen? Would have the closing of the gates felt like the literal closing of the gates, or would it have felt like just something temporary?"

I was disappointed by my fellow fans who were understandably venting their frustration that this season had ended like the previous season, but that, to me, was taking away from the moment, which was, "Ohmygod, we're never going to be sitting here watching a baseball game ever again."

"My reading of it from the broadcast booth as opposed to the stands was clearly a certain percentage of people were just beside themselves and left. A certain percentage of people just couldn't let it go. But I also thought that once the ceremony started, everybody behaved incredibly well and that their emotions shifted. I'd have to guess that at least 80 percent of the people who were there that day did stay.

My mother was one of those who left. She was so upset.

It was actually the perfect catharsis for a fan base that had been left in the lurch two years—and I would argue really three years in a row—in terms of reaching the goal they had presumed was within their reach. It was a perfect way, in some ways, of salving the wound and then helping people with the dual finality of both the season and the ballpark. I thought it worked perfectly considering the upsetting circumstances regarding what happened on the field, the juxtaposition of it helping people in some way by changing the subject."

A lot of people asked later, "How could the Mets hold the ceremony after the game knowing the Mets could have lost it?" I don't see how you could have held it before the game.

"I didn't understand that argument at all. How do you close a stadium and then play the game? It just doesn't make any sense, especially the way that they chose to do it. You can quibble about little pieces of it, who wasn't there, where people walked, was it as all-encompassing as it could have been? However, I have to say the totality of it and the way they decided to finish could not have been more perfect.

You could not have asked for a better way to symbolically close the ballpark than to have the greatest pitcher in the history of the franchise and the greatest position player in the history of the franchise; have the lights go out; and literally close the door on Shea Stadium. It was perfect."

Personally, I could have watched 300 Mets come onto the field.

"That's a whole other subject."

Putting aside the people who may have been holding a grudge and didn't show up, was there a player from any time in Mets history, not obvious, not Mookie Wilson or Nolan Ryan, one guy who you would have just loved to have seen show up?

"There are tons. Everybody has touchstones from their childhood and sometimes they are people others would have ignored. I was a big Jerry Buchek fan for the two years he was a Met. It would have been great to have had Ken MacKenzie, the only winning pitcher from the '62 team. Every living member of the '62 team should have been there.

The fact that Davey Johnson wasn't there and obviously Mookie—that was the negative piece, but the fact that Doc was there made up for a lot because that meant an enormous amount to me."

You did say in the broadcast that that was one of the two times you sort of lost it. I felt the same way. All year in the team store they were selling GOODEN 16 T-shirts.

"Really?"

It's like he was a ghost. He showed up on highlights on Diamond Vision, he showed up on these T-shirts but hadn't been back at Shea since 1994 except for that one game he pitched for the Yankees in 2000 and, I suppose, that World Series.

"The Mets have had a rather ambivalent relationship with Doc over the last decade, and the same was true for Darryl for quite some time. They weren't quite sure how to handle them.

We were in Cincinnati earlier this year and the Reds inducted Barry Larkin into their Hall of Fame, and the Reds have a very active and vital team Hall of Fame. As you know, the Mets Hall of Fame has been largely ignored. The last induction was 2002."

Tommie Agee.

"It's just been allowed to wither and die. At the same time, people occasionally make arguments about whether more players' numbers should be retired, they talk about Gary and Keith and so forth. To me, the guy who is as responsible as anybody for creating that logjam is Doc. To me, other than Seaver, no player has had a greater impact on this franchise than Dwight Gooden did. If you're going strictly on on-field contributions, nobody deserves to have his number retired before Doc. It's almost as though the powers that be have that in the back of their mind, that until Doc is fully rehabilitated as far as the franchise is concerned that those tributes to the team's history have to be kind of put on hold.

I thought it was great they found it within them to put aside whatever hesitation they had had in the past about including Doc as part of their history in inviting him, and hopefully that's the first step in undamming that celebration of their history."

With Shea having gone and the Mets going into a new ballpark, I thought the greatest thing about the 2008 season was the Mets were kind of forced to shine a light on their history. From your perspective, do the Mets do enough, considering they're coming up on fifty years as a franchise? It's not an expansion team anymore; they're not the new kids on the block per se—do the Mets as an organization understand that, that their history means a lot to us?

"I think that's waxed and waned over the years. I think there have been efforts made at times to connect the Mets with their history, such as the establishment of the Mets Hall of Fame. For a number of years they had a Mets alumni group and they would have a couple of former players at the ballpark every weekend to sign autographs, but it's been sporadic.

The troublesome post-playing days of guys like Gooden and Strawberry have made it difficult. They've also had less than friendly relations with some of their other former stars for other reasons sometimes having to do with employment or lack of employment. Those things have provided obstacles, and so the short answer is no, the Mets have not done enough to connect with their history the way their fans connect with their history. There are probably a lot of reasons for that."

We're going into the place built like Ebbets Field. It features a rotunda named after, great American that he is, a Brooklyn Dodger. Shea Stadium was the Mets to people. Citi Field is a new ballpark and it's based on Ebbets Field. How will that translate to the whole Mets mind?

"I don't know. I think that it will be a different-sounding ballpark just by virtue of there being 12,000 fewer people in the ballpark, but I don't know what it will feel like until we get there. I will say this: I certainly hope that Mets history is celebrated in a significant way in Citi Field. It would be a mistake to think Mets history starts again from scratch in 2009 because of the move to a new ballpark."

At those great, historic Mets moments you've called, as professional as you are and as professional as you strive to be, the way all you guys do, are you still thinking, "Ohmygod, the Mets won, this is great!"?

"I think, particularly for me and for Howie growing up as fans of the team, that makes it a little bit different than it is for a lot of the other people who are in the same position. I think that if we weren't broadcasting the games, we'd be sitting in the stands as fans. It's also different on radio than it is on television. On radio, you owe your listeners the description and everything else comes second.

Being in the booth in those moments, there is a piece of fan that comes through in the description and the tone that enables you, as you say, to be a professional, but at the same time channel a little of the emotion and really represent the fans. Let's face it, no matter who pays our paycheck, the people we're serving are the people who are listening or watching, and if they're not getting not only the right information but the right tone, then we're not doing our jobs correctly.

One advantage that both Howie and I have is *you* know the history, *we* know the history. You feel the emotion, we feel some of that same emotion. We're not gonna be screaming and yelling the same way that you're gonna be in the stands, but there's some of that that definitely seeps through."

Do you think Mets fans have changed over the years, whether just being more expectant or less proactive?

"I don't think it's just Mets fans. I think the tone of sports fandom has changed a lot. It's changed because we've changed the culture; it's changed because of sports talk radio; it's changed because of Internet message boards. I think there's a lot more anger than there used to be. The way fans boo is completely different from what I grew up with. It used to be, to me, you booed lack of effort. Now it seems that some fans are ready to boo every incremental failure.

It used to be when we were kids that when Willie Mays or Roberto Clemente or Hank Aaron came to the ballpark you gave them a hand when they came to the plate, even if they were trying to beat your team. I think a lot of the civility has seeped out of being a fan.

That doesn't mean that it can't still be a joyous experience or that there aren't plenty of fans who are gracious and see the game for the game as opposed to seeing the game for an opportunity to win or boo. But there's no doubt that fans have changed as a whole."

Was there anything about Shea, for those of us who only go to the games, yet had our moments with the infrastructure . . . was there anything we the fans who say we're going to miss it don't understand from a standpoint of somebody who worked there, who had to deal with whatever creaked, whatever was too narrow? Is there anything you're just going to be thrilled to be done with?

"There were a lot of things that made working there difficult, starting with the elevator, the slowest elevator in the history of elevators, which made getting from our level to the clubhouse or the field and back excruciating.

The hallway behind the broadcast booth was so narrow that two people walking in opposite directions would have to turn sideways to get past each other, and that made it awfully difficult for the techs to get all their equipment in and out. But those are minor things.

I never really thought about any of that. To me it was just such a thrill to be able to go to work there every day. And I'm sure it still will be in the new ballpark, but there's that certain connection with a place where you spent 500 nights as a fan in the Upper Deck, and all of a sudden they're paying you to come to games.

It's quite a scam."

Did you buy a seat from Shea or anything like that?

"You know, I didn't. I'm not a big memorabilia guy. In fact I'm not a memorabilia guy at all. I thought to myself it would be great to have a couple of seats from the Upper Deck, but I didn't."

Me neither. I did buy a brick, I have to admit that.

"My wife bought us a brick."

A Shea brick or a Citi Field brick?

"A Citi Field brick."

My sister and her husband gave me a gift certificate for a Citi Field brick, but I did buy one of the outfield bricks from Shea.

"Oh really?"

It's much longer than you would realize, widthwise. It takes up an entire bookshelf practically, but I feel better about it being with me than being somewhere else if you know what I mean.

"Have you seen video of the scoreboard coming down?"

Yeah.

"That one made me sick to my stomach."

I had the sense there was nothing wrong with Shea until all these other ballparks started being built.

"Well, there was lots wrong with Shea. If you sat in Section 37, it's a terrible place to watch a game. There are ten- or twenty-thousand good seats and the rest of them are pretty horrid. That's one thing that will be much better; the sightlines at Citi Field are great. And the concession stands at Shea were terrible and the bathrooms were terrible and the concourses were terrible. Think of Shea during a rain delay. There's nothing worse. It would have been nice if they had put a retractable roof on Citi Field, but that's one thing that's gonna be nice about it, that if you get a rain delay, there are places you can go and be comfortable."

Was there something that made Shea Shea in your mind, beyond the cramped concourses and the puddles or, for that matter, beyond the ball going through Buckner's legs? Was there something quintessentially Shea Stadium in your mind that you just never saw anywhere else?

"As a fan, what always struck me was the height of the place, largely that's because I generally sat near the top. My vision of myself at Shea Stadium is always sitting high up in Section 1 of the Upper Deck and watching the game from that straight-down view that you get from up there.

But also, just the expanse beyond the ballpark because it was all so wide open. I still have this vision of the Serval Zippers sign flashing on and off beyond left field. Do you even remember the Serval Zippers sign?"

Yeah.

"That's my vision of Shea. It's that height, it's the permanent out-of-town scoreboard, it's the Serval Zippers sign, it's the things you look at. Now fans are basically directed at what to look at with DiamondVision with all the extraneous sounds and noises and commercials and everything else. When I was going to games, mostly in the '70s and early '80s, those were the things that struck me about Shea: the height and the open expanse, the limitlessness of the horizon. And that will definitely be different at Citi Field. You're not going to have the view beyond the ballpark.

I guess we got used to that this past year."

* * *

Gary and Lynn Cohen have established, in conjunction with Keith Hernandez and Ron Darling, the Pitch In for a Good Cause Foundation, supporting an array of community-minded causes in the Greater Metropolitan Area. For more information, please visit garykeithandron.com.

ACKNOWLEDGMENTS

I have been most fortunate to have had my spirits fortified and my soul uplifted by an All-Amazin' roster of friends, colleagues, and correspondents on my journey to these pages. Leading off in any contemplation of *Faith and Fear in Flushing* is my blog partner Jason Fry, who made writing about the Mets on a daily basis an act of anticipation back when watching them was more a task than a treat. Reading and knowing Jason is decidedly the latter.

An unidentified good samaritan gave my Chicago-based friend Jeff Reiter one free ticket to the 2003 All-Star Game outside U.S. Cellular Field. He called the night "one of my greatest baseball experiences," a phrase that lit a spark in me and led me to think about and write up some of my own greatest baseball experiences. Much of what you've read here has its roots in my ongoing dialogue with Jeff, that rarest breed of baseball fan: someone who doesn't root for the Mets but I like the heck out of anyway.

Every book, I gotta believe, has a person like Sharon Chapman behind it. From the earliest ruminations on this volume becoming a reality through the first rough draft and in a dozen ways large and small, she has been my greatest supporter, and she can count me as one of her ardent admirers.

If I am, as I've suggested in the text, That Guy who's more immersed in his team than anyone anybody knows, surely I have my own version of That Guy I look to in wonder. And I do, in the person of Mark Simon, this Mets fan's Mets fan. His thoughts were most helpful in shaping the final draft, and his supple statistical mind deserves a spot on some list of national treasures.

Navigating fine print that isn't on the back of a baseball card isn't necessarily one of my strong suits. Thankfully, it's something Kevin Chapman does like a pro and he was kind enough to lend me his much-needed expertise and insights. The informal advice of Sydelle Kramer was also helpful and appreciated in this area.

As much of Shea Stadium as I viewed across the thirty-six seasons I spent in its seats, I never saw it resonate as beautifully as it does through the lens of David G. Whitham, a brilliant photographer whose images bring a gorgeous layer of depth to this project.

The flip side of my career, the one not consumed by baseball, would not be a going concern if not aided by the continuing confidence of Larry Jabbonsky, a world-class good guy and the onetime occupant of a Flushing apartment previously leased by Gary Gentry.

The vision of Mark Weinstein at Skyhorse Publishing was essential in bringing *Faith and Fear* to publication. My thanks to him for understanding, in this digital age, that books are still sacred things—and that the story of someone who's built a life around following an intermittently successful baseball franchise is one that is worth telling in this medium.

Profound thanks to Gary Cohen, who was generous with his time, encouragement and perspective. He is truly the Voice of the Mets for all seasons.

My love affair with the printed word and its application in glorifying Mets baseball had its launching pad on the sports shelves of the Long Beach Public Library of my youth. It was from those stacks that I got to know my team and what I was getting myself into through the talents of men like Leonard Koppett, Joe Durso, Dick Schaap, George Vecsey, and Roger Angell. Their seminal works sit on my shelf today and I thank them for the inspiration they unknowingly provided in terms of pastime, profession, and passion.

This Date in New York Mets History, published in 1981, remains the greatest reference book ever penned, Met or otherwise. Long-running gratitude to its author, Dennis D'Agostino, for crafting an ultimate Mets database before there was a Web site called Ultimate Mets Database. Thanks, too, to ultimatemets. com, baseball-reference.com, and retrosheet.com. Each is a fount of information no remotely serious baseball writer could do without.

I value greatly the recent books devoted to this thing of ours by the likes of Dana Brand, Matthew Silverman, and Jon Springer. I appreciate what they've produced as much as the way their efforts helped pave the way for this particular contribution to the category they made that much richer by their participation.

The Mets blogging community makes for a most vibrant home field and I give a special tip of my cap to all of my compatriots who come to play every day. As I retrace my footsteps in pursuing my chronicling of baseball, I think back as well to those with whom I've celebrated Met victories and mourned Met defeats electronically since I figured out you could use a computer for such vital communication: the AOL Grandstand; the Met Cave; Gotham Baseball; the Crane Pool Forum; the New York Baseball Giants Nostalgia Society; and, especially, the core of folks who make up the evolving, enduring e-mail list that one of its members long ago dubbed the Greg Prince All-Stars. I don't know about that name, but it's good to be a part of such a hard-hitting team. Special thanks to the highly creative crew at *Mets Weekly* for providing me an additional platform from which to spout off on Met matters since 2006.

When Jason and I signed on as Faith and Fear in Flushing, it was just us at our URL. We weren't lonely for long. There would be no book and there would be no blog without our readers and our commenters. You are at the heart of what we do at faithandfearinflushing.com. Technically, so is John Keegan of BlogHarbor, who literally keeps us up and running.

I hesitate to start rattling off too many more names, in dread of forgetting at least one, but I have been lucky to have shared Shea Stadium arm rests, rides on the 7 train, and endless Met conversation with some simply incredible people over the years, each of whom has helped inform the content of this book. My eternal love and gratitude to them all, including but by no means limited to Laurie Russo, Dan Gold, Dan Davis, Richie Giustiniani, Rich Porricelli, Jodie Remick, Charlie Hangley, Dave Murray, Joe Figliola, Rob Emproto, Dennis McCarthy, Ray Stilwell, David Corcoran, Emily Bernstein, Joe Dubin, Frank Santopadre, Kevin Connell, John Coppinger, Ben Muschel, John Colella, Andee Joyce, Gary Citro, Taryn Cooper, Mike Steffanos, Gene Sullivan, Dan Ziegler, Jason Mann, Matt Enis, Andrea Foote, Jeff Hysen, Joel Lugo, Fred Bunz, and Larry Russo.

Except for not being related by blood or anything like that, I have two of the best brothers anyone could hope for in Carlos Briceno and Jim Haines. Each of them was, in his own way, the bedeviling angel hovering over my shoulder and whispering insistently in my ear to get moving already yet. Message received, brothers.

I come from a family that didn't and doesn't really care for baseball. But they seem to like me, and that may transcend even the Mets in my eyes. So thank you Suzan Prince, Mark Trost, Florence Bowden, and Charles Prince for that and, well, everything.

Stephanie Prince is the finest person I've ever known. Everything I do is better because she's a part of it.